NUMBERS

WALTER RIGGANS

THE SAINT ANDREW PRESS
EDINBURGH

THE WESTMINSTER PRESS
PHILADELPHIA

Published by
The Saint Andrew Press
Edinburgh, Scotland
and
The Westminster Press ®
Philadelphia, Pennsylvania

Typeset, Printed and Bound in Great Britain
by Thomson Litho Ltd., East Kilbride, Scotland

ISBN (Great Britain) 0 7152 0522 6

Reprinted 1986

GENERAL PREFACE

This series of commentaries on the Old Testament, to which Mr. Riggans' volume on *Numbers* belongs, has been planned as a companion series to the much-acclaimed New Testament series of the late Professor William Barclay. As with that series, each volume is arranged in successive headed portions suitable for daily study. The Biblical text followed is that of the Revised Standard Version or Common Bible. Eleven contributors share the work, each being responsible for from one to three volumes. The series is issued in the hope that it will do for the Old Testament what Professor Barclay's series succeeded so splendidly in doing for the New Testament—make it come alive for the Christian believer in the twentieth century.

Its two-fold aim is the same as his. Firstly, it is intended to introduce the reader to some of the more important results and fascinating insights of modern Old Testament scholarship. Most of the contributors are already established experts in the field with many publications to their credit. Some are younger scholars who have yet to make their names but who in my judgment as General Editor are now ready to be tested. I can assure those who use these commentaries that they are in the hands of competent teachers who know what is of real consequence in their subject and are able to present it in a form that will appeal to the general public.

The primary purpose of the series, however, is *not* an academic one. Professor Barclay summed it up for his New Testament series in the words of Richard of Chichester's prayer—to enable men and women "to know Jesus Christ more clearly, to love Him more dearly, and to follow Him more nearly." In the case of the Old Testament we have to be a little more circumspect than that. The Old Testament was completed long before the time of Our Lord, and it was (as it still is) the sole Bible of the Jews, God's first people, before it became part of the Christian Bible. We must take this fact seriously.

Yet in its strangely compelling way, sometimes dimly and sometimes directly, sometimes charmingly and sometimes embarrassingly, it holds up before us the things of Christ. It should not be forgotten that Jesus Himself was raised on this Book, that He based His whole ministry on what it says, and that He approached His death with its words on His lips. Christian men and women have in this ancient collection of Jewish writings a uniquely illuminating avenue not only into the will and purposes of God the Father, but into the mind and heart of Him who is named God's Son, who was Himself born a Jew but went on through the Cross and Resurrection to become the Saviour of the world. Read reverently and imaginatively the Old Testament can become a living and relevant force in their everyday lives.

It is the prayer of myself and my colleagues that this series may be used by its readers and blessed by God to that end.

New College   JOHN C. L. GIBSON
Edinburgh   General Editor

CONTENTS

B. THE PEOPLE OF ISRAEL AND THE TRIALS OF ADJUSTMENT

Balaam and Balak: An Introduction

C. THE PEOPLE OF ISRAEL AND THE TRIALS OF SETTLEMENT

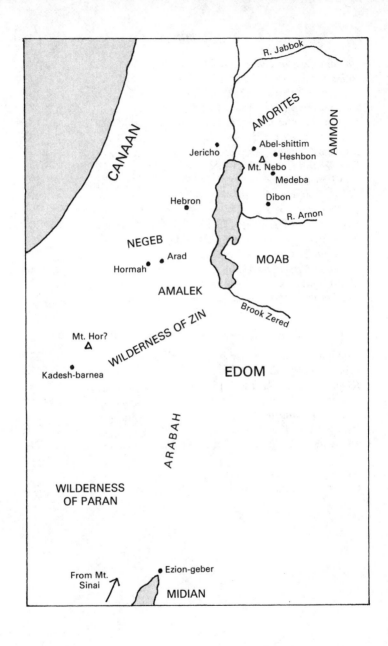

INTRODUCTION

THE TITLE

The title "Numbers" comes via the Latin title "*Numeri*" from the Greek title "*Arithmoi*". The Hebrew title is "In the Wilderness", which is the most significant word (it is one word in Hebrew) in the opening sentences according to the Rabbis. The tradition of calling the book Numbers arose from the number of lists that appear in it, although these are by no means the most important parts of it. There are two main censuses of the people (1:1–4:49; 26) as well as the lists found in 7:10–83; 28:1–29:38; 31:32–52.

AUTHORSHIP AND DATE

According to orthodox tradition the author was Moses. This claim is not part of the sacred text, however. Certain things suggest multiple authorship, and in *Additional Note 1* I mention some that may interest the reader. But here a quotation from W. F. Albright will suffice (it is from his book *The Biblical Period*):

> How much of this ... goes back to Moses himself it would be idle to conjecture in the present state of our knowledge [but] the spirit and much of the detail may be considered as ante-dating the Conquest of Canaan—in other words, as going back to Mosaic origins.

OUTLINE

The book is really about a pilgrimage under God of a fledgling people, and the incidents and reflections fall into three divisions as the story unfolds. They are called here: A. *The People of Israel and the Trials in the Wilderness*; B. *The People of Israel and the Trials of Adjustment*; C. *The People of Israel and the Trials of Settlement*. What is more, there are three general geographical areas involved: I. *Sinai*; II. *South of Canaan*; III. *Moab and*

Edom. So the book may be broken down into two partly overlapping patterns:

A. *The People of Israel and the Trials in the Wilderness*
   I.   *Sinai*, 1:1–10:10 (about 20 days; see 1:1 and 10:11)
   II. *South of Canaan*, 10:11–20:13 (about 38 years; see 10:11 and 33:38)
   III. *Moab and Edom*, 20:14–36:13 (about 5 months; see 33:38 and Deut. 1:3). It was in this area that the final events of division A and all the incidents in divisions B and C took place.

B. *The People of Israel and the Trials of Adjustment*

C. *The People of Israel and the Trials of Settlement*

STRUCTURE

After even a casual reading of the text it will be seen by any student of Numbers that there is only the poorest of literary or theological structure discernible. The basis of the book is a loose narrative of the various trials of the newly-created people of God between the giving of God's *Torah* (his Direction and directions) at Sinai and the camping on the border of the Promised Land opposite Jericho. But from time to time large chunks of disjointed material become prominent—censuses, divine ordinances, cultic-ritual prescriptions, lists of gifts for the sanctuary, etc. Then, in chapters 22–24 appears the cycle of stories centred on the interplay of the desires of the Lord and Balak on the seer Balaam. Moses' brother and sister, Aaron and Miriam, both die in the narrative, and Moses' imminent death is proclaimed. Perhaps the most prominent theme is that of the gracious providence of the Lord in caring for all of Israel's needs—militarily, physically, nutritionally and spiritually—in spite of constant rebellions by the people, both leadership and rank and file.

SUMMARY OF TEACHING

1. *God is always close and caring.* He is involved on his people's behalf in history, as shown by the cloud (9:15–23) and by more

direct means (35:34). We must understand the Old Testament as Israel herself understood it, that is, as concretely rooted in real history and geography.

2. *God will always discipline.* Two aspects are shown here: (a) when the people rebel, mumble against God, or just doubt him; (b) when the Lord tests his people with trials. He demands obedience to his will, and judgment for lack of this is pronounced on the whole people (11:1–3; 21:6; 25:1–5, 6–13), the leaders (14:36–37), the Levites (16), Miriam (12:10), and on Moses and Aaron too (20:12).

3. *God's purpose will always prevail.* Promises made to the patriarchs (32:10–12) would be realized by God in spite of the people's unfaithfulness, the nations' hostilities, the spiritual powers' opposition. His will would be done on earth as it was in heaven.

4. *God's love, discipline and purpose are always holy.* The whole fabric of the book shows this, that he must be served solely and wholly. The laws which it contains are not so much to be seen as automatic formulae for achieving man's holiness as safeguards against taking God's holiness for granted, or letting familiarity breed contempt. Time and care have to be taken to prepare oneself for approaching him in petition or confession. This too is a lesson worth the learning.

We who are drawn by the Father to our calling in Jesus Christ will experience this same care and guidance in our pilgrimages through life. He will look after all our needs in this his very real world; he will discipline us as and when we are in need of it for our maturing in him; he will move both nations and individuals today to fulfil his purposes. What is more, he is still demanding total surrender and obedience (Rom. 12:1–2). In Christ we have full and confident access to the Father, and his holiness must be reflected in our communities as they head towards the true Promised Land, his fundamental promise and purpose.

It can be safely said that the experience and lessons of Israel in her pilgrimage in the book of Numbers parallel those of all the Lord's people everywhere and in every age as they make their pilgrimage to God's own heart.

A. THE PEOPLE OF ISRAEL AND THE TRIALS IN THE WILDERNESS

ISRAEL'S FIGHTING MEN—THE COMMAND!

Numbers 1:1–4

> [1]The Lord spoke to Moses in the wilderness of Sinai, in the tent of meeting, on the first day of the second month, in the second year after they had come out of the land of Egypt, saying, [2]"Take a census of all the congregation of the people of Israel, by families, by fathers' houses, according to the number of names, every male, head by head; [3]from twenty years old and upward, all in Israel who are able to go forth to war, you and Aaron shall number them, company by company. [4]And there shall be with you a man from each tribe, each man being the head of the house of his fathers."

(i)

In the very first verse of this book two points of fundamental importance for understanding the Old Testament, and indeed the New Testament, stand out strongly:

(a) *God has the initiative, and takes the initiative, in his dealings with his people.* This is central to faith. "The Lord spoke to Moses . . . saying . . ." The Bible begins just as assertively: "In the beginning God created . . ." God speaking opens up the book and sets the mood immediately. He is not dependent on our faith to act for us.

(b) *Our relationship with God, based on our encounter with him, is rooted in the here and now.* It is riveted in history—not in imaginative speculation nor in vague mysticism, but in the realities of our common world. "On the first day of the second month, in the second year after they had come out of the land of Egypt". Notice the stress on knowing the times and the places, and on celebrating, remembering, reliving the exact times and places. It is good to remember this when doubts and fears surround us. Even when lost or alone, we can know that God *has* shown himself in certain facts of history and continues to do so. This kept Israel's faith alive for the centuries before the birth of the Jew, Jesus, in Bethlehem.

(ii)

An exciting story is about to unfold in the following chapters. The adventure of the Israelites, which became a pilgrimage, carries on from the stage recorded in Exod. 19:1ff., which locates the people in the wilderness of Sinai after their rescue from Egypt. Several times in the subsequent story the people become despondent and rebellious; but in this book Moses is also seen to lead them into an unexpected pilgrimage with the Living God, the God of their ancestors, the Redeemer from the Burning Bush. This God insists that he has chosen them (Deut. 7:6–11) and proceeds in their pilgrimage to teach them reliance on him alone, and also how to worship him.

The text begins as they are about to set off on their great pilgrimage to the Promised Land. For this journey they needed disciplined preparations for their own individual and communal morale. Part of that discipline involved *having a leader*, appointed and anointed by God, to be the people's representative before God and the mediator of God's word to the people. Moses was that man: "The Lord spoke to Moses". This formula is used over eighty times in the book, suggesting Moses' importance. It is rarely that a man of Moses' godliness and ability emerges from the people of God, but God still does call men to be the shepherds of his people; the prophets to his people; the intercessors for his people.

The communication between God and Moses took place "in the tent of meeting". This is one of the various expressions used for the Tabernacle. It was a sacred, portable tent where God revealed his will to, and lived with, his people. The phrase used here occurs some 140 times in the Old Testament, the English translation deriving from the Latin version. The Hebrew term for *meeting* carries with it a sense of meeting by appointment, so this sacred place was the place where Moses came to be given direction and directions from his Lord, when called by him, or when needing him. A closer look at the significance of the Tabernacle will be given in the commentary to 9:15–23.

This tent of meeting was to be the heart of the pilgrim people (see Exod. 33:7ff., where the people follow Moses' every movement as he approaches it), and was therefore to be protected during the journey, as were the people themselves. Thus a second part of their discipline involved *the establishing of an efficient dynamic structure*. The Old Testament is clear that Israel is more than a collection of individuals and tribes. She is a unity of peoples, truly a nation; even before she occupies Canaan, and even after she is conquered and scattered into exile. She must learn to live as a unity under God: a long and painful process, as Numbers and the rest of the Old Testament and the New Testament too show.

(iii)

So the people needed to take stock and prepare themselves. They needed to assess their resources, human, livestock, physical, spiritual. In other words, a census was called for. According to ancient records, there were usually two reasons for a census: (a) *for taxation purposes* (as in Exod. 38:24ff.); (b) *for military purposes*, as here. God calls the census, and wants it detailed. The phrase, "the congregation of the people of Israel", is peculiar to this strand of the writings of the Old Testament. The same Hebrew term is behind it as lies behind the tent of "meeting", and is used some seventy times. It means that Israel is a people called to a destiny, a divine appointment in history.

The count then is taken: (a) *by families*, or as the Scots would well understand it, by clans; (b) *by fathers' houses*, i.e. smaller, closer units; (c) *every male, head by head*. This literally is "to their skulls", the same word appearing as Golgotha in the New Testament. The males are counted from the fighting age of twenty years and upward. This formula, with the idea that they must be "able to go forth to war", is used fourteen times in the chapter, so there is no doubt that the census was intended to determine the

Israelites' military potential. The Levites, who are non-military, received a separate census (1:47ff.; 3:14–51).

The first few verses of the book, then, promise action and strategy, trial and maturing. They also speak of a certain need for shared leadership. Moses is helped by his brother Aaron, and the senior heads of the tribes. These men play vital roles in their society, such as sheikhs in bedouin society. Aaron's dominant role unveils as the book goes on. It is a lesson well learned to really share leadership.

ISRAEL'S FIGHTING MEN—THE MEN

Numbers 1:5–19

⁵"And these are the names of the men who shall attend you. From Reuben, Elizur the son of Shedeur; ⁶from Simeon, Shelumi-el the son of Zurishaddai; ⁷from Judah, Nahshon the son of Amminadab; ⁸from Issachar, Nethanel the son of Zuar; ⁹from Zebulun, Eliab the son of Helon; ¹⁰from the sons of Joseph, from Ephraim, Elishama the son of Ammihud, and from Manasseh, Gamaliel the son of Pedahzur; ¹¹from Benjamin, Abidan the son of Gideoni; ¹²from Dan, Ahiezer the son of Ammishaddai; ¹³from Asher, Pagiel the son of Ochran; ¹⁴from Gad, Eliasaph the son of Deuel; ¹⁵from Naphtali, Ahira the son of Enan." ¹⁶These were the ones chosen from the congregation, the leaders of their ancestral tribes, the heads of the clans of Israel.

¹⁷Moses and Aaron took these men who have been named, ¹⁸and on the first day of the second month, they assembled the whole congregation together, who registered themselves by families, by fathers' houses, according to the number of names from twenty years old and upward, head by head, ¹⁹as the Lord commanded Moses. So he numbered them in the wilderness of Sinai.

(i)

An account is now given of the actual men chosen to be Israel's representatives. The same stress is shown here on the importance of knowing the historical side to the coin whose other side is spiritual. Knowing names is important—these were real people. From the twelve tribes are given the names of the heads of the tribes and their ancestors, to further identify and guarantee them. It is a form of spiritual pedigree.

Of the twenty-four names here, nine carry the divine name for God, "El": Elizur, *My God is a Rock*; Shelumiel, *God is my Peace*; Nethanel, *God gives*; Eliab, *My God is a Father*; Elishama, *My God listens*; Gamaliel, *God is my Reward* (this name became popular with the later Rabbis, e.g. Saul of Tarsus' teacher, Acts 22:3); Pagiel, *God is my Fortune*; Eliasaph, *My God adds*; Deuel, which is probably an easily made error in the manuscript tradition for Reuel (as in 2:14), *God is a Friend*.

Also, three of the names carry the divine title of God, "Shaddai", probably meaning something like *Powerful Protection*. The names are: Shedeur, *Shaddai is a Light*; Zurishaddai, *Shaddai is my Rock*; Ammishaddai, *Shaddai is my Kinsman*.

Finally, there are three names which carry another divine title of God, "Zur". This means *Rock*, referring to God's power, but more so to his care for his people like the restful shade given by large rocks from the blistering heat of the sun (see Isa. 32:2). The first two have already been given, and the third is Pedahzur, *The Rock redeems*.

Of them all, six are compounded with terms for relationships commonly used with respect to God, i.e. "Abi", *My Father*; "Ahi", *My Brother*; "Ammi", *My Kinsman*. These are all ancient names and reflect the types of relationships the people believed they had with their God. For this reason, they are most important in understanding popular piety in Israel's early life.

Modern Western methods for choosing names for children hardly ever involve seriously checking the actual meanings of the names. But the custom in the East is to choose names according to experiences in having the children; or according to wishes for their future; or according to intuition of their character or personality. Therefore knowing someone's name gives insight into their character and pedigree, and this explains the Bible's love of genealogies and family connections. Therefore the Gospel according to Matthew begins with a rooting of Jesus of Nazareth in Israel's life and times. As a matter of interest, two of the persons recorded here, Amminadab and Nahshon, are said to be ancestors of Jesus (Matt. 1:4).

(ii)

There are also strict rules of protocol within the tribal hierarchies. Tribes from Jacob's legitimate wives take precedence over those from his handmaids. In this list we have the Leah tribes first, followed by the Rachel tribes, with the Bilhah and Zilpah tribes last (see Gen. 29:31–30:24 for the sequence of birth). Levi, a Leah tribe, is not included because of its "ministerial" function; but the number is made up to twelve by the tribe of Joseph being represented by its two half tribes, Ephraim and Manasseh, Ephraim taking precedence because of the blessing in Gen. 48:13ff. In the next list (vv. 20ff.) the order is the same, except that Gad is strangely promoted to third place. But that list is looking forward to chapter 2, which describes the positioning of the tribes around the "tent of meeting" in the Israelite camp. There Gad takes the slot among the Leah tribes vacated by Levi; see the diagram in the commentary on 2:1–34.

A glance at the major English translations will show that in v. 16 there is much variation. The RSV text says these leaders were heads of "the clans of Israel". The AV has a literal translation with "the thousands", followed more cautiously perhaps by the Jerusalem Bible's "hosts". The Hebrew has the term for the number 1,000, but there is evidence from sources outside the Old Testament, as well as inside, that this term came to have a technical meaning as well. Usually the context is a military one, and it perhaps originally signified a unit of 1,000 men (see especially 1 Sam. 8:12); yet the impression is that it came to be the term for a set unit within the armed forces. Hence the translation of the New American Standard Bible, "divisions". Perhaps better would be "battalions", "brigades", or the like.

So Moses carried out the command of God and "numbered the people". A richer translation would be that he *mustered the troops*, since the root meaning of the verb conveys a sense of gathering, seeking, appointing. What God commands, Moses does. In Genesis there is a recurrent phrase in chapter 1, "And God said . . . and there was", i.e. God's word is as good as his bond. If he says he will do something then it will be done (compare Isa. 55:11). Here we find that God says to his servant that something must be done, and such is the faith and obedience of this exemplary servant that it is simply stated as having been done.

ISRAEL'S FIGHTING MEN—THE COUNT

Numbers 1:20–46

[20]The people of Reuben, Israel's first-born, their generations, by their families, by their fathers' houses, according to the number of names, head by head, every male from twenty years old and upward, all who were able to go forth to war: [21]the number of the tribe of Reuben was forty-six thousand five hundred.

[22]Of the people of Simeon, their generations, by their families, by their fathers' houses, those of them that were numbered, according to the number of names, head by head, every male from twenty years old and upward, all who were able to go forth to war: [23]the number of the tribe of Simeon was fifty-nine thousand three hundred.

[24]Of the people of Gad, their generations, by their families, by their fathers' houses, according to the number of the names, from twenty years old and upward, all who were able to go forth to war: [25]the number of the tribe of Gad was forty-five thousand six hundred and fifty.

[26]Of the people of Judah, their generations, by their families, by their fathers' houses, according to the number of names, from twenty years old and upward, every man able to go forth to war: [27]the number of the tribe of Judah was seventy-four thousand six hundred.

[28]Of the people of Issachar, their generations, by their families, by their fathers' houses, according to the number of names, from twenty years old and upward, every man able to go forth to war: [29]the number of the tribe of Issachar was fifty-four thousand four hundred.

[30]Of the people of Zebulun, their generations, by their families, by their fathers' houses, according to the number of names, from twenty years old and upward, every man able to go forth to war: [31]the number of the tribe of Zebulun was fifty-seven thousand four hundred.

[32]Of the people of Joseph, namely, of the people of Ephraim, their generations, by their families, by their fathers' houses, according to the number of names, from twenty years old and upward, every man able to go forth to war: [33]the number of the tribe of Ephraim was forty thousand five hundred.

³⁴Of the people of Manasseh, their generations, by their families, by their fathers' houses, according to the number of names, from twenty years old and upward, every man able to go forth to war: ³⁵the number of the tribe of Manasseh was thirty-two thousand two hundred.

³⁶Of the people of Benjamin, their generations, by their families, by their fathers' houses, according to the number of names, from twenty years old and upward, every man able to go forth to war: ³⁷the number of the tribe of Benjamin was thirty-five thousand four hundred.

³⁸Of the people of Dan, their generations, by their families, by their fathers' houses, according to the number of names, from twenty years old and upward, every man able to go forth to war: ³⁹the number of the tribe of Dan was sixty-two thousand seven hundred.

⁴⁰Of the people of Asher, their generations, by their families, by their fathers' houses, according to the number of names, from twenty years old and upward, every man able to go forth to war: ⁴¹the number of the tribe of Asher was forty-one thousand five hundred.

⁴²Of the people of Naphtali, their generations, by their families, by their fathers' houses, according to the number of names, from twenty years old and upward, every man able to go forth to war: ⁴³the number of the tribe of Naphtali was fifty-three thousand four hundred.

⁴⁴These are those who were numbered, whom Moses and Aaron numbered with the help of the leaders of Israel, twelve men, each representing his fathers' house. ⁴⁵So the whole number of the people of Israel, by their fathers' houses, from twenty years old and upward, every man able to go forth to war in Israel—⁴⁶their whole number was six hundred and three thousand five hundred and fifty.

(i)

This section may seem rather inconsequential to the modern reader, but again the stress is unswervingly on the historicity of the events. Israel's God is not remote; neither does he work only in the inner souls or deepest psyches in ways that are incommunicable from person to person. He does this, but more, he also changes people, nations, governments. He is at work in nature. There is evidence of his existence and his presence, according to Israel. So here there is given a prosaic list of tribes and totals, in a stubborn formula. But it shows the fruit of God's will, as a result of the census he ordered.

The tribal totals for men fit for action are as follows:

Reuben	: 46,500	Simeon	: 59,300
Gad	: 45,650	Judah	: 74,600
Issachar	: 54,400	Zebulun	: 57,400
Ephraim	: 40,500	Manasseh	: 32,200
Benjamin	: 35,400	Dan	: 62,700
Asher	: 41,500	Naphtali	: 53,400
	Total	: 603,550	

These are the adult males over twenty years of age and fit for war. From comparisons with the percentage of other communities, ancient and modern, of the militarily capable to the rest of society, estimates have been given for the whole camp of between two and three million people. This figure adds to the 603,550 for the likely numbers of the Levites (see next section), the women, those under twenty years of age, the aged, the unfit for war.

Commentators have pointed out that this would be far too many for the movements and survival of Israel as recorded in Numbers. It also seems too large a number to survive in a relatively small area. Again, we read in 10:1ff. that the whole camp could be encompassed within the distance covered by the sound of only two trumpets. Finally, according to Exod. 23:29–30 and Deut. 7:7 ("It was not because you were more in number than any other people that the Lord set his love upon you and chose you, for you were the fewest of all peoples"), the Israelites who fled from slavery in Egypt were too few to occupy Canaan. Therefore some believe the figures are just exaggerations to impress others with Israel's history and power. The question also arises as to how much glory would go to God for miraculously saving Israel in her wars, if she had such numbers.

(ii)

It is unnecessary to make such an assumption. It is also unnecessary to try to replace the figures in another context, e.g. the census of Sam. 24, taken of course much later. If the interpretation of the number 1,000 as a military term for an armed unit of men is correct (see last section), then the picture is clearer. Say the term is translated *battalion*. This would involve different numbers per tribe. Then the numbers are as follows:

Reuben	: 46 battalions with 500 men
Simeon	: 59 battalions with 300 men
Gad	: 45 battalions with 650 men
Judah	: 74 battalions with 600 men
Issachar	: 54 battalions with 400 men
Zebulun	: 51 battalions with 400 men
Ephraim	: 40 battalions with 500 men
Manasseh	: 32 battalions with 200 men
Benjamin	: 35 battalions with 400 men
Dan	: 62 battalions with 700 men
Asher	: 41 battalions with 500 men
Naphtali	: 53 battalions with 400 men
Total	: 592 battalions with 5,550 men.

Working as before, this would give an estimated size for the whole camp of between 25,000 and 30,000 people. This seems a number more fitting to the narratives of the desert wanderings, and also "makes sense" of the wonderful works of God on behalf of such a small group in the face of the natural odds and the established armies which it encountered.

This was Israel's God, the One who "chose what is foolish . . . what is weak . . . what is low and despised in the world . . . to bring to nothing things that are, so that no human being might boast in the presence of God" (1 Cor. 1:26–29).

ISRAEL'S FIGHTING MEN—THE BALANCE

Numbers 1:47–54

[47]But the Levites were not numbered by their ancestral tribe along with them. [48]For the Lord said to Moses, [49]"Only the tribe of Levi you shall not number, and you shall not take a census of them among the people of Israel; [50]but appoint the Levites over the tabernacle of the testimony, and over all its furnishings, and over all that belongs to it; they are to carry the tabernacle and all its furnishings, and they shall tend it, and shall encamp around the tabernacle. [51]When the tabernacle is to set out, the Levites shall take it down; and when the tabernacle is to be pitched, the Levites shall set it up. And if any one else comes near, he shall be put to death. [52]The people of Israel shall

pitch their tents by their companies, every man by his own camp and every man by his own standard; [53] but the Levites shall encamp around the tabernacle of the testimony, that there may be no wrath upon the congregation of the people of Israel; and the Levites shall keep charge of the tabernacle of the testimony." [54]Thus did the people of Israel; they did according to all that the Lord commanded Moses.

(i)

Not all of the eligible warriors were actually to fight. "The Levites" were not included in the census because they were not free for military service (in chapter 3 is recorded a separate census just of the sons of Levi). This is the first of three census-takings of Israel in the Old Testament: (a) Num. 1:17–46, with the Levites separate, 3:14–39; (b) Num. 26:2–51, with the Levites separate, 26:62; (c) 2 Sam. 24:1–9, repeated in 1 Chron. 21:1–5 (where Satan is said to have inspired it, not God), with the Levites not included, 1 Chron. 21:6.

The phrase for "counting heads" in Hebrew is literally, to *lift up each head*, i.e. to God, and reflects the belief that it was God's prerogative alone to count the seed of Israel. For men to count was to try to set limits on God, to reduce him to numbers. The People of God were—and are—to trust him to increase them as he saw fit. The numerical size of God's Israel is his concern. At least this was the belief that developed in Israel and is reflected in the fact that, rather than declare that the Lord punished David for obeying him in counting Israel's population (2 Sam. 24), the Chronicler says that the notion was put into David's mind by Satan. It was sin.

(ii)

How many tribes were there? Here in Num. 1 there are thirteen, including the Levites. 1 Kings 11:31–32 speaks of eleven tribes. Gen. 46:8–27 has thirteen tribes including the Levites. Even when lists agree as to the number of tribes, the constituent tribes can vary. Most lists have the tradition of twelve tribes (Gen. 32:22–26; Deut. 27:12–13; 1 Chron. 2:1–2; Ezek. 48:1ff.), but this may speak more of an arrangement made much later in the ordering of Israel's structures rather than of a fact that exactly twelve well-defined tribal groups were involved in the formation of Israel right from the beginning. There may have been a merging of tribes at points, or a splitting of tribes. However that may be, the tribes we have are witnessed to very early on in Israel's records.

One theory is that before the Levites were set apart as here, to care for the sanctuary, all the tribes shared the duty on a rota basis. The celebration of the New Moon was important to Israel from early on (see the commentary on 28:11–15), and perhaps each new month saw a different tribe taking over responsibility. Thus the number settled on for the number of tribes was twelve. After the Levites became the caretakers of the sanctuary, the symbolism of the whole year being represented was kept by preserving the number twelve as the representative number for Israel. This was surely reinforced during Israel's Exile in Babylon where she came into contact with astrology, since the twelve signs of the zodiac have been found in mosaic form in several ancient synagogues, notably at Beth Alpha in modern Israel.

Evidence of this desire to keep the number twelve can be seen in Gen. 29–30 where there are twelve divisions only if Dinah becomes a leader, since Benjamin is not mentioned. Again, in 1 Chron. 2:1–3 Levi is mentioned in the group, but the number twelve is preserved by having Joseph in place of his sons Manasseh and Ephraim. In Deut. 33:6ff. and Judg. 5:14ff, there is no mention of Simeon. Even in the New Testament it can be seen in Rev. 7:1–8 that Levi is included at the expense of Dan to maintain the number twelve. This number became the symbol for Israel.

That is why Jesus spoke of the twelve disciples ruling the twelve tribes, i.e. Israel (Matt. 19:28). In other words they were the sign of a new beginning for Israel in Jesus, undergoing renewal on behalf of them, until such time as all Israel would be renewed. For the same reason James wrote to the twelve tribes dispersed in the world, i.e. all God's Israel, those in the Messiah, whether Jew or Gentile. So important indeed was the symbol of twelve tribes that after the death of Judas Iscariot the eleven disciples of Jesus felt the strong need to replace him to restore that exact number (Acts 1:15–26).

THE LEVITES

Numbers 1:47–54 (*cont'd*)

(iii)

On looking specifically at the tribe of Levi, it is clear that they were specially consecrated to God's service. The exact origin and meaning of the name is unknown, but it may be connected with the Hebrew verb "to join". It has been suggested that this tribe was not at first a member of the Israelite confederacy, but "joined" it later; or that they were "joined" to God as a kind of special people within the chosen people. But the most plausible theory is that the name draws attention to their being "joined" to the *liturgy* and the sanctuary. This would suit all the Biblical references to their functioning. There is, moreover, a very similar Arabic term for the custodians of the sanctuaries and the helpers at worship in South Arabia in the period before Muhammad. Certainly the Levites are commanded here to care for the Tabernacle and its furnishings.

This is beautifully summed up in the phrase that they were to "tend" or "minister" to it. This term means to do a worthy service for someone, and is especially used in the context of the worship of God (Exod. 28:35; Deut. 10:8). We must all take care to tend to our worship and those aids to worship we, or others, find valuable. In this book the reverence in which the people of Israel held God will become obvious, and the care they took to do only the very best of work for his Tabernacle. It is sadly commonplace to caricature the faith of Israel as remote, legalistic, cold; this is far from the truth. It is also commonplace to caricature her worship as such; this is especially done by those groups who might equally well be caricatured as being too familiar and comfortable in the presence of the Father, who is also the Holy God. Both emphases are necessary, God's holiness and his Fatherhood, in order that men may worship him in spirit and in truth.

(iv)

Verse 50 preserves the tradition that the Tabernacle was called "the tabernacle of the testimony", since it was said to contain the second set of two stone tablets of God's testimony to Israel, i.e. the tablets of the Ten Commandments (Exod. 31:18; 32:19; 34:1; 40:20). Wherever the Tabernacle was, with these holy objects, it was too holy, and thus too dangerous for non-authorized, unprepared people to approach. It was seen as the very place where God lived with his people. So it is not misrepresenting the case to say that the Tabernacle mediated God's presence, and was therefore a *sacrament* of the presence of God. It was the fundamental mediator of God to his people in the camp. The Levites therefore protected it from unconsecrated people; and vice versa. The Tabernacle was placed in an open area in the centre of the camp, and the tribes pitched their tents around it. No one could now accidentally stumble in on it, thereby contaminating it or endangering themselves.

Several times in the book this function of the Levites is stressed again (e.g. 8:19; 16:46), and the belief of Israel regarding unconsecrated handling of, or approach to, the holy things of God is reflected clearly in 2 Sam. 6:6ff., where even a helpful yet unauthorized hand is punished by death. It is summed up at the end of this passage by the call on the Levites to "keep charge of" the Tabernacle. This is a technical term for guarding and acting as guardian (2 Kings 11:5–6). They protect and look after it.

The Israelites, and later the Jews, kept alive this belief that somehow God lives with his people, but it was to be a long time before God fully entered into the life of Israel, or fully pitched his tent/tabernacle with them. Saint John captures the significance of the Incarnation of Jesus in this way, by asserting at the beginning of his Gospel, "And the Word became flesh and dwelt among us . . ." (John 1:14), where the term for "dwelt" means *to pitch a tent*, referring to God's full tabernacling with us. God cannot be limited by time and space, but we can rejoice that for a time he was fully revealed and located in the man, Jesus of Nazareth. What is more, we do not need to "keep charge of" this Tabernacle—rather he is our Protector and Shepherd.

ISRAEL'S FIGHTING MEN—THE CAMP

Numbers 2:1–34

¹The Lord said to Moses and Aaron, ²"The people of Israel shall encamp each by his own standard, with the ensigns of their fathers' houses; they shall encamp facing the tent of meeting on every side. ³Those to encamp on the east side toward the sunrise shall be of the standard of the camp of Judah by their companies, the leader of the people of Judah being Nahshon the son of Amminadab, ⁴his host as numbered being seventy-four thousand six hundred. ⁵Those to encamp next to him shall be the tribe of Issachar, the leader of the people of Issachar being Nethanel the son of Zuar, ⁶his host as numbered being fifty-four thousand four hundred. ⁷Then the tribe of Zebulun, the leader of the people of Zebulun being Eliab the son of Helon, ⁸his host as numbered being fifty-seven thousand four hundred. ⁹The whole number of the camp of Judah, by their companies, is a hundred and eighty-six thousand four hundred. They shall set out first on the march.

¹⁰"On the south side shall be the standard of the camp of Reuben by their companies, the leader of the people of Reuben being Elizur the son of Shedeur, ¹¹his host as numbered being forty-six thousand five hundred. ¹²And those to encamp next to him shall be the tribe of Simeon, the leader of the people of Simeon being Shelumi-el the son of Zurishaddai, ¹³his host as numbered being fifty-nine thousand three hundred. ¹⁴Then the tribe of Gad, the leader of the people of Gad being Eliasaph the son of Reuel, ¹⁵his host as numbered being forty-five thousand six hundred and fifty. ¹⁶The whole number of the camp of Reuben, by their companies, is a hundred and fifty-one thousand four hundred and fifty. They shall set out second.

¹⁷"Then the tent of meeting shall set out, with the camp of the Levites in the midst of the camps; as they encamp, so shall they set out, each in position, standard by standard.

¹⁸"On the west side shall be the standard of the camp of Ephraim by their companies, the leader of the people of Ephraim being Elishama the son of Ammihud, ¹⁹his host as numbered being forty thousand five hundred. ²⁰And next to him shall be the tribe of Manasseh, the leader of the people of Manasseh being Gamaliel the son of Pedahzur, ²¹his host as numbered being thirty-two thousand two hundred. ²²Then the tribe of Benjamin, the leader of the people of Benjamin being Abidan

the son of Gideoni, [23]his host as numbered being thirty-five thousand four hundred. [24]The whole number of the camp of Ephraim, by their companies, is a hundred and eight thousand one hundred. They shall set out third on the march.

[25]"On the north side shall be the standard of the camp of Dan by their companies, the leader of the people of Dan being Ahiezer the son of Ammishaddai, [26]his host as numbered being sixty-two thousand seven hundred. [27]And those to encamp next to him shall be the tribe of Asher, the leader of the people of Asher being Pagiel the son of Ochran, [28]his host as numbered being forty-one thousand five hundred. [29]Then the tribe of Naphtali, the leader of the people of Naphtali being Ahira the son of Enan, [30]his host as numbered being fifty-three thousand four hundred. [31]The whole number of the camp of Dan is a hundred and fifty-seven thousand six hundred. They shall set out last, standard by standard."

[32]These are the people of Israel as numbered by their fathers' houses; all in the camps who were numbered by their companies were six hundred and three thousand five hundred. [33]But the Levites were not numbered among the people of Israel, as the Lord commanded Moses.

[34]Thus did the people of Israel. According to all that the Lord commanded Moses, so they encamped by their standard, and so they set out, every one in his family, according to his fathers' house.

(i)

Instructions are now given for the order of the camp when it is at rest. The twelve tribes are to camp in a square formation around the "tent of meeting", three to each side. The tribes therefore cover the compass points (vv. 3, 10, 18, 25). In 3:21–39 the picture is filled out further, with the sons of Levi and of Aaron surrounding the Tabernacle more immediately. They therefore stand between the Tabernacle and the tribes. The Lord's presence is not only the spiritual, but also the physical, centre of Israel. The east side is the most honoured, as it faces the rising sun in front of the sanctuary. With the physical positioning of the tribes, there also therefore comes their relative status, working from east to north.

Perhaps it is as well to put it into a diagram:

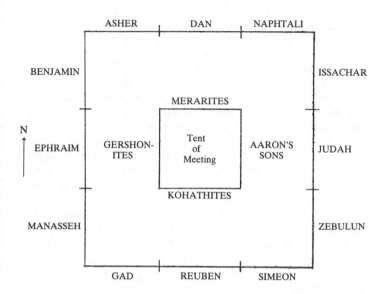

This pattern was accepted by Ezekiel for his plan for the court around the Temple in the New Age (Ezek. 40:47). Again it formed the basis of John's revelation in his vision of the New Jerusalem (Rev. 21:16). God's principles and plans remain, though they may need to be adapted for specific purposes or situations. In the realm of the revelations of God regarding moral matters, we see the affirmation of this by Jesus when he insists that "not an iota, not a dot, will pass from the law until all is accomplished" (Matt. 5:18)

(ii)

Each tribe has to camp around the "ensigns" of their ancestors. The Rabbis have a tradition that each had also a piece of cloth identifying the tribal leader under whom all the various clan chiefs were united, the colours of which were the same as their particular stones in the High Priest's breastplate (Exod. 28:21). The RSV also has them camped "each by his own standard", i.e. flag. The Hebrew term is usually rendered this way, but a translation of "company" instead of "standard" is also possible; there is a similar term meaning a "large group of men". The Greek and Syriac versions early on saw this possibility also, and translated accordingly.

The actual word is used in the sense of "army division" on a papyrus found at the Jewish colony at Elephantine in Egypt (5th century B.C.). It is used in the same sense in the War scroll found at Qumran (2nd century B.C.). At Qumran such a "division" seems to contain about 1,000 men, but in the colony many fewer are involved. If the word is translated as such here in vv. 2, 3, 10, 17, 18, 25, 31, 34, then the result makes excellent sense.

The impression given then is that the Lord is preparing his people for a battle. The need is for discipline, strategy, method, so that the Lord's goal may be realized. The Church, God's Israel, needs the same. How can we obey Christ's commands to "heal the sick, raise the dead, . . . cast out demons" (Matt. 10:8) without them? To enter into the spiritual realm as one of God's priests, one of his soldiers, without them is to be immature and a liability.

(iii)

There were four main tribal groups, each later associated with a symbol: Judah, represented in Jewish tradition by a lion (see Gen. 49:9); Reuben, represented by a human face; Ephraim, represented by an ox; Dan, represented by an eagle. The lion was a symbol of ferocious power and irresistibility in the ancient East; the ox one of strength and reliability and fertility; the eagle one of nobility and swift, clean movement.

These traditions arose from the vision of Ezekiel's "four living creatures" (Ezek. 1:4-14, especially v. 10), and were carried on in mystical circles in Judaism. They are to be seen in John's vision of the "four living creatures" around Christ's throne (Rev. 4:6-8). By the middle of the second century A.D. there was a

Christian tradition which represented the Gospels in this fashion too: Matthew, by the face of a man; Mark, by a lion; Luke, by an ox; John, by an eagle.

So the tribes are mustered in their divisions, around the Tabernacle, and the scene is set. At the close of the chapter the text states again that the people did as God commanded them. This is in striking contrast to much of the rest of the pilgrimage. We shall see ourselves too in the changing fortunes of this people, and in their fickle attitude towards God and his leading.

AARON'S SONS—THE PRIESTS

Numbers 3:1–4

[1]These are the generations of Aaron and Moses at the time when the Lord spoke with Moses on Mount Sinai. [2]These are the names of the sons of Aaron: Nadab the first-born, and Abihu, Eleazar, and Ithamar; [3]these are the names of the sons of Aaron, the anointed priests, whom he ordained to minister in the priest's office. [4]But Nadab and Abihu died before the Lord when they offered unholy fire before the Lord in the wilderness of Sinai; and they had no children. So Eleazar and Ithamar served as priests in the lifetime of Aaron their father.

(i)

"These are the generations of . . ." Here we have a phrase which is typical of priestly circles in Israel. In this section Aaron comes before Moses, since the priests are responsible for its transmission, and since Aaron was the High Priest. There are ten such phrases in the Pentateuch: Gen. 5:1; 6:9; 10:1; 11:10; 11:27; 25:12; 25:19; 36:1; 37:2; and this one, Num. 3:1. For many modern readers they introduce tables of "dull facts", but for the purpose of establishing and rooting in human history the saving purposes of God, they are important. They show God choosing and planning and having his way with his people.

Aaron's four sons are now named (see also Exod. 6:23; Lev.

10:1ff.) and given tasks, having been specially anointed for those tasks. Israel's priesthood was seen until the destruction of the Temple as absolutely fundamental to Israel's spiritual life. More will be discovered later about the office of priest, but it is helpful to note in outline here what happened to Aaron's line. There are several stages.

(a) *In the earliest period* there were cases of non-priests offering sacrifices, e.g. Cain and Abel (Gen. 4:4), Noah (Gen. 8:20), Abraham (Gen. 12:7–8). There are references to foreign priests, e.g. Melchizedek (Gen. 14:18), Jethro (Exod. 2:16; 3:1; 18:1). But there is also a passage suggesting a Levite was preferred (Judg. 17:5–13).

(b) *In early monarchy times* Zadok, who belonged to Aaron's line, emerged (2 Sam. 8:17; 15:24–29) as the chief priest in the new kingdom (1 Kings 2:35). Yet at the same time the king could act as priest on occasion, e.g. David in 2 Sam. 6:12–19, and Solomon in 1 Kings 8:62. Note, however, that Saul is rebuked for doing the same thing (1 Sam. 13:8–14).

(c) *In King Josiah's reign* there was a great reform (2 Kings 23:1–25), and sacrificing was limited to priests, and then only at Jerusalem. The Levites, however, are counted among the priests. This is the situation reflected in the book of Deuteronomy (see 10:8; 18:1; 21:5; 33:8).

(d) *By Ezekiel's time* things had again changed. He had a vision of how things in the future should be, and the priesthood was to be restricted to those descended from Aaron. The Levites were seen as apostates (Ezek. 44:9–14) and therefore were to perform only menial tasks. Only Zadokite priests of Jerusalem who stayed faithful could offer sacrifices (Ezek. 44:15–16).

(e) *After the Exile* it was not possible to arrange things quite according to Ezekiel's vision. A distinction was made between priests and Levites upon the return to the land (Ezra 2:36–42; Neh. 7:39–43), but though they did not offer sacrifice, the Levites acted as singers and gatekeepers, a class above the Temple servants. It is a situation something like this final one, obviously regarded as "ideal", that has been read back into the book of Numbers.

(ii)

Aaron's sons are here said to be "ordained" into their ministries. The expression is literally to *fill one's hand,* i.e. to give in trust into someone's hand some office or responsibility. This is how God works with his people, by trusting them to trust him and serve him. The two elder sons die tragically (see Lev. 10:1–3 for the story), and so the younger brothers provide the only legitimate line of descent. Both branches of the family were still functioning in King David's time (1 Chron. 24:1–4), though it was then that Eleazar's branch (Zadok belonged to this) began to have pre-eminence.

They are also "anointed" by God. God commonly anoints people in the Old and New Testaments for tasks and offices. It is always to be a servant, never to be a someone special to be served. If these people neglect their tasks or abuse their offices or their authority then God deals severely with them (e.g. Hos. 5:8–10; 9:7–9; 1 Kings 21:17–19), as he does with any who presume to do the task or fulfil the office without God's anointing. Work for God cannot be begun without his permission, even more, without his anointing. The root of this essential term means "to smear" with oil or ointment or the like. The custom was to pour oil on the head of someone set apart for a particular office. We see it done e.g. over King Saul (1 Sam. 10:1); King David (1 Sam. 16:12f.); King Jehu (1 Kings 19:16); the prophet Elisha(1 Kings 19:16); the prophet in Isa. 61:1; Aaron and his priestly sons (here; Exod. 28:41).

The Hebrew title *Messiah* derives from this term, meaning "the anointed one". It is used of the Persian King Cyrus in Isa. 45:1 who, probably beyond his knowledge, was chosen by the Lord to carry out the great ministry to Israel of letting them return to Zion. However, in time it became a unique term, "*the* Anointed One", for God's chosen Redeemer and Restorer of Israel. He would be the ideal King that Israel had never had, the ideal sovereign. Orthodox Judaism still awaits his coming, as expressed in the twelfth of the thirteen articles in its "creed": *I declare faith with complete trust in the coming of the Messiah— though he may tarry, nevertheless, I do daily wait for him to come* (Standard Siddur Prayer Book).

The Greek term for Messiah is *Christos,* which becomes the New Testament word for this person. Those who know Jesus of Nazareth to be this anointed one therefore take their name from the term. In other words, to follow Christ is to be a Christ-ian. He is the Prophet, the Priest, the King. And even he came to serve, not to be served, to give his life as a ransom. In so doing, he fulfilled his mission to serve God: "I glorified thee on earth, having accomplished the work which thou gavest me to do . . . and the word which you hear is not mine but the Father's who sent me . . . If you keep my commandments, you will abide in my love, just as I have kept my Father's commandments and abide in his love" (John 17:4; 14:24; 15:10).

It is only by a life of active service; only by asking for the grace to see God's plan for the world around us, and by asking to be allowed to "join in"; only by sacrificial loving care to each other, that we can begin to understand Jesus. In imitating him we become like him, like the priests, set apart from the rest to serve the rest.

LEVI'S SONS—THE SERVANTS

Numbers 3:5–39

[5]And the Lord said to Moses, [6]"Bring the tribe of Levi near, and set them before Aaron the priest, that they may minister to him. [7]They shall perform duties for him and for the whole congregation before the tent of meeting, as they minister at the tabernacle; [8]they shall have charge of all the furnishings of the tent of meeting, and attend to the duties for the people of Israel as they minister at the tabernacle. [9]And you shall give the Levites to Aaron and his sons; they are wholly given to him from among the people of Israel. [10]And you shall appoint Aaron and his sons, and they shall attend to their priesthood; but if any one else comes near, he shall be put to death."

[11]And the Lord said to Moses, [12]"Behold, I have taken the Levites from among the people of Israel instead of every first-born that opens the womb among the people of Israel. The Levites shall be mine, [13]for all the first-born are mine; on the day that I slew all the first-born in the land of Egypt, I consecrated for my own all the first-born in Israel, both of man and of beast; they shall be mine: I am the Lord."

[14] And the Lord said to Moses in the wilderness of Sinai, [15] "Number the sons of Levi, by fathers' houses and by families; every male from a month old and upwards you shall number." [16] So Moses numbered them according to the word of the Lord, as he was commanded. [17] And these were the sons of Levi by their names: Gershon and Kohath and Merari. [18] And these are the names of the sons of Gershon by their families: Libni and Shime-i. [19] And the sons of Kohath by their families: Amram, Izhar, Hebron, and Uzziel. [20] And the sons of Merari by their families: Mahli and Mushi. These are the families of the Levites, by their fathers' houses.

[21] Of Gershon were the family of the Libnites and the family of the Shimeites; these were the families of the Gershonites. [22] Their number according to the number of all the males from a month old and upward was seven thousand five hundred. [23] The families of the Gershonites were to encamp behind the tabernacle on the west, [24] with Eliasaph, the son of Lael as head of the fathers' house of the Gershonites. [25] And the charge of the sons of Gershon in the tent of meeting was to be the tabernacle, the tent with its covering, the screen for the door of the tent of meeting, [26] the hangings of the court, the screen for the door of the court which is around the tabernacle and the altar, and its cords; all the service pertaining to these.

[27] Of Kohath were the family of the Amramites, and the family of the Izharites, and the family of the Hebronites, and the family of the Uzzielites; these are the families of the Kohathites. [28] According to the number of all the males, from a month old and upward, there were eight thousand six hundred, attending to the duties of the sanctuary. [29] The families of the sons of Kohath were to encamp on the south side of the tabernacle, [30] with Elizaphan the son of Uzziel as head of the fathers' house of the families of the Kohathites. [31] And their charge was to be the ark, the table, the lampstand, the altars, the vessels of the sanctuary with which the priests minister, and the screen; all the service pertaining to these. [32] And Eleazar the son of Aaron the priest was to be chief over the leaders of the Levites, and to have oversight of those who had charge of the sanctuary.

[33] Of Merari were the family of the Mahlites and the family of the Mushites: these are the families of Merari. [34] Their number according to the number of all the males from a month old and upward was six thousand two hundred. [35] And the head of the fathers' house of the families of Merari was Zuriel the son of Abihail; they were to encamp on the north side of the tabernacle. [36] And the appointed charge of the

sons of Merari was to be the frames of the tabernacle, the bars, the pillars, the bases, and all their accessories; all the service pertaining to these; [37]also the pillars of the court round about, with their bases and pegs and cords.

[38]And those to encamp before the tabernacle on the east, before the tent of meeting toward the sunrise, were Moses and Aaron and his sons, having charge of the rites within the sanctuary, whatever had to be done for the people of Israel; and any one else who came near was to be put to death. [39]All who were numbered of the Levites, whom Moses and Aaron numbered at the commandment of the Lord, by families, all the males from a month old and upwards, were twenty-two thousand.

(i)

In this section the focus of attention is again on the Levites, i.e. on the sanctuary and its functionaries. This was a tribe set apart by God to serve him in the sanctuary, and Numbers is a priestly work, which we can see from the stress throughout the book on priestly concerns and interpretations. The Levites are brought physically to the very presence of the Lord (v. 6), symbolic of the fact that the Lord has asked the other tribes to let go of them to have this special ministry, without pressure on them to serve militarily or agriculturally or as shepherds, etc. They were totally dedicated to their tasks, and this is expressed in v. 9, where the RSV has it that they were "wholly given" to God. The Hebrew is literally "given given", i.e. the verb is used twice for emphasis. Because of this distinct service, they receive a distinct census from the rest of Israel.

It must be noted that v. 9 shows that the Levites were subordinate to Aaron's priestly family. In 18:2 it is said to Aaron by God that he must bring forward the Levites "that they may join you", i.e. that they may link with you in service to you. This is confirmation of the meaning of the term from the root "to join". Since Aaron's family were anointed and appointed by God, to serve them was not idolatry, but rather a case of ministering to the ministers—a godly and much-needed ministry. How congregations and fellowships need to learn that lesson today: to

constantly intercede for and support the elders and teachers and
pastors and prophets! And also how those called to full-time or
fuller-time ministry need to realize *their* need for ministry: to be
humble enough to ask for prayer and support!

(ii)

Israel is called by God into a special relationship with him; to
worship and obey him and carry his name to all other nations.
This relationship is not theirs by right (see especially Deut.
7:6–11), but by the grace of God. There are conditions to be met,
commands to be obeyed, promises to be trusted, if the benefits of
that grace are to be experienced and sealed. The language of
"rights" is not appropriate for Israel's calling—all is of grace from
the Lord who chose her. So the relationship is, in short, a covenant one. Not a contract, with double initiative and mutual
rights, but a covenant, with a unilateral claim by the Lord on
Israel's life and destiny.

So at the fundamental level the whole people are to be channels
of God's special grace to the world. Israel, and all her people, is a
sacrament in human history of God's presence. They are all holy
and priests in this sense. As God says through Moses: "Now,
therefore, if you will obey my voice and keep my covenant, you
shall be my own possession among all peoples; for all the earth is
mine, and you shall be to me a kingdom of priests and a holy
nation" (Exod. 19:5–6). Much later on this is re-presented as
God's plan for Israel after the second Exodus, i.e. the return from
Exile in Babylon: "you shall be called the priests of the Lord, men
shall speak of you as the ministers of our God" (Isa. 61:6).

On a second level, however, there is a priesthood not of all of
Israel, but of those called out by God to minister to all Israel. This
is a representative office, never ordained by God to selfishly
monopolize or control knowledge of or access to him. The Levites are not holy in themselves. They are "consecrated" by God,
which is to say, according to the literal meaning of this crucial
Hebrew term, "separated" or "set apart" for special use. In much
the same way, in the celebration of the Lord's Supper, the cele-
brant sets apart the common bread and wine from all common use

to their special use in that wonderful mystery. No one save God himself has innate holiness. Israel is the "Holy Land" to modern pilgrims, not because there is something special about its soil or air or water, but because God chose it as the Promised Land.

MINISTERS AND CARETAKERS

Numbers 3:5–39 (cont'd)

(iii)

Within this priesthood, this ordained priesthood, there was a three-fold hierarchy: (a) *Levites*, who were servants at the sanctuary; (b) *Priests*, consecrated specifically to minister to the people; and (c) *High Priest*, in whom the separate character and dedication of the priesthood was gathered up. He represented the priesthood of all the Israelites in that he wore a symbolic breastplate with twelve precious and semi-precious stones to represent the twelve tribes (Exod. 28:15ff.). He also represented the Levites and priests in that only he could enter the "Holy of Holies", i.e. the holiest room of the Temple, and that only once per year, to make atonement sacrifices for the nation's sinful nature (Lev. 16). See *Additional Note* 2.

The priests, then, represented the people before God, by offering their sacrifices and leading them in prayer; and they represented God before the people, by guarding his revelations and traditions and administering justice (see, e.g., Deut. 17:8–9). This is the two-fold calling.

We can therefore now understand the excitement of the writer inspired to write the letter in the New Testament to the "Hebrews", when he discovered the depth of Jesus' ministry in the whole plan of God. Jesus is the True Priest, the great High Priest of our faith. He alone can totally represent God before us, and interpret his ways for us since he "bears the very stamp" of God's nature (Heb. 1:3; see also Col. 1:19, "in him all the fulness of God was pleased to dwell"). And what is incomparably more, he can totally represent us before God and express our needs to him, since with respect to human nature "he himself likewise

partook of the same nature . . . made like his brethren in every respect" (Heb. 9:11–28). He has made atonement for us "once for all" (Heb. 9:12). In short, he is the Mediator of a new covenant relationship, bringing us to a new and full experience of the presence of God (Heb. 10:19–25).

At one point, Paul speaks of his ministry to and for Jesus as a "priestly service" (Rom. 15:16), and the teaching of the New Testament is that we are all God's Israel, priests and holy living sacraments of his grace: "you are a chosen race, a royal priesthood, a holy nation, God's own people" (1 Pet. 2:9); see also Rev. 1:6; 5:10; 20:6. Again and again we must notice how much of the depth and beauty of God's Word we let go by unheeded when we do not appreciate, even in part, the Jewishness of Jesus and his early followers.

(iv)

In vv. 11–13 the Levites are consecrated to represent the first-born males of Israel in commemoration of the miracle and demonstration of God's claim on his people when he slew the Egyptian first-born, but spared the Israelites by passing over their homes (Exod. 12:1–13). As a constant and faithful sign of God's claim and of Israel's gratitude the first-born sons and livestock were specially dedicated to the Lord from that time on (Exod. 22:29–30; 34:19–20). For this, see the next section. Here the claim is further made by God on the Levites as substitutes for Israel in this actual dedication. Those whom God has delivered he has consecrated. What an eternal truth! Those delivered by the Lord belong to the Lord.

So the census of the Levites is carried out, and the spiritual potential is assessed. Verse 15 states that they were numbered from the age of one month, not from twenty years as the other tribes. Why? Partly because to know if a man is fit and "able to go forth to war" (1:3) it is necessary to see the mature specimen, whereas to serve the Lord in the sanctuary needs no such physical strength. Partly because it is best to begin to be nurtured and disciplined and trained for service of the Lord in spiritual matters from the youngest age. There is a word to parents here.

Subdivisions are even made within the tribe according to the three sons of Levi: Gershon, Kohath, Merari. The Gershonites, on the west of the Tabernacle (see on 2:1-34), are in charge of coverings and curtains and the like. The Merarites, on the north of the Tabernacle, are responsible for the frames, bases, etc. The Kohathites, to the south of the Tabernacle, take care of the most sacred furniture—the ark, the table, the lampstand, the altars, the various vessels, the separation screen from the Holy of Holies—all too holy for any but consecrated hands to touch (4:15; 7:9). Presumably the numbers should be revised in accordance with the table given in the commentary to 1:20-46, which would yield, counting only the hundreds, a total of 1,300. If the Greek translation is followed in v. 28 (300 instead of 600), the total becomes 1,000 which, since it includes all males from babyhood, is not greatly different from the numbers of the other tribes.

ISRAEL'S SONS—THE FIRST-BORN

Numbers 3:40-51

40 And the Lord said to Moses, "Number all the first-born males of the people of Israel, from a month old and upward, taking their number by names. 41 And you shall take the Levites for me—I am the Lord—instead of all the first-born among the people of Israel, and the cattle of the Levites instead of all the firstlings among the cattle of the people of Israel." 42 So Moses numbered all the first-born among the people of Israel, as the Lord commanded him. 43 And all the first-born males, according to the number of names, from a month old and upward as numbered were twenty-two thousand two hundred and seventy-three.

44 And the Lord said to Moses, 45 "Take the Levites instead of all the first-born among the people of Israel, and the cattle of the Levites instead of their cattle; and the Levites shall be mine: I am the Lord. 46 And for the redemption of the two hundred and seventy-three of the first-born of the people of Israel, over and above the number of the male Levites, 47 you shall take five shekels apiece; reckoning by the shekel of the sanctuary, the shekel of twenty gerahs, you shall take

them, [48]and give the money by which the excess number of them is redeemed to Aaron and his sons." [49]So Moses took the redemption money from those who were over and above those redeemed by the Levites; [50]from the first-born of the people of Israel he took the money, one thousand three hundred and sixty-five shekels, reckoned by the shekel of the sanctuary; [51]and Moses gave the redemption money to Aaron and his sons, according to the word of the Lord, as the Lord commanded Moses.

(i)

At the command of the Lord, Moses proceeds to count the first-born male children in Israel's camp. These are the ones regarded symbolically as representing the actual children spared by the Lord in Egypt, when the angel of the Lord passed over the houses of the people of the Lord as he slew the Egyptian first-born. These physical first-born were therefore in a special relationship with the Lord. Even before the "passing through" of the Red Sea, that singular act of Israel's redemption, these first-born could say (assuming they could speak) that they had been redeemed from the general death in Egypt at the "passing over" of the angel. This shows that the Lord had been seen to be at work on behalf of his people, had been experienced as a Redeemer, before they set out on their pilgrimage. By the time we see God doing great things for us, he has already been at work. By the time we see him working wonders in the lives of other people, he has been active for a long time.

Part of the Israelite genius for seeing how God works with his people is shown here. In the same way that fathers were told to say to their sons that they celebrated the Feast of Passover because the Lord had brought *them* out of Egypt, whether all had been *physically* present or not (Exod. 13:14ff.); in the same way that to this day first-born Jewish sons fast on the evening of the day of the Passover Feast, to show their distinction from the others since they were redeemed by the Lord, and still are taught to regard the Lord's redemption as being for them personally; so the first-born are regarded here as being the Lord's even though not all by any means had actually been in Egypt physically.

Spiritually and morally they had. The Negro spiritual declares a similar belief when it asks: "Were you there when they crucified my Lord?" Physically no, but spiritually and morally yes!

(ii)

The number of the male first-born comes to the same total as the Levites, plus 273 extra. It may seem strange to some readers to find cattle referred to. But cattle meant wealth, prosperity, security. So they were very important. They are also mentioned in the narrative of the Exodus: "At midnight the Lord smote all the first-born in the land of Egypt, from the first-born of Pharaoh who sat on his throne to the first-born of the captive who was in the dungeon, and all the first-born of the cattle" (Exod. 12:29; see also 13:15). Even the cattle, then, are to be seen as an integral part of the Lord's caring concern for Israel.

The Levites were to be substituted in service and dedication to the Lord for the first-born. But what of the extra 273? It was not possible to make them Levites, therefore a system of compensation was devised. Instead of being substituted for by a Levite, they could be substituted for by a sum of money given for the care of the sanctuary. This was reckoned as five shekels apiece, giving 1,365 shekels.

The root meaning of this monetary term is "to weigh", and the shekel was at first a weight, then a measure of value or worth, and only later a coin in our sense. There were various standards and practices in its use. Here it is the "shekel of the sanctuary" as opposed to the "weights current among the merchants" (Gen. 23:16). Examples of shekels have been discovered by archaeologists and there are no two of exactly the same weight. By Jesus' time there was a silver coin called a shekel weighing about half an ounce. The "gerah" was worth one twentieth of such a shekel.

This sum of five shekels is called "redemption money", from a term borrowed from commercial law meaning "to ransom", i.e. to free something which has fallen under the control of someone else. This term will be further examined in 5:5–10. This imagery immediately takes us to the New Testament. We think of the One who was substituted for us in death that we might be delivered from the control of those forces fighting against God, and against his people. Two things are reversed though. Firstly, *he* is the first-born, indeed the only begotten, Son of God, substituted for us. Secondly, he was not substituted for us after our redemption to show God's claim on us, but was substituted *as* our redemption, coming out of God's claim on us. So he is our righteousness before God, and God sees us in and through Jesus, as we see God in and through Jesus (1 Cor. 1:30; 2 Cor. 5:21). The image finds its most beautiful expression in a passage that speaks of how we are freed by payment from the control of an enemy, but freed by one whose claim on us is more radical and total: "You are not your own; you were bought with a price" (1 Cor. 6:19–20).

THE LEVITICAL WORK-FORCE

Numbers 4:1–49

[1]The Lord said to Moses and Aaron, [2]"Take a census of the sons of Kohath from among the sons of Levi, by their families and their fathers' houses, [3]from thirty years old up to fifty years old, all who can enter the service, to do the work in the tent of meeting. [4]This is the service of the sons of Kohath in the tent of meeting: the most holy things. [5]When the camp is to set out, Aaron and his sons shall go in and take down the veil of the screen, and cover the ark of the testimony with it; [6]then they shall put on it a covering of goatskin, and spread over that a cloth all of blue, and shall put in its poles. [7]And over the table of the bread of the Presence they shall spread a cloth of blue, and put upon it the plates, the dishes for incense, the bowls, and the flagons for the drink offering; the continual bread also shall be on it; [8]then they shall spread over them a cloth of scarlet, and cover the same with a covering of goatskin, and shall put in its poles. [9]And they shall take a cloth of blue, and cover the lampstand for the light, with its lamps, its snuffers, its trays, and all the vessels for oil with which it is supplied: [10]and they shall put it with all its utensils in a covering of goatskin and put it upon the carrying frame. [11]And over the golden altar they shall spread a cloth of blue, and cover it with a covering of goatskin, and shall put in its poles; [12]and they shall take all the vessels of the service which are used in the sanctuary, and put them in a cloth of blue, and cover them with a covering of goatskin, and put them on the carrying

frame. [13] And they shall take away the ashes from the altar, and spread a purple cloth over it; [14] and they shall put on it all the utensils of the altar, which are used for the service there, the firepans, the forks, the shovels, and the basins, all the utensils of the altar; and they shall spread upon it a covering of goatskin, and shall put in its poles. [15] And when Aaron and his sons have finished covering the sanctuary and all the furnishings of the sanctuary, as the camp sets out, after that the sons of Kohath shall come to carry these, but they must not touch the holy things, lest they die. These are the things of the tent of meeting which the sons of Kohath are to carry.

[16] "And Eleazar the son of Aaron the priest shall have charge of the oil for the light, the fragrant incense, the continual cereal offering, and the anointing oil, with the oversight of all the tabernacle and all that is in it, of the sanctuary and its vessels."

[17] The Lord said to Moses and Aaron, [18] "Let not the tribe of the families of the Kohathites be destroyed from among the Levites; [19] but deal thus with them, that they may live and not die when they come near to the most holy things: Aaron and his sons shall go in and appoint them each to his task and to his burden, [20] but they shall not go in to look upon the holy things even for a moment, lest they die."

[21] The Lord said to Moses, [22] "Take a census of the sons of Gershon also, by their families and their fathers' houses; [23] from thirty years old up to fifty years old, you shall number them, all who can enter for service, to do the work in the tent of meeting. [24] This is the service of the families of the Gershonites, in serving and bearing burdens: [25] they shall carry the curtains of the tabernacle, and the tent of meeting with its covering of goatskin that is on top of it, and the screen for the door of the tent of meeting, [26] and the hangings of the court, and the screen for the entrance of the gate of the court which is around the tabernacle and the altar, and their cords, and all the equipment for their service; and they shall do all that needs to be done with regard to them. [27] All the service of the sons of the Gershonites shall be at the command of Aaron and his sons, in all that they are to carry, and in all that they have to do; and you shall assign to their charge all that they are to carry. [28] This is the service of the families of the sons of the Gershonites in the tent of meeting, and their work is to be under the oversight of Ithamar the son of Aaron the priest.

[29] "As for the sons of Merari, you shall number them by their families and their fathers' houses; [30] from thirty years old up to fifty years old, you shall number them, every one that can enter the service,

to do the work of the tent of meeting. ³¹And this is what they are charged to carry, as the whole of their service in the tent of meeting: the frames of the tabernacle, with its bars, pillars and bases, ³²and the pillars of the court round about with their bases, pegs, and cords, with all their equipment and all their accessories; and you shall assign by name the objects which they are required to carry. ³³This is the service of the families of the sons of Merari, the whole of their service in the tent of meeting, under the hand of Ithamar the son of Aaron the priest."

³⁴And Moses and Aaron and the leaders of the congregation numbered the sons of the Kohathites, by their families and their fathers' houses, ³⁵from thirty years old up to fifty years old, every one that could enter the service, for work in the tent of meeting; ³⁶and their number by families was two thousand seven hundred and fifty. ³⁷This was the number of the families of the Kohathites, all who served in the tent of meeting, whom Moses and Aaron numbered according to the commandment of the Lord by Moses.

³⁸The number of the sons of Gershon, by their families and their fathers' houses, ³⁹from thirty years old up to fifty years old, every one that could enter the service for work in the tent of meeting—⁴⁰their number by their families and their fathers' houses was two thousand six hundred and thirty. ⁴¹This was the number of the families of the sons of Gershon, all who served in the tent of meeting, whom Moses and Aaron numbered according to the commandment of the Lord.

⁴²The number of the families of the sons of Merari, by their families and their fathers' houses, ⁴³from thirty years old up to fifty years old, every one that could enter the service, for work in the tent of meeting—⁴⁴their number by families was three thousand two hundred. ⁴⁵These are those who were numbered of the families of the sons of Merari, whom Moses and Aaron numbered according to the commandment of the Lord by Moses.

⁴⁶All those who were numbered by the Levites, whom Moses and Aaron and the leaders of Israel numbered, by their families and their fathers' houses, ⁴⁷from thirty years old up to fifty years old, every one that could enter to do the work of service and the work of bearing burdens in the tent of meeting, ⁴⁸those who were numbered of them were eight thousand five hundred and eighty. ⁴⁹According to the commandment of the Lord through Moses they were appointed, each to his task of serving or carrying; thus they were numbered by him, as the Lord commanded Moses.

(i)

Duties are now delegated to the Levitical work-force. The age range for full and active service is given as from thirty years to fifty years, a good spread of maturity and health and fitness. It must be remembered that during the journeying they were responsible for the dismantling, transporting, and re-assembling of the sanctuary and its furniture. In Num. 8:23ff. the range is from twenty-five years to fifty years, giving responsibility at an earlier stage to the young men. In later times still, perhaps reflecting the shortage of Levites able to carry out the work, the bottom age was lowered to twenty years (1 Chron. 23:24, 27; 2 Chron. 31:17; Ezra 3:8).

The term used for their active "service" is a very interesting one. It is used in other passages for other pursuits, e.g. military service (Num. 1:3; it is the word in modern Hebrew for army service too); hard labour (Job 7:1); severe hardship under foreign domination (Isa. 40:2). In short, it was hard work with terrible responsibility. Being a Levite or a priest was not seen as an easy option in life by God. Indeed, he expects more from his chosen servants than from others. The books of Amos and Hosea and early Isaiah are particularly harsh in condemnation of priests (and prophets) who neglect their holy calling and pander either to their own selfish interests or to the easy way of telling people only what they want to hear. It is a difficult and often lonely calling to be a servant of God.

In Ezek. 3:16–21; 33:1–9, the prophet is given the situation in a nutshell. If God's spokesmen are faithful, then the people will shoulder the awful responsibility of neglecting God's ways revealed to them; if, however, the spokesmen prove negligent, they themselves will shoulder that responsibility. Ministry to God's people; caring for them in his name; claiming his promises for them and proclaiming his commands to them; all this necessarily involves the servant of God in full commitment to those people. Costly involvement indeed! So the Levites are called by God to this "service". Discipline again comes through as a must for any pilgrimage. Paul writes similar words of advice and encouragement to Timothy that he "may wage the good warfare" in his ministry (1 Tim. 1:18).

THE WORK

Numbers 4:1–49 (*cont'd*)

(ii)

The most prestigious furniture is cared for by the Kohathites, as the text has it, "the most holy things". It is all wrapped in cloths of blue, perhaps symbolic of heaven (see Exod. 24:10). There is also a "covering of goatskin" for protection. But what was it exactly? The word is rare in Hebrew and was interpreted in several ways by the ancient translators and commentators. Some took it as a colour, but that is undoubtedly wrong; the traditions of the Rabbinic schools take it as referring to an animal, hence the AV "badgers' skins", the RV "sealskin" and the RSV "goatskin". There is a parallel Arabic term for a dolphin, so it may have been that rare skin. There is also a related Arabic term for a process of tanning, a process that would be known in Egypt, so it may refer to a processed leather. In fact the term only occurs again in Ezek. 16:10, where something grand is also being described, and there the RSV translates as "leather".

Why should this be important? Because whatever the material was, it was rare and splendid, and its rarity and splendour testify to the Israelites' love and reverence for the dwelling-place of God. Nothing less than the best should be offered to God by any who belong to him. A "woman of the city" came to Jesus and anointed his feet with her precious box of alabaster, giving all she could (Luke 7:36–50). To give all we can means to give everything we have. As Isaac Watts puts its:

> Were the whole realm of nature mine,
> That were an offering far too small;
> Love so amazing, so divine,
> Demands my soul, my life, my all.

(iii)

In the sanctuary there were different tables, one of which was the "table of the bread of the Presence". Literally it is the bread of "the face", i.e. the face of God, used symbolically of the fact that God is "face to face" with Israel, present with her. This bread is referred to as the "shewbread" in the AV, but the other term used in v. 7 is more helpful. See Lev. 24:5–9, where we are told that it was "continually" spread out on the table before the Lord. The adjective used in the Hebrew can mean "always" or "for ever". However, perhaps an even better translation of the Hebrew would be "regular", since in fact the High Priest changed the loaves each sabbath. They are the daily evidence of the people's devotion to the Lord. When they were changed, the "old loaves" were seen as "most holy", and the Talmud reveals that half of the bread was eaten by the outgoing priests, and half by those coming in to serve.

Other tables were for sacrifices and storage. Then in Mal. 1:12 comes the expression "the table of the Lord" for the table of the burnt offering, which was the sacrifice of the whole animal accompanying confession of sin and guilt. Here is the background to the New Testament concept of "the table of the Lord" that we find in 1 Cor. 10:21 for the table around which the sacrament of the Lord's Supper is celebrated. But this is not our table, our altar. It is not the Church's altar. It is God's altar, commemorating the offering of his Son. It is the Son's altar, commemorating his offering of himself (John 10:18). In short, it is the Lord's Table.

Another of the most sacred and most important pieces of furniture was the "lampstand", but discussion of this will be kept for the section 8:1–4.

When we are in danger of taking God's presence with us for granted, of taking our access to the Father for granted, of letting familiarity breed contempt, we must remember that he is not only our Father but also a Holy God. This is said so clearly for us in v. 20, where even to *see* the "holy things" brings death. The Hebrew of the phrase "even for a moment" is very colourful, meaning "at a swallowing": no one may see the holy things even for as long as it would take for a sincere gulp in awe and wonder. To be close enough to God's presence as mediated through his sanctuary to be awestruck, is to be too close for comfort. This follows in the

Hebrew tradition that man cannot come into the presence of God or, as it is put literally, see his face and live (Exod. 33:20).

God's presence with us in Jesus is much more intimate than through any sanctuary ritual. As Paul says: "For it is the God who said, 'Let light shine out of darkness', who has shone in our hearts to give light of the knowledge of the glory of God in the face of Christ" (2 Cor. 4:6). We have nothing to fear provided we have repented and surrendered ourselves totally to God in Christ—yet we do well to remember his holiness. We are also advised in the New Testament to "offer to God acceptable worship, with reverance and awe; for our God is a consuming fire" (Heb. 12:28–29).

(iv)

In vv. 21–28 the Gershonites are given their tasks, which are less grand, and in vv. 29–33 the Merarites are accorded even humbler tasks and responsibilities. Yet God is insistent that they also must be able and diligent (vv. 23, 30), and that their tasks are as necessary as those of the Kohathites. If one part of the sanctuary is defiled or damaged, the sanctuary is defiled or damaged. For God's people to be all they are called to be, they must work as a family, and as a team. Each is as necessary and therefore as important as the other. Paul gives the message very clearly in 1 Cor. 12:12–31. We are "the body of Christ and individually members of it . . . the eye cannot say to the hand, 'I have no need of you' . . .".

SEPARATE THE UNCLEAN!

Numbers 5:1–4

[1]The Lord said to Moses, [2]"Command the people of Israel that they put out of the camp every leper, and every one having a discharge, and every one that is unclean through contact with the dead; [3]you shall put out both male and female, putting them outside the camp, that they may not defile their camp, in the midst of which I dwell." [4]And the people of Israel did so, and drove them outside the camp; as the Lord said to Moses, so the people of Israel did.

(i)

The presence of the Tabernacle and the ark in the camp stands for the very presence of the Lord in the camp. So he is there in their centre. This makes the camp holy ground, and unclean, impure, unworthy people and things are to be removed as being incompatible with this. These include people with a "discharge", i.e. any form of haemorrhageing or leakage from the sexual organs, including menstruation discharge, and they include people who have been in contact with a dead person. For the details of those "offences" see Lev. 13; Lev. 15; Num. 19. Menstruant women are still shunned by religious men in the East. This taboo probably arises from the fact that the very life of a living creature is seen to reside in the blood (e.g. Lev. 17:14: "For the life of every creature is the blood of it"), and at such times women are discharging blood. The author has walked with strictly religious men in Jerusalem who cross to the other side of the street rather than pass close to a young woman who, for all they know, may be menstruant. Early on, special ritual baths were created for women to cleanse themselves during this time. A mediaeval Jewish philosopher, Maimonides, tells us that it was common in his day for menstruant women to be kept in separate rooms from their families. But the taboo is based on a reverence for life. As is the shunning of discharges from the sexual organs.

All manner of superstitions grew up in antiquity around the subject of death, and especially regarding contact with the dead. They range from general distaste to a belief that the evil spirits of death (and they were always evil) lurked nearby to corpses ready to capture those in range. Leprosy was always regarded as the most contagious and deadly of diseases. All three forms of uncleanness given here were seen as contagious, i.e. contact with someone who had become unclean made one as unclean oneself as contact with an unclean object. See Lev. 13:45f.; 15:4ff.; Num. 19:22. For the actual war camps there was even greater strictness (Deut. 20:1–9; 23:10–15; 1 Sam. 21:1ff.; 2 Sam. 11:11ff.) The men who formulated these rules were not particularly harsh, nor did they wield authority arbitrarily, but were concerned to preserve at all costs the ceremonial purity of the people.

Indeed, for the faith of the Old Testament, questions of clean or unclean were of fundamental importance. To be clean, especially with regard to the sanctuary and its ceremonials, was seen as an integral part of Israel's response in worship and service to her Holy God. It is summed up well in Lev. 15:31, "Thus you shall keep the people of Israel separate from their uncleanness, lest they die in their uncleanness by defiling my tabernacle that is in their midst." If God sees uncleanness when he looks at Israel, he will turn away from her (Ezek. 39:24).

Seen in a broader context, it can be stated in this way: Israel believed that, being God's chosen people, she had to reflect in her life and worship the very nature and character of the God whose she was. So this involved justice (Amos 5:21–24), covenant love (Hos. 4:1–2; 11:1–4) and holiness (Exod. 19:6; Deut. 14:21; Num. 15:40). This holiness was seen as inseparable from ritual cleanliness. The Rabbis had a saying which has come down to the modern Western world via the preaching of John Wesley and Matthew Henry, "Cleanliness is next to godliness", which catches this suggestion of inseparability.

(ii)

In the New Testament there is the revelation that there will be no uncleanness in heaven (Rev. 21:27). By Jesus' day the belief was well developed that unclean people or situations were, if not created by the powers of darkness, at least being used by them. This lies behind the calling of demons "unclean spirits" (e.g. Matt. 10:1) in the Gospels. Heb. 10:21–22 shows the belief that Jesus' crucifixion was a cleansing sacrifice for mankind. So the stress on cleanliness before God is still there. It is too easy to criticize it and say it is all negative—cleanliness *from* impurity, *from* contamination. But it must be seen positively to understand the Biblical emphasis. It was a movement, a decision *for* holiness, *for* closeness with God, *for* adopting his standards and ways. What is fascinating is that not only what was unclean was un-touchable (as in the present passage), but also that what was holy was untouchable (e.g. Num. 3:10, 38; 2 Sam. 6:6–9). The people of the Bible lived between two extremes. Or to put it better, they lived in the interplay between two dimensions, the wholly other dimension of God's Spirit and the utterly profane dimension of human selfishness and achievement. They were always—and as the book of Numbers will show, quite painfully so—human, yet they were claimed by God to be his people witnessing to him and his glory among the nations.

None of us lives as God wants us to. We cannot get fully past our selfishness to surrender totally to God. We all live in that interplay, that tension between God's ways and the world's ways, between God's way and our way. And Jesus exposes us to ourselves constantly in this matter. He even exposes that hypocrisy which can act in the right way but from the wrong attitude or motivation. It is not what comes to us, or what we get close to, that makes us clean or unclean, but what comes from our hearts, our desires and motives (Matt. 15:10–20). Just as he cleansed the disciples by his word, "You are already made clean by the word which I have spoken to you" (John 15:3), and symbolically by washing their feet (John 13:10), so he cleanses all of us, his Church, by water and the word (Eph. 5:25–26). Most important of all, we read in 1 John 1:7 that "the blood of Jesus his Son cleanses us from all sin".

COMPENSATIONS AND DUES

Numbers 5:5–10

⁵And the Lord said to Moses, ⁶"Say to the people of Israel, When a man or woman commits any of the sins that men commit by breaking faith with the Lord, and that person is guilty, ⁷he shall confess his sin which he has committed; and he shall make full restitution for his wrong, adding a fifth to it, and giving it to him to whom he did the wrong. ⁸But if the man has no kinsman to whom restitution may be made for the wrong, the restitution for wrong shall go to the Lord for the priest, in addition to the ram of atonement with which atonement is made for him. ⁹And every offering, all the holy things of the people of Israel, which they bring to the priest, shall be his; ¹⁰and every man's holy things shall be his; whatever any man gives to the priest shall be his."

(i)

After cheating someone, or slandering someone, or lusting after someone, the offending person has a few options open: to try to cover it up and go on unrepentant; to repent and confess to the sin; to go one further and not only confess but actually try to compensate for the wrong done or the character defamed. This act of compensation after repentance is called restitution. In Israel's law God demands the honesty of repentance from his people, and the sacrifice of restitution also. In fact, the person who has been wronged has not only to be reimbursed for what he lost, but also to be awarded a true compensation to the value of one fifth again of what he lost.

Such restitution, a disincentive to crime in itself, marks the Israelite community out from all others. What is more, it was so important that if for any reason it proved impossible to pay it back to the original person, it was to be paid back to that person's next of kin. If there were not even a next of kin to be found, the guilty person must still restore the payment plus the compensation, and in that case it went to God's representative, the priest.

God's demands, then, are seen to be radical and total. Israel was not a nation like all the others. To be born into the camp or into the nation was to have no arbitrary future before one. No birth was outside God's control or knowledge or plan (see Jer. 1:5) and no child escaped God's claim on his or her life. To grow in the faith of and to faith in the God of Moses, of Abraham, Isaac and Jacob, was to experience God's claim on one's life and to be expected to live the kind of life that would give glory to him.

(ii)

The term next of kin, or as the RSV has it, "kinsman", is very important for understanding the Old Testament idea of Israel's solidarity. The term originally meant the nearest blood relative of a person, and in Israel this relationship brought with it a terribly strong bond. It had civil and criminal law ramifications. This next of kin had to buy the property of a relative in straitened circumstances, and even to marry his widow if he died childless; and if need be, he had to buy or "redeem" him from slavery, or avenge his death if he were murdered.

It is not surprising that so strong a term was used to illumine the Lord's relationship to Israel, his power to save and re-save Israel. The Lord is referred to profoundly and beautifully as Israel's *go-el*, her Next of Kin, her Redeemer, in the context of the Exodus from Egypt (Exod. 6:6; Ps. 106:10); and in the context of the return from the Exile in Babylon (Isa. 43:1; 44:22–24; 47:4; 52:9). The Lord is also seen as the Next of Kin of individuals (e.g. Gen. 48:16; 2 Sam. 4:9; Pss. 26:11; 49:15). Most famously the title is found in the book of Job where the hero cries out of his despair, "I know that my Redeemer lives" (Job 19:25).

In the New Testament we find the imagery used just as powerfully. Jesus himself says he came "to give his life as a ransom for many" (Matt. 20:28), a way of interpreting Jesus' death picked up in Titus 2:14 and especially in 1 Pet. 1:18–19. Paul uses the idea in Rom. 3:24 and 1 Cor. 1:30, but especially in that celebrated passage 1 Cor. 6:19–20, where he says clearly: "You are not your own; you were bought with a price". Such is Jesus, our Next of Kin, our *go-el*.

Another important thing to notice in this section is the relationship between sin and crime. It is possible to sin against God without sinning against people. That is to say not all sins are crimes, or a breaking of social conventions. People can blaspheme (a crime in some societies) or envy or covet or hate. However, we *cannot* sin against people without it also being a sin against God too (see Matt. 5:23–24). It is put categorically in Lev. 6:1–7 that all such sins as cheating, stealing, slander, etc., are "proxy" sins against the Lord. Such sins against one another are called "breaking faith with the Lord". This is further shown by the fact that the ram used for sacrifice in the process of confession—restitution—forgiveness is there called the "ram of atonement", indicating quite clearly that a sin against God and his will is involved. Atonement is a central concept to be examined in the commentary on 8:5–26; it always reflects a situation where there has been an alienation from God through sin against him.

John puts it succinctly when he says to us: "If any one says 'I love God' and hates his brother, he is a liar; for he who does not love his brother whom he has seen, cannot love God whom he has not seen" (1 John 4:20).

TRIAL OF SUSPECTED WIVES

Numbers 5:11-31

[11]And the Lord said to Moses, [12]"Say to the people of Israel, If any man's wife goes astray and acts unfaithfully against him, [13]if a man lies with her carnally, and it is hidden from the eyes of her husband, and she is undetected though she has defiled herself, and there is no witness against her, since she was not taken in the act; [14]and if the spirit of jealousy comes upon him, and he is jealous of his wife who has defiled herself; or if the spirit of jealousy comes upon him, and he is jealous of his wife, though she has not defiled herself; [15]then the man shall bring his wife to the priest, and bring the offering required of her, a tenth of an ephah of barley meal; he shall pour no oil upon it and put no frankincense on it, for it is a cereal offering of jealousy, a cereal offering of remembrance, bringing iniquity to remembrance.

[16]"And the priest shall bring her near, and set her before the Lord; [17]and the priest shall take holy water in an earthen vessel, and take some of the dust that is on the floor of the tabernacle and put it into the water. [18]And the priest shall set the woman before the Lord, and unbind the hair of the woman's head, and place in her hands the cereal offering of remembrance, which is the cereal offering of jealousy. And in his hand the priest shall have the water of bitterness that brings the curse. [19]Then the priest shall make her take an oath, saying, 'If no man has lain with you, and if you have not turned aside to uncleanness, while you were under your husband's authority, be free from this water of bitterness that brings the curse. [20]But if you have gone astray, though you are under your husband's authority, and if you have defiled yourself, and some man other than your husband has lain with you, [21]then' (let the priest make the woman take the oath of the curse, and say to the woman) 'the Lord make you an execration and an oath among your people, when the Lord makes your thigh fall away and your body swell; [22]may this water that brings the curse pass into your bowels and make your body swell and your thigh fall away.' And the woman shall say, 'Amen, Amen.'

[23]"Then the priest shall write these curses in a book, and wash them off into the water of bitterness; [24]and he shall make the woman drink

the water of bitterness that brings the curse, and the water that brings the curse shall enter into her and cause bitter pain. [25]And the priest shall take the cereal offering of jealousy out of the woman's hand, and shall wave the cereal offering before the Lord and bring it to the altar; [26]and the priest shall take a handful of the cereal offering, as its memorial portion, and burn it upon the altar, and afterward shall make the woman drink the water. [27]And when he has made her drink the water, then, if she has defiled herself and has acted unfaithfully against her husband, the water that brings the curse shall enter into her and cause bitter pain, and her body shall swell, and her thigh shall fall away, and the woman shall become an execration among her people. [28]But if the woman has not defiled herself and is clean, then she shall be free and shall conceive children.

[29]"This is the law in cases of jealousy, when a wife, though under her husband's authority, goes astray and defiles herself, [30]or when the spirit of jealousy comes upon a man and he is jealous of his wife; then he shall set the woman before the Lord, and the priest shall execute upon her all this law. [31]The man shall be free from iniquity, but the woman shall bear her iniquity."

(i)

This passage does seem to modern western sense and sensibility to be somewhat unsavoury. Here are regulations about what is called in v. 18 an "offering of jealousy", i.e. an offering made to the Lord which was made necessary by a husband's jealousy. More specifically, the case is one of suspected adultery—a man suspects his wife. Regulations for the reverse situation do not occur. This is further reflected in the terms used: the word for "husband" is the same as the word for "lord, master", and the word for "wife" is simply the word for "a woman". The situation in its eastern context is not nearly so black, though, as is often suspected in the West. But the fact remains that only the husband has such rights as these.

When no immediate proof of adultery can be produced, and therefore normal judicial procedures are useless, then these are the measures resorted to. Something must be done, even if there is only suspicion of adultery, since the legitimacy of a man's heirs will be at stake. In the commentary on 1:5–19 it was seen how vital to Israelite society was the accreditation and purity of family and heirs. Therefore suspicion itself is seen as ground enough for the testing of a wife's faithfulness and purity. However, the legislation became more lenient as the people grew and matured. The Mishnah, which is the codified body of revelations and laws held as bindingly authoritative by the Jews, has a section devoted to this subject. According to this, first of all a man must, before two witnesses, forbid his wife to see the suspected lover again, and also refrain from all sexual intercourse with her himself till it be known whether she has conceived. Only if the wife refuses all this can she be brought to the ordeal described here.

At this earlier period only a "spirit of jealousy" is necessary to bring the case to trial. The word for "spirit" is the same as that used for the Spirit of God. It is also used of powerful emotions. So this section is talking about a man who is eaten up by his suspicions and too powerfully upset to let them go unremarked. It is not just a fleeting pang of jealousy. See *Additional Note* 3.

(ii)

The sacrifice involved requires neither oil nor frankincense, and so indicates that it was seen as a sin offering, as these were always dry (Lev. 5:11). Oil and frankincense suggest joy and plenty. The sacrifice is also called in v. 15 an "offering of remembrance". This cannot mean literally to remind God, but may mean rather to bring the situation out into the open, i.e. it is an offering to make it known. Or it may be that this is an idiom for urging God to make an act of justice. When he acts on the bringing to mind of a sin, the sinner is punished (1 Kings 17:18), but when it is not brought to his mind, the sinner goes unpunished (Ps. 25:7).

The woman's hair was to be untied so that it hung long and loose. This was to remove the dignity attached to braided hair, and to show shame and uncleanness (compare Lev. 13:45, dealing with lepers). Then the priest was to take some "holy water", v. 17, which according to the Mishnah means only that it was taken from the sacred brass dish, and mix it with dust from the ground. At the appropriate time the wife must drink this. The Hebrew for this mixture which was to be drunk may be translated "water of bitterness", or perhaps better, "water of ordeal". A modern Jewish translation is "the water which brings the guilt to light", which captures the meaning.

As well as drinking this, she had to take a powerful oath. At the end of the oath she says, "Amen, Amen". This is used casually nowadays as a way to close a prayer, but it is actually a commitment to the prayer. The word comes from a root that suggests absolute dependability. To say "Amen" after a statement or a prayer means that the message received is totally reliable and sound, and that the person saying it is in total agreement and shares the conviction. To say "Amen" is to commit oneself to doing what can be done to ensure that the sentiments expressed become realized in the life of God's people. There is a saying in the Talmud that "whosoever says Amen with all his strength, to him the gates of Paradise will be opened". Such is its power. In Matt. 5:18, 26 etc., the AV reports Jesus as introducing his teachings by saying, "Verily I say unto you . . ."; the RSV has "truly". The Greek, following the Hebrew, has "Amen". Jesus prefixed his teachings by saying, "I say to you, 'Amen . . .' ". In other words, he began his teachings by saying it was all utterly dependable and true.

The saying of this "Amen, Amen" combined with the drinking of the water would produce strong psychosomatic changes in the woman. The pressure on an innocent woman would be great, but that on a guilty woman would be enormous. What is envisaged is that the "thigh" will "fall away" (vv. 21, 22, 27), i.e. that there will be a miscarriage or abortion. The thigh is often used as a euphemism for the sexual organs. Such an event was seen as a form of "poetic justice". Jewish traditions of justice are largely based on a principle (made popular by Gilbert and Sullivan in their song from the Mikado) "to let the punishment fit the crime", which says: "with what measure a man measures out, it is measured to him". So the Mishnah says: "She began transgression with the thigh first and afterwards with the belly—therefore the thigh shall suffer first and afterwards the belly". Adding to the testing character of the trial was the fact that the curses and the oath were written in ink which was then blotted with the water so

that it ran with it, and the very words of the curse were symbolically transferred to the water.

(iii)

This principle of retributive justice (for such it is, having the
punishment balance the sin) runs through the New Testament
too: "for whatever a man sows, that he will also reap" (Gal.
6:7–9; 2 Cor. 9:6). Jesus expresses it more positively when he
says: "whatever you wish that men would do to you, do so to
them; for this is the law and the prophets" (Matt. 7:12). This cuts
across all the human barriers of creed, race, sex, status, etc.
There is a prayer in the morning service for each young Jewish
man in which he thanks God that he is neither a Gentile, nor a
slave, nor a woman. Paul must have had this negative approach in
mind when he asserted positively and boldly: "There is neither
Jew nor Greek, there is neither slave nor free, there is neither
male nor female; for you are all one in Christ Jesus"
(Gal. 3:28).

DEDICATION OF THE NAZIRITE

Numbers 6:1–21

[1]And the Lord said to Moses, [2]"Say to the people of Israel, When
either a man or a woman makes a special vow, the vow of a Nazirite, to
separate himself to the Lord, [3]he shall separate himself from wine and
strong drink; he shall drink no vinegar made from wine or strong drink,
and shall not drink any juice of grapes or eat grapes, fresh or dried.
[4]All the days of his separation he shall eat nothing that is produced by
the grapevine, not even the seeds or the skins.

[5]"All the days of his vow of separation no razor shall come upon his
head; until the time is completed for which he separates himself to the
Lord, he shall be holy; he shall let the locks of hair of his head grow
long.

[6]"All the days that he separates himself to the Lord he shall not go
near a dead body. [7]Neither for his father nor for his mother, nor for
brother or sister, if they die, shall he make himself unclean; because his
separation to God is upon his head. [8]All the days of his separation he is
holy to the Lord.

⁹"And if any man dies very suddenly beside him, and he defiles his consecrated head, then he shall shave his head on the day of his cleansing; on the seventh day he shall shave it. ¹⁰On the eighth day he shall bring two turtledoves or two young pigeons to the priest to the door of the tent of meeting, ¹¹and the priest shall offer one for a sin offering and the other for a burnt offering, and make atonement for him, because he sinned by reason of the dead body. And he shall consecrate his head that same day, ¹²and separate himself to the Lord for the days of his separation, and bring a male lamb a year old for a guilt offering; but the former time shall be void, because his separation was defiled.

¹³"And this is the law for the Nazirite, when the time of his separation has been completed: he shall be brought to the door of the tent of meeting, ¹⁴and he shall offer his gift to the Lord, one male lamb a year old without blemish for a burnt offering, and one ewe lamb a year old without blemish as a sin offering, and one ram without blemish as a peace offering, ¹⁵and a basket of unleavened bread, cakes of fine flour mixed with oil, and unleavened wafers spread with oil, and their cereal offering and their drink offerings. ¹⁶And the priest shall present them before the Lord and offer his sin offering and his burnt offering, ¹⁷and he shall offer the ram as a sacrifice of peace offering to the Lord, with the basket of unleavened bread; the priest shall offer also its cereal offering and its drink offering. ¹⁸And the Nazirite shall shave his consecrated head at the door of the tent of meeting, and shall take the hair from his consecrated head and put it on the fire which is under the sacrifice of the peace offering. ¹⁹And the priest shall take the shoulder of the ram, when it is boiled, and one unleavened cake out of the basket, and one unleavened wafer, and shall put them upon the hands of the Nazirite, after he has shaven the hair of his consecration, ²⁰and the priest shall wave them for a wave offering before the Lord; they are a holy portion for the priest, together with the breast that is waved and the thigh that is offered; and after that the Nazirite may drink wine.

²¹"This is the law for the Nazirite who takes a vow. His offering to the Lord shall be according to his vow as a Nazirite, apart from what else he can afford; in accordance with the vow which he takes, so shall he do according to the law for his separation as a Nazirite."

(i)

God called all Israel to be set apart for himself (Exod. 19:6); within Israel he called out the priesthood to be especially consecrated to him (see commentary on ch. 3). But it was also possible for lay people to make a special vow of dedication to God for a set purpose and time. Such people were called "Nazirites", from a verb meaning "to separate" or "consecrate". The most famous one in the Bible was Samson (Judg. 13–16).

The abstentions demanded of a Nazirite are the striking things, but they are not the vow, and the vow made the Nazirite, all else stemming from it. He was to abstain from "wine and strong drink"; also from "vinegar", since this was produced from wine that had soured; even raisins had to be rejected. The abstention was probably not so much from alcohol as such as an abstention from and rejection of the Canaanite urban cultivation of the grape, symbolic of delicacy and fine living and even degeneracy (Hos. 3:1; 1 Sam. 25:18, 36), in favour of the simplicity and trust in the Lord typical of the wilderness experience. John the Baptist is a good case in point, with the command given to his parents (Luke 1:14ff.) and his subsequent wilderness existence (Luke 3:1–20).

Nazirites were also prohibited from cutting their hair. Samson's notorious strength, however, was not magically in his hair, but in the dedication behind it. So when he despised the vow he lost his strength. Only living hair grows, so it became a symbol of the Nazirites' life before God. If this life was defiled in any way then the hair had to be shaved off and the process begun again. The apostle Paul had taken this vow (Acts 18:18) as, according to an early historian of the Church, had Jesus' brother, James, who became a leader of the church in Jerusalem. To this day religious orders are called by the modern equivalent of "Nazirites" in Israel.

A lesson to be learned is that if we do make vows before the Lord then we must honour them, otherwise the blessing of the Lord will leave us, as it did Samson. Generally speaking, on the subject of vows and oaths Jesus gives us sound advice in Matt. 5:33–37: don't make great promises or vows, and "Let what you say be simply 'Yes' or 'No' ". It is a common source of amusement how often our New Year's resolutions are broken by February, yet when we make vows before the Lord we must realize that we are walking on *holy ground*.

The further abstention mentioned here is having no contact with the dead, even the closest of relatives. It is recorded elsewhere only of the High Priest (Lev. 21:11). This reinforces the preciousness of the vow to the Lord. We are reminded of Jesus' words to those who wanted to make a great commitment to him but who first wanted to bury their dead relatives or say goodbye to them. He said: "Leave the dead to bury their own dead; but as for you, go and proclaim the kingdom of God" (Luke 9:59–60). To walk after Jesus is to walk on holy ground, which necessarily means taking up a cross and following him. This is costly, but wonderful. The basic meaning of the verb "to make a vow" in v. 2 is in fact *to do something wonderful or extraordinary*. Such is our Father that when we make costly commitment to him it turns out to be the most wonderful thing we have done.

(ii)

The various sacrifices and offerings to be made when a Nazirite accidentally broke one of these taboos and when the time for which he had made his vow came to an end (13ff.) are not of great significance to us nowadays. But the reference in v. 20 to a "wave offering" is especially interesting. The priest took the offering and literally waved it back and forth in the direction of the altar while standing in front of the altar (see Lev. 7:30). He would be swaying as he did so. This represented the fact that the offerer was giving back to God what God had already given to him, thus the movement towards the altar and back from the altar. The words of W. W. How's hymn come to mind:

> We give Thee but Thine own,
> Whate'er the gift may be;
> All that we have is Thine alone,
> A trust, O Lord, from Thee.

God's is the initiative at all times and in all dimensions of life. So whatever is offered to him is based on his prior offer. Our genuine sacrifice, then, in response to God's giving of his own Son, is one of praise and thanksgiving. Even the love we have for God and one another is a gift from God. The AV in 1 John 4:19

has a serious mistranslation when it puts: "We love God, because he first loved us." This is true, but the text actually reads: "We love, because he first loved us." This is even more radical. The very fact we can love at all is thanks to God who is himself Love (1 John 4:8). Our own offerings are all wave offerings.

BLESS YOU AND KEEP YOU!

Numbers 6:22–27

> [22]The Lord said to Moses, [23]"Say to Aaron and his sons, Thus you shall bless the people of Israel: you shall say to them, [24]The Lord bless you and keep you: [25]The Lord make his face to shine upon you, and be gracious to you: [26]The Lord lift up his countenance upon you, and give you peace.
> [27]"So shall they put my name upon the people of Israel, and I will bless them."

The Aaronic blessing, as it is called, is one of the best-known and most loved passages in the Bible, though many people may be unaware that it is part of the book of Numbers. It is a powerful and beautiful benediction, used particularly by us in the celebration of baptism and ordination. There are only fifteen words in the Hebrew text and yet they portray a world of trust and faith in God. They are partially quoted in Pss. 4:6; 67:1, and tradition has it that in the Temple the priests would chant these verses boldly and joyfully, even using the personal name of God revealed to Moses from the burning bush, a name otherwise shunned because of its intrinsic holiness. The blessing became very popular in Protestant churches after the Reformation.

Reference is made to the Lord's "face", metaphorically of course, and most expressively too. The face of God is the source of light. His character and attitudes are most clearly seen there as with human beings. Several idioms therefore occur in Hebrew. For him to turn his face away or hide his face from someone is to show his displeasure (e.g. Ezek. 39:23); for him to set his face against someone is to be hostile (e.g. Jer. 21:10). Similarly for a man to set his face to a task is to fasten his will to accomplishing it (e.g. Jer. 42:17; see also Luke 9:51 where Jesus sets his face to Jerusalem as he prepares for that last week of his life before the crucifixion). Here the idiom is one of blessing someone. The Lord is called on to "bless" Israel, i.e. to give his good gifts of crops, herds, fertile seasons, children, general prosperity, and to "keep" Israel, i.e. to protect from bad harvests, enemies, childlessness, etc. Some Rabbis have interpreted this as: may the Lord bless Israel with good possessions, yet also keep her from becoming a slave to them.

So in this context he is called on to "make his face to shine" on Israel. A shining face is a sign of pleasure in the company of those it shines on (Pss. 31:16; 80:3, 7, 19). In other words, the Lord is called on to accept Israel straight to his heart. Perhaps the expression arose from association with the joy of the dawn shining at the start of a new day (2 Sam. 2:32), or from the joy of seeing lightning flashes from the skies signalling the welcome rain after the hot dry summer (Pss. 77:18; 97:4). He is also called on to "be gracious", i.e. to show undeserved favour. The word "countenance" is the same as the word "face", and the Lord is called on to "lift up his face" on Israel.

Finally, the Lord is called on to "give peace". In modern Hebrew this term has been terribly debased. It is of course in Hebrew *shalom*, perhaps along with *Amen* and *Hallelujah* the Hebrew words we know best. It is the word learned by all tourists who come to Israel, being printed on the sun hats they buy. Nowadays, it is used conventionally for "Hello" and also for "Goodbye". In the Bible, however, the word carries a profound meaning of security in life from hardships and curses; of completeness and wholeness in life's experiences; of inner harmony and balance. In short, it is one of the fundamental words of the Old Testament. To wish someone *shalom* might be to want the very best for him in life. For it is the Lord's own *shalom*. This is not something which appears when war or argument stops, but only when people are tuned in to the will of God for their lives and are doing it. For Israel, *shalom* was only possible when she lived in harmony with the values and promises of the covenant. A great Jewish scholar, Montefiore, once commented on this peace as being:

... the peace which alone reconciles and strengthens, which calms us and clears our vision, which frees us from restlessness and from the bondage of unsatisfied desire, which gives us the consciousness of attainment, the consciousness of permanence even amid the transitoriness of ourselves and of outward things.

In John's Gospel, Jesus speaks words of peace to us three times in his last week on earth:

Peace I leave with you; my peace I give to you; not as the world gives do I give to you (14:27)

I have said this to you, that in me you may have peace (16:33)

Jesus came and stood among them and said to them, "Peace be with you" (20:19,21,26).

Here is the key to victorious living! Paul tells us in Gal. 5:22 that peace is one of the marks of a follower of Jesus; it is one of the "fruits of the Spirit".

INTRODUCING ISRAEL'S ELDERS

Numbers 7:1–89

[1]On the day when Moses had finished setting up the tabernacle, and had anointed and consecrated it with all its furnishings, and had anointed and consecrated the altar with all its utensils, [2]the leaders of Israel, heads of their fathers' houses, the leaders of the tribes, who were over those who were numbered, [3]offered and brought their offerings before the Lord, six covered wagons and twelve oxen, a wagon for every two of the leaders, and for each one an ox; they offered them before the tabernacle. [4]Then the Lord said to Moses, [5]"Accept these from them, that they may be used in doing the service of the tent of meeting, and give them to the Levites, to each man according to his service." [6]So Moses took the wagons and the oxen, and gave them to the Levites. [7]Two wagons and four oxen he gave to the sons of Gershon, according to their service; [8]and four wagons and eight oxen he gave to the sons of Merari, according to their service, under the direction of Ithamar the son of Aaron the priest. [9]But to the sons of Kohath he gave none, because they were charged with the care of the holy things which had to be carried on the shoulder. [10]And the

leaders offered offerings for the dedication of the altar on the day it was anointed; and the leaders offered their offering before the altar. [11]And the Lord said to Moses, "They shall offer their offerings, one leader each day, for the dedication of the altar."

[12]He who offered his offering the first day was Nahshon the son of Amminadab, of the tribe of Judah; [13]and his offering was one silver plate whose weight was a hundred and thirty shekels, one silver basin of seventy shekels, according to the shekel of the sanctuary, both of them full of fine flour mixed with oil for a cereal offering; [14]one golden dish of ten shekels, full of incense; [15]one young bull, one ram, one male lamb a year old, for a burnt offering; [16]one male goat for a sin offering; [17]and for the sacrifice of peace offerings, two oxen, five rams, five male goats, and five male lambs a year old. This was the offering of Nahshon the son of Amminadab.

. . . .

[78]On the twelfth day Ahira the son of Enan, the leader of the men of Naphtali: [79]his offering was one silver plate, whose weight was a hundred and thirty shekels, one silver basin of seventy shekels, according to the shekel of the sanctuary, both of them full of fine flour mixed with oil for a cereal offering; [80]one golden dish of ten shekels, full of incense; [81]one young bull, one ram, one male lamb a year old, for a burnt offering; [82]one male goat for a sin offering; [83]and for the sacrifice of peace offerings, two oxen, five rams, five male goats, and five male lambs a year old. This was the offering of Ahira the son of Enan.

[84]This was the dedication offering for the altar, on the day when it was anointed, from the leaders of Israel: twelve silver plates, twelve silver basins, twelve golden dishes, [85]each silver plate weighing a hundred and thirty shekels and each basin seventy, all the silver of the vessels two thousand four hundred shekels according to the shekel of the sanctuary, [86]the twelve golden dishes, full of incense, weighing ten shekels apiece according to the shekel of the sanctuary, all the gold of the dishes being a hundred and twenty shekels; [87]all the cattle for the burnt offering twelve bulls, twelve rams, twelve male lambs a year old, with their cereal offering; and twelve male goats for a sin offering; [88]and all the cattle for the sacrifice of peace offerings twenty-four bulls, the rams sixty, the male goats sixty, the male lambs a year old sixty. This was the dedication offering for the altar, after it was anointed.

[89]And when Moses went into the tent of meeting to speak with the Lord, he heard the voice speaking to him from above the mercy seat that was upon the ark of the testimony, from between the two cherubim; and it spoke to him.

(i)

This is perhaps the longest chapter in the Old Testament (excluding Ps. 119), and certainly for modern readers it must seem the longest (even including Ps. 119). It is based on the fairly tedious repetition of a formula twelve times (only two of which have been included in the text above). The various leaders of the tribal groups bring offerings to the Tabernacle for its upkeep and beautification after Moses has completed the anointing and consecration. Of course, the offerings are also an indication of the willingness of the people to give, so that the Lord's presence may be glorified. This term for "leaders of Israel" is translated by some as "princes", a meaning it has elsewhere, but here it is really the priestly term for "elders". The phrase is used generally by Ezekiel (21:12; 22:6; 45:9), but only of these twelve people in the Pentateuch. They were seen as special elders under Moses (Num. 1:44; 4:46), representing the people in much the same way as Moses himself.

The men and tribes are listed according to the order of the march in 2:1–34. A minor point to note is that the "covered wagons" they brought for carrying the Tabernacle and its furniture may be simply straightforward functional wagons, or may in fact be the type used for military purposes. So the Tabernacle may be seen as of primary value in *battle* with Israel's enemies, who are the Lord's enemies. This all takes place chronologically a month before the census of 1:1–4, on the first day of the first month in the second year after the Exodus (Exod. 40:17).

The offerings are for:
(a) transport for the Tabernacle
(b) vessels for the sanctuary
(c) animals for sacrificing

It is probably true to say that the formula is repeated fully so often, rather than just listing the names, so that, on the one hand, the Israelites could enjoy the memory of the days when there was much to give and much joy in giving it, and so that, on the other hand, the leaders in every succeeding generation could drive home the example of generosity to their contemporaries.

(ii)

The word for "offering" is very interesting. Its root meaning is "to draw close", to someone or something; thus here something brought to the altar, brought "close" to God. Israel knew that God was not domesticated in the Tabernacle, yet they also knew that his special meeting place with his people was there. There were more than a dozen types of offering known to Israel (see *Additional Note* 4), each for a specific purpose (Lev. chs. 1–5), but the special word here, *corban*, is one that in later Judaism developed a certain notoriety. Technically speaking a *corban* could be anything dedicated to the service of the Lord for any reason, or for a fixed time. The Mishnah reflects the situation in Jesus' time when it says that anything set aside as a *corban*, even rashly, could never be used for any other purpose, not even in a drastic change of circumstances. In this sense it parallels the dedication of the Nazirites in 6:1–21. This is by no means an ignoble concept. Yet it was open to abuse, if family circumstances demanded help and it was refused on grounds of service to a higher cause. This is the ground of Jesus' criticism in Mark 7:9–13.

Such absoluteness on our part is not gracious. Nothing is holy in itself, save God himself; not even vows or duties or laws. Such are holy only inasmuch as they are inspired by love for God and then his people, and inasmuch as they are carried out to promote that love. If not, they do not glorify God and cannot be said to reflect his will. Much "righteous" activity is carried out, sadly, without being rooted in God's kind of love, costly and compassionate. This, according to Jesus, is unacceptable to God, even with respect to that most fundamental and holy of commands, the institution of the Sabbath: "The sabbath was made for man, not man for the sabbath" (Mark 2:23–27). Martin Luther King Jnr. served the world well when he reminded us of this fact even with respect to national laws. They must be weighed consciously against God's revealed will. As he wrote from Birmingham Jail:

> ... there are two types of laws: just and unjust ... I would agree with St. Augustine that "an unjust law is no law at all".... A just law ... squares with the moral law or the law of God.

However, in this case, the offerings were pleasing to God. And so Moses carried out the "dedication of the altar" (vv. 10, 88). This term is equally interesting. The basic meaning is "to train up". The name of faithful Enoch, who "walked with God" (Gen. 5:21ff.) but later was not, for God took him, is connected with this term. Abraham's most "seasoned" men are associated with it (Gen. 14:14). The noun is used in the title of Ps. 30 of the "dedication" of the Temple; in 2 Chron. 7:9 of the "dedication" of the altar in the Temple; then again in Neh. 12:27 of the "dedication" of Jerusalem's rebuilt wall. Most famously it is used in 1 Maccabees 4:52ff., in the Apocrypha, of the "dedication" of the Temple after its recapture by Judas Maccabeus in 165 B.C. To this day there is a feast of the Jews to celebrate this great victory and rededication of the Temple, and its name is this term used here: *Chanukkah*. Such a dedication would be then, as now, the cause of marvellous excitement and joy.

(iii)

In the last verse, mention is made of the "mercy seat". The word comes from a verb "to cover". A related noun appears in the Hebrew original of the phrase the Day of "Atonement". The concept of atonement, meaning "covering", will be discussed at 8:5–26. In Lev. 16:14–15 it is set out how on that day the High Priest must sprinkle the blood of sacrifice onto the "mercy seat". It was on the top of the ark and distinct from it. So Moses (in v. 89) goes into the tent to speak with the Lord, and he hears his voice speaking to him. Why this should be reported at this particular juncture is not certain, unless it be simply to remind us that all the instructions Moses was receiving were from God. The fact is, however, that God did speak to him, in fulfilment of Exod. 25:22. God promises to come to his people, and does come to them. What is more, both the Exodus passage and this one stress that God spoke "from above the mercy seat", i.e. he was not in it nor in any way identified with it. God was in the *voice*.

When God wants us to meet him he speaks to us. Christians now believe that the true Word of God, Jesus Christ, is God's necessary and sufficient means of communicating with men. Jesus is our meeting-place with God. He brings God's Word to us and takes our word to God.

THE GOLDEN LAMPSTAND

Numbers 8:1–4

[1]Now the Lord said to Moses, [2]"Say to Aaron, When you set up the lamps, the seven lamps shall give light in front of the lampstand." [3]And Aaron did so; he set up its lamps to give light in front of the lampstand, as the Lord commanded Moses. [4]And this was the workmanship of the lampstand, hammered work of gold; from its base to its flowers, it was hammered work; according to the pattern which the Lord had shown Moses, so he made the lampstand.

This was one of the most sacred pieces of furniture, the "lampstand", or to give it its full title, "the lampstand for the light", as in 4:9 and Exod. 35:14. The Hebrew term has come down into English usage: *Menorah*. It is one of the common modern symbols for Judaism, and the Jewish communities of Great Britain and Northern Ireland donated a commanding and striking one to the Israeli parliament, which was erected opposite the parliament building in Jerusalem. The original golden one stood on the south side of the Tabernacle, and is fully described in Exod. 25:31–40. There was a tripod base and a triple branch structure on either side of the central shaft. Each branch culminated in a cup shaped like the flower of the almond tree. So there were seven branches in all. The Jewish historian, Josephus, says that the number seven represented the sun and the moon and the five planets known to antiquity, and was therefore symbolic of God's sovereign creativity. We do not know for sure.

Typically of the Israelites' care and devotion, it was cast in one piece of beaten gold. It is probably right to see the roots of this symbol in the ancient concept of the "tree of life" which is found in the sacred literature of many eastern cultures as well as in the

Old Testament (Gen. 2:9; 3:22). Light and life are very closely allied in the thought of the East. The number seven is also the sacred symbolic number for wholeness, completeness. Perhaps then the *menorah* represents the fulness of God's life-giving, light-giving presence among his people, and from them to the whole world? Zechariah (ch. 4) interprets the lamps as the seven eyes of the Lord watching all the world, again the number seven suggesting that the Lord sees everything.

In John's vision (Rev. 1:12–20) the Church of Christ, represented symbolically by the seven churches "in Asia", is further represented by seven such lampstands. We too are the work of the Lord, to minister life and light to the world, to bring light to bear on the sacrifice of our Lord Jesus Christ so that the world can see him and his Gospel. Jesus himself says to us: "You are the light of the world . . . Let your light so shine before men, that they may . . . give glory to your Father who is in heaven" (Matt. 5:14–16). And of course in the middle of Revelation's seven lampstands, Christ was walking. He is the source of our light and life: "I am the light of the world; he who follows me will not walk in darkness but will have the light of life" (John 8:12).

CONSECRATION AND RETIREMENT

Numbers 8:5–26

⁵And the Lord said to Moses, ⁶"Take the Levites from among the people of Israel, and cleanse them. ⁷And thus you shall do to them, to cleanse them: sprinkle the water of expiation upon them, and let them go with a razor over all their body, and wash their clothes and cleanse themselves. ⁸Then let them take a young bull and its cereal offering of fine flour mixed with oil, and you shall take another young bull for a sin offering. ⁹And you shall present the Levites before the tent of meeting, and assemble the whole congregation of the people of Israel. ¹⁰When you present the Levites before the Lord, the people of Israel shall lay their hands upon the Levites, ¹¹and Aaron shall offer the Levites before the Lord as a wave offering from the people of Israel, that it may be theirs to do the service of the Lord. ¹²Then the Levites shall lay their hands upon the heads of the bulls; and you shall offer the

one for a sin offering and the other for a burnt offering to the Lord, to make atonement for the Levites. [13] And you shall cause the Levites to attend Aaron and his sons, and shall offer them as a wave offering to the Lord.

[14] "Thus you shall separate the Levites from among the people of Israel, and the Levites shall be mine. [15] And after that the Levites shall go in to do service at the tent of meeting, when you have cleansed them and offered them as a wave offering. [16] For they are wholly given to me from among the people of Israel; instead of all that open the womb, the first-born of all the people of Israel, I have taken them for myself. [17] For all the first-born among the people of Israel are mine, both of man and beast; on the day that I slew all the first-born in the land of Egypt I consecrated them for myself, [18] and I have taken the Levites instead of all the first-born among the people of Israel. [19] And I have given the Levites as a gift to Aaron and his sons from among the people of Israel, to do the service for the people of Israel at the tent of meeting, and to make atonement for the people of Israel, that there may be no plague among the people of Israel in case the people of Israel should come near the sanctuary."

[20] Thus did Moses and Aaron and all the congregation of the people of Israel to the Levites; according to all that the Lord commanded Moses concerning the Levites, the people of Israel did to them. [21] And the Levites purified themselves from sin, and washed their clothes; and Aaron offered them as a wave offering before the Lord, and Aaron made atonement for them to cleanse them. [22] And after that the Levites went in to do their service in the tent of meeting in attendance upon Aaron and his sons; as the Lord had commanded Moses concerning the Levites, so they did to them.

[23] And the Lord said to Moses, [24] "This is what pertains to the Levites: from twenty-five years old and upward they shall go in to perform the work in the service of the tent of meeting; [25] and from the age of fifty years they shall withdraw from the work of the service and serve no more, [26] but minister to their brethren in the tent of meeting, to keep the charge, and they shall do no service. Thus shall you do to the Levites in assigning their duties."

(i)

The Levites are now taken and ritually cleansed to mark their dedication to the Lord. They wash themselves with water to separate themselves from sin, and shave their bodies so that future growth of hair is clean and pure. Thereafter the people "lay their hands" on the Levites (v. 10). This would probably be done, of course, by a representative number, not all the camp literally. Interestingly, the noun from the verb "to lay hands" is the technical Rabbinic term for "ordination". In the Old Testament, laying hands on an animal or a person either accompanies or transfers a blessing (e.g. Gen. 48:14ff.; Num. 27:18, 23); or it marks the transfer of sin and the burden of guilt (e.g. Lev. 1:4; 16:21–22). Here it is a blessing.

In the New Testament the "laying on of hands" always conveys a blessing. It is found:

(a) *When Jesus very simply blesses the children who run to him* (Matt. 19:13ff.). This is a "symbolic expression of what was essentially an act of prayer" (J. C. Lambert).

(b) *When people are being healed* (Mark 6:5; Luke 4:40; Acts 9:12; 17; 28:8).

(c) *When people are baptized in the early Church* (Acts 9:17–18; 19:5–6; see also Heb. 6:2).

(d) *When people are ordained in the early Church* (Acts 6:6; 13:3; 1 Tim. 4:14; 2 Tim. 1:6).

Look again at the statement of Lambert's. These instances of laying on of hands always come in the context of prior prayer and trust in God. In other words, it is not to be seen as in any way implying a position of power or authority on the part of the person who lays hands on another. Here it was still the Lord who chose, anointed and consecrated the Levites, even though he also used the "people of Israel" to pass on his blessing. God uses us; we don't use him. Sadly, many believers seem today to have lost sympathy with the ministries of laying on of hands. It is based in Scripture, and we need to believe in and practise it more than we do—as long as we remember that only the Lord blesses, and we are only part of that blessing when we submit all to him.

(ii)

In v. 12 the other sense of laying on hands is seen. Here animals are substituted for the Levites as sacrifices. This is done "to make atonement" for them. The English word here is made up of the syllables AT-ONE-MENT, i.e. being in a state of oneness, of reconciliation. This is just what the term actually does mean, a process of reconciling. In the Old Testament the term is used of getting rid of the blockages of sin so that restoration with God becomes possible. In other words, it denotes a restored union, a reconciliation of what was apart, not a continuous union. It is usually necessary to sacrifice an animal to achieve this, as here, the victim taking the burden of sin and punishment.

The Bible teaches clearly that man is alienated from God due to his selfish rebellion against him and his ways, and that man needs to be reconciled to God. Something had to be done about the barrier of sin, so in Old Testament times God inspired a system of sacrifices to remove the burden of sin and guilt (Exod. 29:36; Lev. 4:20). And the verb used for these reconciling acts is the one translated here to make "atonement", which in the Hebrew is literally "to cover".

Originally there may have been a partly natural, partly inherited idea that God had a fearful anger which had to be appeased before he could forgive and accept, but gradually Israel learned that even when he was angry it was out of love and a desire to bless. It is properly therefore the barrier of sin that is removed, not the barrier of God's fury.

In v. 19 it is further stated that the Levites protect the people from disaster due to unholy acts that may be committed in the sanctuary. In this sense they themselves act as an "atonement". They "cover" the people on God's behalf, acting as a kind of buffer. The text says they protected the people from a possible "plague", the same word as is used in the account of the death of the first-born, the last plague, in Egypt (Exod. 11:1ff.). By a beautiful poetic touch, then, the Levites are shown to be taking the place of the first-born of Israel, and protecting them from death.

In the New Testament the corresponding word is found in Rom. 5:11, with respect to the death of Jesus for us on the cross. This substitutionary death once and for all wipes out the debt owed to God, covers the sin, and establishes reconciliation. The means of atonement is, in the New Testament as in the Old, given by God, with its source in God alone.

Following on from this line of thought, the basic point of v. 18 is that God has "taken" the Levites in place of the first-born, and the basic point of v. 19 is that he has "given" them back for service. He takes to give. This spiritual movement of taking and giving was in fact reflected in the physical movement back from and forward to the altar called "waving" the offering (see the commentary on 6:1–21). When God takes from his people it is never from selfish motive, and will never impoverish his people. All that is needed—and it is a hard thing to learn—is grace to wait until he gives back what he has planned. Then we can know the richness of his blessing.

(iii)

Those paying attention to the text will notice that the evidence of v. 24 clashes with that of Num. 4:35. Here the Levites may serve for five more years, from the age of twenty-five rather than thirty. It may simply be that the two texts reflect different times of writing, and that in the course of time the ages varied with the availability of suitable men. Or it may be that there developed a five year period of training, a form of apprenticeship.

In v. 26 it is suggested that *retired* Levites (those above fifty) could volunteer to help younger men in their learning. The uses we make of retirement are very important. It is a chance to get involved with the younger community without feelings of threat on either side; to pass on skills and insights; to share lessons learned from mistakes and successes. But, of course, in the truest sense there is no retirement for the "priests" of God. The call to proclaim the Gospel and live it is lifelong. Even after physical death there is no retirement from praising God and proclaiming the glory of Jesus Christ (Rev. 5).

THE PASSOVER—STANDARD

Numbers 9:1–5

[1]And the Lord spoke to Moses in the wilderness of Sinai, in the first month of the second year after they had come out of the land of Egypt,

saying, [2]"Let the people of Israel keep the passover at its appointed time. [3]On the fourteenth day of this month, in the evening, you shall keep it at its appointed time; according to all its statutes and all its ordinances you shall keep it." [4]So Moses told the people of Israel that they should keep the passover. [5]And they kept the passover in the first month, on the fourteenth day of the month, in the evening, in the wilderness of Sinai; according to all that the Lord commanded Moses, so the people of Israel did.

(i)

The people of Israel are reminded of their obligation to commemorate the Passover feast. According to these verses the celebration took place after setting up the Tabernacle, one month before the census at Sinai. The original Passover was celebrated when the people came out of Egypt, and was then regularly celebrated in the first month of the year (Exod. 12; Deut. 16). In the East the days are reckoned from evening to evening rather than from midnight to midnight, so the feast begins in the evening, or, as the Hebrew says, "between the two evenings" (v. 3). It is still, of course, celebrated by Jews the world over and is likely to be the oldest of all rituals of this type in the world still observed. It has an "appointed time", and to disobey the call to remember its foundation is to flout God himself, the Redeemer. It must be remembered that although the Old Testament opens with the Creator God, Israel's first experience of him was not as Creator, but as Redeemer at the Red Sea. The Passover feast, then, celebrates Israel's first and decisive meeting with the Lord.

Shortly after the liberation from Egypt, the nation Israel was created at Sinai, and it is at that point that the book of Numbers begins. The free nation under the Lord is on the move to occupy the land promised to them by him. The modern Passover service is a mixture of traditions and interpretations ranging from ancient times to the Middle Ages. However, certain elements are constant. There is always the unleavened bread, that is to say bread without yeast or any other similar agent. This recalls the flight from Egypt, when there was no time to wait for the bread to be leavened before leaving. There is also part of the shankbone of a lamb, roasted, to commemorate the lamb once slaughtered in the Temple, or before that in the Tabernacle, which in its turn commemorated the lamb slaughtered at the coming of the angel of death in Egypt. There is a roasted egg to symbolize new life emerging even from the fires of the worst disasters, new life like that given by the Lord to the Israelites. Then there are also bitter herbs to symbolize the people's bitter slavery, and a sweet fruit mixture to modify the bitter taste, recalling God's lovingkindness to Israel.

The faith of Israel grows, and in fact self-consciously grows, as the people of Israel appreciate that theirs is an historic faith, rooted in history, therefore subject to change and development. So in Passover meals there is a place prepared and left for Elijah, in case he should choose that time to come to prepare for the advent of the Messiah (Mal. 4:5–6). The Messiah is expected to come to carry out the once and for all liberation of Israel.

(ii)

Jesus himself was a good Jew, and celebrated the Passover with his family, and then later with his own disciples (Matt. 26:2, 17ff.; Luke 2:41; John 2:13). He knew the redemption traditions, the longing after God to come again as his people's Redeemer, the Messianic hopes for deliverance. It was important to him, and must be to us also. Even more so since he is called "our paschal lamb", i.e. "our passover", by Paul, also a good Jew (1 Cor. 5:7). Once we begin to appreciate the powerful imagery of the Passover, we can better appreciate the power of the celebration of the sacrament of Holy Communion, the Eucharist. There is now no doubt that what we call the "Last Supper" was a Passover meal. Jesus is the Bread of Life; he is the Lamb of God sacrificed for us; his is the blood that protects and redeems us. When he broke the bread and lifted one of the four cups of wine drunk at the meal, then he took potent symbols and made them even more potent. This was not the casual use of bread and wine, nor even just an inspired parable of the basic food of life as a symbol for himself. This was the deliberate choice of the feast of the redemption of God's people to reaffirm once and for all his own act of redemption, that was soon to come for all the world. Jesus even spoke of Elijah coming before him in the person of John the Baptist (Matt. 11:11–14; 17:12–13).

THE PASSOVER—ALTERNATIVE

Numbers 9:6–14

> 6And there were certain men who were unclean through touching the dead body of a man, so that they could not keep the passover on that day; and they came before Moses and Aaron on that day; 7and those men said to him, "We are unclean through touching the dead body of a man; why are we kept from offering the Lord's offering at its appointed time among the people of Israel?" 8And Moses said to them, "Wait, that I may hear what the Lord will command concerning you."
>
> 9The Lord said to Moses, 10"Say to the people of Israel, If any man of you or of your descendants is unclean through touching a dead body, or is afar off on a journey, he shall still keep the passover to the Lord. 11In the second month on the fourteenth day in the evening they shall keep it; they shall eat it with unleavened bread and bitter herbs. 12They shall leave none of it until the morning, nor break a bone of it; according to all the statute for the passover they shall keep it. 13But the man who is clean and is not on a journey, yet refrains from keeping the passover, that person shall be cut off from his people, because he did not offer the Lord's offering at its appointed time; that man shall bear his sin. 14And if a stranger sojourns among you, and will keep the passover to the Lord, according to the statute of the passover and according to its ordinance, so shall he do; you shall have one statute, both for the sojourner and for the native."

In one sense there was no alternative to the feast. And there were no variations of emphasis allowed within the feast. But a problem did arise out of the command to and the desire to keep the Passover, a problem that would prove common enough. What was to be done about ritually unclean people who wanted to celebrate their redemption? And what about those who were clean ritually but unclean spiritually in that they didn't want to remember? Or even visitors to the camp? Real practical issues. Moses seeks the will of God.

Presumably Moses went to the tent of meeting (Exod. 25:22) to await God's word. Later on in Numbers (15:34) it is shown that people could be held in custody, as it were, until the answer came from the Lord about them. This is truly waiting on the Lord. And he speaks. For the ritually unclean comes a concession that they will not be punished for their inability to celebrate the Passover at the "appointed time" (v. 2). A supplementary celebration was sanctioned for one month later, which allowed enough time for the purification process to be completed. In this sense we can speak of an alternative Passover, with its own ordained, appointed time. An example of this taking place can be found in 2 Chron. 30:1–22, where King Hezekiah arranged for the feast in Jerusalem in the second month, as all the people, priests included, were unclean and had neglected the Lord's commands and forgotten his redemption from Egypt.

For those who were able to but chose not to claim the feast as their own and celebrate it, the matter was naturally much more serious. They were to be "cut off" from fellowship with the people of God. This expression represents a terrible judgement on the offender. But what does it really mean? Does it refer to execution or to excommunication? Would these amount to much the same thing in the hostile desert? Other examples of the verb show that it was used of the death of people, e.g. Gen. 9:11 of all the earth at the Flood; Isa. 29:20 of the wicked in Israel. Furthermore, an examination of the cases where the full phrase is used, "cut off from his people", shows that the offences are of the gravest nature, disobeying the Lord's commands and denying his sovereignty (Gen. 17:14; Lev. 7:20,21,25,27; 19:8; here). Most scholars therefore accept that the phrase means ritual killing to remove the person from the face of the earth (compare the story of Achan in Josh. 7).

Finally there is a ruling in v. 14 for visitors to the camp, i.e. non-Israelites who chose to live in the camp for set times, perhaps proselytes wishing to accept the faith of the Lord. In Exod. 12:48–49 it is laid down that such are to be welcomed as long as the males are circumcised. That stipulation is not stated here. But the important thing is that such well-intentioned people are to be welcomed into the fellowship under the one Lord and commandments. See Deut. 10:19.

There is kindness and openness in this section, then, as well as cruelty (even if it is in a good cause). Christians would be well advised to concentrate on the kindness and openness and to welcome to the Lord's Table—our Passover—all who wish to be there.

THE CLOUD AND THE TABERNACLE

Numbers 9:15–23

15On the day that the tabernacle was set up, the cloud covered the tabernacle, the tent of the testimony; and at evening it was over the tabernacle like the appearance of fire until morning. 16So it was continually; the cloud covered it by day, and the appearance of fire by night. 17And whenever the cloud was taken up from over the tent, after that the people of Israel set out; and in the place where the cloud settled down, there the people of Israel encamped. 18At the command of the Lord the people of Israel set out, and at the command of the Lord they encamped; as long as the cloud rested over the tabernacle, they remained in camp. 19Even when the cloud continued over the tabernacle many days, the people of Israel kept the charge of the Lord, and did not set out. 20Sometimes the cloud was a few days over the tabernacle, and according to the command of the Lord they remained in camp; then according to the command of the Lord they set out. 21And sometimes the cloud remained from evening until morning; and when the cloud was taken up in the morning, they set out, or if it continued for a day and a night, when the cloud was taken up they set out. 22Whether it was two days, or a month, or a longer time, that the cloud continued over the tabernacle, abiding there, the people of Israel remained in camp and did not set out; but when it was taken up they set out. 23At the command of the Lord they encamped, and at the command of the Lord they set out; they kept the charge of the Lord, at the command of the Lord by Moses.

As the people were about to leave Sinai they were given instructions when to camp and when to break camp—and, we are told, they responded. So in daylight hours a "cloud" led them: when it lifted and moved off, they broke camp and followed; when it settled, they made camp. By night a flame, or fire of sorts, covered the Tabernacle. This cloud was very important in Israel's life and traditions. It was a guiding system from God (Exod. 13:21–22) and also a sign of the presence of his glory (Exod. 16:10; 20:21; 40:34ff.). See also Lev. 16:2; 1 Kings 8:10. The repetitions in this simple story stress the importance of waiting for God's guidance, as much a message for today as then. And the spelling out in v. 22 that the people waited precisely the time indicated further shows that this passage "represents the profoundest convictions of the Hebrews about what actually happened to them in the desert—God himself led them" (John Marsh).

It will be remembered that at the Transfiguration of our Lord before his disciples "a bright cloud overshadowed them, and a voice from the cloud said, 'This is my beloved Son'..." (Matt. 17:5). The glory of the Father was still represented by the cloud at the time of the glorifying of the Son. The cloud's presence shows the presence of the holy God, and paradoxically, its opaqueness protects his glory from defilement and the people from contact with the holy God. It is recorded in 2 Chron. 6:1 that "The Lord has said that he would dwell in thick darkness". When the triumphant Son of Man comes, Jesus says, he will come "in clouds with great power and glory" (Mark 13:26; compare Rev. 1:7)— just as the Lord came at Sinai in power and glory (Exod. 19:9).

It is worth noting here that the word "the tabernacle" itself comes from a root meaning "to settle down" (hence the word for a "neighbour") or "to pitch a tent". And of course it was of a tent form. So the picture presented is of God camping with his people who formed a camp around him and centred on him. The Jewish traditions by Jesus' time had taken this root and developed a new term, *Shekinah*, for the closeness of God's presence with his people. There is a passage in the Jewish book, *The Sayings of the Fathers*, which reads: ".... if two sit together and the words of the law are spoken between them, the Shekinah rests between them". So Jesus can have the last word: "Where two or three are gathered in my name, there am I in the midst of them" (Matt. 18:20).

TWO SILVER TRUMPETS

Numbers 10:1–10

¹The Lord said to Moses, ²"Make two silver trumpets; of hammered work you shall make them; and you shall use them for summoning the congregation, and for breaking camp. ³And when both are blown, all the congregation shall gather themselves to you at the entrance of the tent of meeting. ⁴But if they blow only one, then the leaders, the heads of the tribes of Israel, shall gather themselves to you. ⁵When you blow an alarm, the camps that are on the east side shall set out. ⁶And when you blow an alarm the second time, the camps that are on the south side shall set out. An alarm is to be blown whenever they are to set out. ⁷But when the assembly is to be gathered together, you shall blow, but you shall not sound an alarm. ⁸And the sons of Aaron, the priests, shall blow the trumpets. The trumpets shall be to you for a perpetual statute throughout your generations. ⁹And when you go to war in your land against the adversary who oppresses you, then you shall sound an alarm with the trumpets, that you may be remembered before the Lord your God, and you shall be saved from your enemies. ¹⁰On the day of your gladness also, and at your appointed feasts, and at the beginnings of your months, you shall blow the trumpets over your burnt offerings and over the sacrifices of your peace offerings; they shall serve you for remembrance before your God: I am the Lord your God."

(i)

This is a lovely little passage on the two silver trumpets of the camp. Commissioned by God, they were again of the finest workmanship (v. 2) to honour him. There are three types of trumpet mentioned in the Old Testament, two for the signalling of events and calling to repentance, and the third type, which is referred to here. This was a long slender tube with flaring end, estimated at between one and one half to three feet long. It is represented on several coins and in the Roman Forum carved into the Arch of Titus.

The two trumpets had each two uses:

1(a) to assemble the camp, or its leaders
 (b) to signal the time to march
2(a) to call on the Lord for help in battle (see also 2 Chron. 13:12–15)

(b) to call on the Lord's presence at festivals (see also Ps. 98:6) There were two techniques in use also: firstly, a regular blast on the trumpet, and second, a staccato rhythm of three short blasts. Much of what we know of this comes from the writings of later times (e.g. the Mishnah). The short blasts naturally carried a note of urgency; compare 1 Cor. 14:8.

It was the priests who blew the trumpets, further stressing God's control over the camp. As in the section 5:11–31, there is the thought that God can be called upon to remember his people (vv. 9, 10). This is not a fear that he may forget his people, but rather an expression of humility before him. He must not be taken for granted, nor his blessing presumed. There were times when the people felt as if God had forgotten them, a common feeling among all of us, when like the Psalmist, we cry out: "Rouse thyself! Why sleepest thou, O Lord? Awake! Do not cast us off forever!" (Ps. 44:23). But to call on him in humility is to find him near. The Psalmists often ask God to "remember" them, and "remind" him of all he has done for them so far, anticipating similar care in the future (e.g. Pss. 25:6; 74:2, 18). Israel's confidence that the Lord really was always near is best expressed perhaps in the confidence of Elijah when sarcastically he criticizes Baal, the chief god of the Canaanites, who cannot answer. He mocks Baal's priests with the words: "Cry aloud, for he is a god; either he is musing, or he has gone aside [i.e. to the toilet!], or he is on a journey, or perhaps he is asleep and must be awakened" (1 Kings 18:27).

(ii)

Recalling the Lord's mercies is one of the best antidotes to the sickness of depression and cynicism, in ourselves or in others. Paul's letters to the churches were in large part responses to unhealthy situations there. They were sent to discipline and correct when it was necessary. And what Paul does time and again to get his own perspective and that of the church right, is to *remember:*

First, I thank my God through Jesus Christ for all of you . . . (Rom. 1:8).

I give thanks to God always for you ... (1 Cor. 1:4–8).
I thank my God in all my remembrance of you ... (Phil. 1:3–5).

It is an example worth following. Before we consider criticizing someone, or disciplining them, let us first pause long enough to remember what there is to give praise for; then thank God; then give them encouragement; and then speak with grace and truth about what needs to be spoken about.

We have come to the end of the record of the events that took place in the Sinai region as the people of Israel began their struggles in the wilderness. The story picks up again as they move off to the area of Paran.

ORDER OF THE MARCH

Numbers 10:11–28

[11]In the second year, in the second month, on the twentieth day of the month, the cloud was taken up from over the tabernacle of the testimony, [12]and the people of Israel set out by stages from the wilderness of Sinai; and the cloud settled down in the wilderness of Paran. [13]They set out for the first time at the command of the Lord by Moses. [14]The standard of the camp of the men of Judah set out first by their companies; and over their host was Nahshon the son of Amminadab. [15]And over the host of the tribe of the men of Issachar was Nethanel the son of Zuar. [16]And over the host of the tribe of the men of Zebulun was Eliab the son of Helon.

[17]And when the tabernacle was taken down, the sons of Gershon and the sons of Merari, who carried the tabernacle, set out. [18]And the standard of the camp of Reuben set out by their companies; and over their host was Elizur the son of Shedeur. [19]And over the host of the tribe of the men of Simeon was Shelumiel the son of Zurishaddai. [20]And over the host of the tribe of the men of Gad was Eliasaph the son of Deuel.

[21]Then the Kohathites set out, carrying the holy things, and the tabernacle was set up before their arrival. [22]And the standard of the camp of the men of Ephraim set out by their companies; and over their host was Elishama the son of Ammihud. [23]And over the host of the

tribe of the men of Manasseh was Gamaliel the son of Pedahzur. ²⁴And over the host of the tribe of the men of Benjamin was Abidan the son of Gideoni.

²⁵Then the standard of the camp of the men of Dan, acting as the rear guard of all the camps, set out by their companies; and over their host was Ahiezer the son of Ammishaddai. ²⁶And over the host of the tribe of the men of Asher was Pagiel the son of Ochran. ²⁷And over the host of the tribe of the men of Naphtali was Ahira the son of Enan. ²⁸This was the order of march of the people of Israel according to their hosts, when they set out.

The total time spent in the "wilderness of Sinai" seems to have been just under a year. According to Exod. 19:1 the people arrived at Sinai at the start of the third month of their first year of freedom, and according to v. 11 here, they left the area on the twentieth day of the second month of their second year of freedom. The first ten chapters of Numbers deal with the final twenty days of that period. A year of waiting on the Lord at the place where they received confirmation of his commitment to them and his demand for commitment from them; at the place where Moses received the revelation of God's will for them; at the place where having been liberated they were now created a nation! Constantly in the book of Numbers Israel is shown as having to wait on the Lord for revelation of his will; constantly she becomes impatient; so constantly Moses and Aaron have to wait on the Lord in the face of rebellion, grumbling and discouragement. It is a lesson hard to learn, but vital for a life with the Lord. We find it repeated many times outside this book too, but nowhere more poignantly than in Acts 1:1–5 where the risen Jesus tells the disciples to wait in Jerusalem, the place of the revelation, until he sends the promised Holy Spirit. There, as here, God's people are preparing to advance and take the Promised Land.

The cloud lifts from the "tabernacle of the testimony" and they move off. Having broken camp they set out according to the instructions already given (see 2:1–34), except that the Levites (2:17) are split; the Gershonites and Merarites set out with the Tabernacle immediately after the men of Judah, followed by the men of Reuben, and then come the Kohathites, with the "holy things". Thus by the time the latter arrived at the next camping site the Tabernacle would already be erected.

The camp moved "by stages", i.e. it took some days, until it came to the "wilderness of Paran". The name survives to this day in the names of some bedouin tribes. It is not known exactly where this area lay, but it was west of the Dead Sea/Aqaba Gulf rift and south of the Negeb. In short, it was another wilderness. How disheartening for the people! To experience such a solemn revelation of God's will around the bleak peaks of Sinai; to be prepared so thoroughly for warfare and adventure; and then to be led to a wilderness! Soon enough (see 11:1–3) the people grumble and rebel. It is so like the Lord to give an immediate test of faith and love after preparing for a great move with him. It is, sadly, so like us to misunderstand and lose heart.

At the back of the camp came the "men of Dan" as a "rear-guard". In Isa. 52:12 the same term is found of the Lord who is about to guide his people home from their bondage in Babylon: "the Lord will go before you, and the God of Israel will be your rear-guard". It is a wonderful picture of the Lord all around, leading and protecting. Just as wonderful is the fact that the related verb means to "gather up"; so Ps. 27:10 gives the beautiful picture of the Lord gathering up in his arms the Psalmist in the way that mothers and fathers cuddle their children close to them for warmth and security: "For my father and my mother have forsaken me, but the Lord will take me up".

Finally, there is an important word used in v. 28, where Israel is said to march according to her "hosts". Later on in Israel's life there emerged a title for the Lord which fast became a firm favourite with his people—"Lord of Hosts" (e.g. Isa. 9:7; Hos. 12:5). In different contexts this refers to God's leadership of:

(a) *the angelic armies*—for which see Ps. 148:2; Isa. 6:1–3; and especially Josh. 5:13–15. These are the warriors of heaven who fight the supernatural forces opposed to God's work.

(b) *the warrior armies of Israel*—for which see here; Exod. 7:4; 12:41, 51; Ps. 60:10; and especially 1 Sam. 17:45. These are the Lord's human warriors, who fight against his enemies on earth. This image does not have the attractiveness and warmth of the "rear-guard" image, but it also has its necessary lesson.

For the next forty years (all but) Israel will be constantly on the move in the areas south and east of Canaan.

GUIDED BY HOBAB

Numbers 10:29–32

> [29]And Moses said to Hobab the son of Reuel the Midianite, Moses' father-in-law, "We are setting out for the place of which the Lord said, 'I will give it to you'; come with us, and we will do you good; for the Lord has promised good to Israel." [30]But he said to him, "I will not go; I will depart to my own land and to my kindred." [31]And he said, "Do not leave us, I pray you, for you know how we are to encamp in the wilderness, and you will serve as eyes for us. [32]And if you go with us, whatever good the Lord will do to us, the same will we do to you."

Moses turns to another man for help. He has humility enough and wisdom enough to seek someone the Lord has sent Israel's way and who knows the lie of the land and will be able to lead their company through the treacherous wilderness. So what of the cloud that led them? Was that not enough? We are never given a picture of how the cloud moved; did it, for instance, move over the ground as an army might so that all that was necessary was to copy its movements? Perhaps it is sound to assume it moved as a normal cloud, high over the ground, so that all the camp could see it. Therefore it would move "as the crow flies", leaving the Israelites to negotiate the terrain and the route. In this sense, a guide would not be inconsistent with the cloud. Once again, Moses shows his humanity in its weakness (needing help) and in its strength (seeking help).

There is some difficulty in identifying the man he asked to help them. Here it is "Hobab the son of Reuel the Midianite, Moses' father-in-law"; but according to Judg. 4:11 Moses' father-in-law was Hobab himself. Exod. 2:18 tells us that Moses' father-in-law *was* Reuel who was a "Midianite"; however, in Exod. 18:1 the story is that it was "Jethro, the priest of Midian" who was Moses' father-in-law. It is all very confusing, and the scholars have many theories to account for these discrepancies. But this is not the place to discuss them. Of more interest is that we are not told what Hobab's final decision was. However, there is a hint in Judg. 1:16, which mentions descendants of Moses' father-in-law accompanying the people of Judah, that Moses succeeded in persuading Hobab to go with them as guide. The text puts it beautifully in saying he was to be Israel's "eyes". We are reminded of Job's description of himself as he had been before his disasters overtook him (29:15).

ARISE, O LORD!

Numbers 10:33–36

[33]So they set out from the mount of the Lord three days' journey; and the ark of the covenant of the Lord went before them three days' journey, to seek out a resting place for them. [34]And the cloud of the Lord was over them by day, whenever they set out from the camp.

[35]And whenever the ark set out, Moses said, "Arise, O Lord, and let thy enemies be scattered; and let them that hate thee flee before thee." [36]And when it rested, he said, "Return, O Lord, to the ten thousand thousands of Israel."

(i)

Why would the ark precede Israel by three days? Some scholars say the phrase "three days' journey" was accidentally repeated by a scribe copying the text and therefore should not be there the second time; in other words the ark was just in front of the people. The translators of the Syriac text could make no sense of it, so they changed the text to say that the ark preceded them only "one day", presumably to be able to say that it was close enough to them to be a guide. It is probably a careless repetition. The ark's function however, is clear and deliberate. No confusion there. The verb used for "to seek out" is the one used of the "spies" in Num. 13, chosen to confirm the glorious promise of the Lord to them that the land was in fact full of promise. The ark is leading them to that very place. It is a magnificent picture— behind them the "mount of the Lord", where they received their call and revelation, and before them the "ark of the covenant of the Lord", where was enshrined the revelation and presence of the Lord, taking them "home" to the Promised Land.

The word "resting place" gives an equally beautiful picture. This is a term used primarily of the Promised Land (e.g. Deut. 12:9; Ps. 95:11), the Israelites' real place of rest, of comfort and security, of ease and plenty, the dream of Israel right down the centuries. But it was a term too rich in meaning to be kept to one context. In Ps. 132:8ff. it is used for the ark's "resting place" in the Temple; in Ruth 1:9 Naomi wishes such a "home" for Ruth and Orpah; in Isa. 32:18 it describes the state of peace and security for God's people in the last days, when the Lord is finally triumphant; then in Isa. 66:1 it is used daringly of the very "place of . . . rest" of the Lord himself. Such a rest is the Lord's plan for all of us, his people: "Come to me, all who labour and are heavy laden, and I will give you rest" (Matt. 11:28). See also Heb. 4:9.

(ii)

Verses 35–36 seem strangely out of context here, being so martial in character. Especially is this true of the call for the ark to "return", since on the march it did not return, rather the Israelites caught up with it and camped around it. There seems little doubt that this is a text introduced here from elsewhere to further define the function of the ark. The Hebrew text actually has two giant letters "N" bracketing the verses, and the Talmud speculates that this indicates the verses were taken from another source (e.g. the "Book of the Wars of the Lord", Num. 21:14). They are triumphant verses, speaking hyperbolically of the 10,000,000 Israelites, or perhaps (see commentary on 1:16) their 10,000 "battalions". The Lord was their Warrior God.

These verses are still used at the opening and closing of the "Ark", i.e. the receptacle for holding the scrolls of the Old Testament, in the synagogue when the scrolls are taken out to be read. Yet they are very, very old indeed. They reflect a time when the ark was the focus of the Lord's power, and when the purpose of Israel as the army of the Lord was to occupy the Promised Land (see 1 Sam. 4:1–10; 2 Sam. 11:11). Some scholars see Ps. 24 as a song of celebration for the ark returning after victory in battle. This cry to the Lord to "rise" was a common war chant; see Ps. 68:1: "Let God arise, let his enemies be scattered..."; Isa. 28:21: "For the Lord will rise up as on Mount Perazim...". In Obad. 1 the Lord tells Israel to prepare for war and "Rise up!...".

At 10:28 we were reminded that the Lord was the "Lord of hosts", chief of the angelic and Israelite armies. There was a book, noted above, of the "Wars of the Lord". The idea of a people's god, or gods, being warriors was not, of course, unique to Israel (the Canaanite Baal was a warrior too), but the Lord proved himself the irresistible Warrior. Constantly he came to Israel as her Redeemer, and was celebrated as Conqueror. Study should be made by the reader of several key passages: Exod. 15:1–18, "The Lord is a man of war; the Lord is his name"; Deut. 33:1–3, 26–29; Josh. 5:13–15; Judg. 5:1–9; Pss. 24:7–10; 68:1, 7, 11ff.; Hab. 3:2–15. Clearly Israel saw her wars as the Lord's wars: "my lord is fighting the battles of the Lord" ... "Fear not, and be not dismayed at this great multitude; for the battle is not yours but God's" (1 Sam. 25:28; 2 Chron. 20:15).

Needless to say, she was not always right in thinking this. There are instances scattered throughout the Old Testament of the Lord not blessing Israel's campaigns because of her sins of disobedience or self-sufficiency; e.g. Num. 14:39–45; Josh. 7. Sometimes the Lord even wages war against Israel in judgement; e.g. Jer. 21:4ff., "I myself will fight against you with outstretched hand and strong arm, in anger, and in fury, and in great wrath." See also Isa. 10:5–27, where the Lord chooses to use Assyria for his purposes with Israel, although the Assyrians believe that the move is their idea. In short, the Lord will not put up with wickedness, nor with ingratitude for what he has done, nor with an ignoring of what he has revealed, whether among those opposed to his people or among his people themselves. We may be uncomfortable with it today, but very close to the centre of the Gospel of the Old Testament is the idea of God as a Warrior.

The New Testament is more circumspect, but it still makes rich use of military metaphors. The Lord is still fighting for his people.

Paul insists that we surround ourselves with "the whole armour of God" so that we can stand with Jesus in his fight against the "devil" and all wickedness wherever we find it. With Jesus, and in his might, ourselves protected by him, "we are ... contending against ... the principalities, against the powers, against the world rulers of this present darkness, against the spiritual *hosts* of wickedness in the heavenly places" (Eph. 6:10–17).

We must not forget that there is a battle to be waged against evil, and that faith sometimes needs to be encouraged, in the words of John Monsell's hymn, to:

> Fight the good fight
> With all thy might;
> Christ is thy strength,
> and Christ thy right.

There are even times when we should be praying with Israel of old: "Arise, O Lord, and let thy enemies be scattered; and let them that hate thee flee before thee."

BURNING: TABERAH

Numbers 11:1–3

¹And the people complained in the hearing of the Lord about their misfortunes; and when the Lord heard it, his anger was kindled, and the fire of the Lord burned among them, and consumed some outlying parts of the camp. ²Then the people cried to Moses; and Moses prayed to the Lord, and the fire abated. ³So the name of that place was called Taberah, because the fire of the Lord burned among them.

(i)

This is the first of several times the people begin grumbling and asserting themselves. They show themselves willing to wait on the Lord when everything is going well, or when at least they have a glimpse of how the Lord is working or about to work. But when they have nothing to look at then they begin to despair and fall away. It is a true characteristic of human nature that we need to be able to hold on to something tangible, or some dream of our own making, or someone of our acquaintance in order to feel secure. To be part of a situation where no help or familiarity is available or imaginable is to panic or to lose heart, or to grumble. What little faith we have in the Lord's providential care of us! After Jesus calmed the storm (*through which he himself was sleeping peacefully*) by commanding: "Peace! Be still!", he turned to his disciples with the sad words: "Why are you afraid? Have you no faith?" (Mark 4:35–41). He often has to say that to us.

It is the sin of ingratitude that looms so large on God's horizon. Right after the word of faith that Moses gave to Hobab in 10:29, that "the Lord has promised good to Israel", the people complain about their "misfortunes", the word being in fact the Hebrew for the opposite of "good", i.e. "evil". As Job had to learn, it is the Lord who sends all life's experiences, all working together for his "good" (Job 2:10). But what may be "good" for us may often be not what we want to hear, so it comes across as something "bad", as in the slightly comic figure of the king of Israel who was obviously not prepared to hear the word of God from the prophet Micaiah when it didn't suit him (1 Kings 22:8). The Israelites needed to learn properly, as we do, that "in everything God works for good with those who love him, who are called according to his purpose" (Rom. 8:28).

We are not told what they were actually complaining about. The Rabbinic tradition has it that, as on the next occasion, they complained of hunger, and so some suggest that the word for "hunger" was the original text, not "evil". This requires only a slight change in the Hebrew. However, the play on ideas with the "good" of 10:29 seems much more powerful and original. It is enough for the writer's purpose to point out that when faced with actual problems, the people started to complain rather than to praise God and seek a chance to serve him and learn more about him.

(ii)

To express the Lord's anger and punishment, the "fire of the

Lord" falls on the camp. This image of "fire" is a consistent one in the Old Testament. God's glorious presence is often conveyed by the presence of fire, as at Sinai (Exod. 13:21; 24:17); it is a manifestation of his purging power (e.g. Lev. 9:22ff.; Num. 16:19ff.; Ps. 18:8ff.); it is seen as God's distinct way of judgement (Amos 1:4; Lam. 1:12–13; Ezek. 10:1–2); it is a symbol of God's wrath (e.g. Isa. 30:27ff.; Jer. 15:14; 17:4). God himself can be described as "a devouring fire, a jealous God" (Deut. 4:24; compare Heb. 12:29). The image speaks of his irresistibility, his purity, his fascination. But more than that, it tells of his power to refine and help his people to maturity and cleanness: "For he is like a refiner's fire . . . and he will purify the sons of Levi and refine them . . ." (Mal. 3:2ff.). In fact his judgement is his purification: "Behold I have refined you . . . in the furnace of affliction" (Isa. 48:10).

Here is the Gospel of God's judgement—his anger is at the sin not the sinner. Any time he punishes, it is seen by him as a disciplining, an educating, a refining; it is a rooting out of all that is not godly in us, of all that hinders us from being who God wants us to be, of all that is not part of the harvest of the Spirit. It is for our good. As long as we turn always to God, even in the middle of disciplining, then we will be "being changed into his likeness from one degree of glory to another; for this comes from the Lord who is the Spirit" (2 Cor. 3:18).

(iii)

Finally, mention must be made of Moses as the great intercessor for Israel. The narration of v. 2 is very simple and low-key, beautifully so. Many times we read of him praying for them, but sometimes, as here, the people came to him. This is found again in Num. 21:7: "And the people came to Moses, and said, '. . . pray to the Lord . . .'". Even though they grumbled about him and sometimes even plotted against him, the people knew that he was the Lord's man. Wouldn't it be wonderful if that could be said about us?

MANNA PROVIDED

Numbers 11:4–9

> [4]Now the rabble that was among them had a strong craving; and the people of Israel also wept again, and said, "O that we had meat to eat! [5]We remember the fish we ate in Egypt for nothing, the cucumbers, the melons, the leeks, the onions, and the garlic; [6]but now our strength is dried up, and there is nothing at all but this manna to look at."
>
> [7]Now the manna was like coriander seed, and its appearance like that of bdellium. [8]The people went about and gathered it, and ground it in mills or beat it in mortars, and boiled it in pots, and made cakes of it; and the taste of it was like the taste of cakes baked with oil. [9]When the dew fell upon the camp in the night, the manna fell with it.

The Old Testament is a wonderfully "human" book, meaning that although it is the Word of God to his people, it shows that people to be no more nor less than what they are. There is no feeling given that faults are hushed up or that inadequacies are glossed over. There is no evidence that only the good stories are related about the characters who feature among the people. No bones are made about Jacob being a twister; or about Samson being a womanizer; or about Saul being disobedient to God's explicit commands; or about David having lust for Bathsheba and arranging for the death of her husband. Absalom comes across as a schemer and a coward; Ahab as a corrupt and weak man; Israel as a people constantly wrestling with her God. She could never make up her mind whether to commit absolutely everything to the Lord, or whether to hold something in reserve for other lords; she did not always see the need for the prophets to insist on total surrender to only one Lord; undoubtedly it took a long time before she believed there were no other gods. There really was no uniformly responsive entity "Israel"—she was made up of human beings like ourselves.

Under the influence of some who were worse than the rest ("the rabble"), the whole people lost heart. They let the moans of a dissatisfied minority speak louder to them than the promises of God. And they "wept again", presumably referring to vv. 1–3.

One of the greatest Jewish commentators, Rashi, asked pointedly why did they cry out for meat when they were surrounded by their own sheep and cattle (Exod. 12:38; 17:3; and v. 22 in this very chapter). Perhaps these were being kept for sacrificial purposes. But even if from time to time they ate some of their animals, it was clearly the fish and the vegetables and fruit and herbs of Egypt that they missed. Instead of this varied diet, they now had only the manna as a staple daily food. And they had to work hard to gather and prepare it, whereas in Egypt they had all these different dishes "for nothing". In Exod. 16:1–21 a parallel account is given of this episode and of the one concerning the quails recorded in 11:31–35. In that passage it is said that the "whole congregation" moaned and grumbled about the lack of food until the Lord sent daily "bread from heaven" (v. 4), which they found on the ground as "a fine flakelike thing" (v. 14). Here, however, it is only stated that it was there all the time. In Exodus the manna was part of the miracle of food provided where there was none; here it is part of the problem needing a miracle; there, the "quails" were the other part of the miracle; here they are the miraculous provision altogether.

But what was it, this "manna"? Bread? Not according to this passage, nor indeed to the Exodus passage, where "bread" means simply "food". Most scholars agree that it was in fact a gum-like substance from a shrub called the *Tamarix gallica*. At night the juice that builds up during the day drops onto the ground, and this then melts in the morning sun. The bedouin still put it onto bread as a form of jam. The name of the substance in Arabic is *"mann"*, hence the Hebrew term "manna". This is further corroborated by the fact that they gathered it in the morning, with the dew. Exod. 16:15 gives a more fanciful explanation of the name. On seeing it for the first time the Israelites asked, "What is it?", which in Hebrew is *"man hu"*, thus suggesting the similar-sounding name "manna".

The RSV translation in v. 6 is a bit misleading. The complaint is not that they are weak from hunger ("our strength is dried up") but rather, "there is nothing at all to whet our appetite". In other words, they are experiencing wilderness living with none of the varied luxuries they had known, and are sickened by the constant necessity to eat this nutritious but boring food.

Here is God's sovereign way: to work great and glorious wonders, to do mighty miracles on a vast incomprehensible scale; and yet also to arrange for all the regular and equally wonderful workings of his creation to serve his people just at the time they are needed—the arrival of a message in a letter, for example, or a telephone call, or a personal visit, just when we need it; a chance meeting with someone just when it is necessary for us to be moved in another direction; that personal word to us in a sermon when the rest of the congregation hears something else; the daily food and security so often taken for granted. All are miracles of God's providential care for us. So here in the wilderness, in the desert lands, God gave his people food, and, a point often missed, daily water: "When the dew fell upon the camp in the night, the manna fell with it" (v. 9).

MOSES CONFESSES I

Numbers 11:10–15

[10]Moses heard the people weeping throughout their families, every man at the door of his tent; and the anger of the Lord blazed hotly, and Moses was displeased. [11]Moses said to the Lord, "Why hast thou dealt ill with thy servant? And why have I not found favour in thy sight, that thou dost lay the burden of all this people upon me? [12]Did I conceive all this people? Did I bring them forth, that thou shouldst say to me, 'Carry them in your bosom, as a nurse carries the sucking child, to the land which thou didst swear to give their fathers?' [13]Where am I to get meat to give to all this people? For they weep before me and say, 'Give us meat, that we may eat.' [14]I am not able to carry all this people alone, the burden is too heavy for me. [15]If thou wilt deal thus with me, kill me at once, if I find favour in thy sight, that I may not see my wretchedness."

(i)

This is an important little section about the life of Moses. As was said in the last section, the Old Testament never backs away from showing its heroes in their full humanity. Here, in the context of an ungrateful and complaining Israel, Moses is shown to be complaining too. When the text says that Moses was "displeased", it means just that. This was no time of quiet, humble, confident prayer, trusting in the Lord to fulfil all that he had promised. There is no sense of thankfulness here at all for the Lord's commission to him, for the privilege of being his minister. Instead it is a time of confession that the responsibility is too great, that the demands made are too much for him.

So the question begs to be asked: what is the difference at this point between Moses and the people of Israel? Or more acutely put: what is the difference between Moses and the rabble? Of course he had an appreciation of God that far outstripped the others; of course he had a vision that the others only guessed at or saw in part; of course God himself had called him out to be his man; of course he was experiencing pressures far beyond the understanding of the others. But the more God gives, the more he expects. Moses was given gifts to enable him to be God's man. It was perhaps always in God's plan to delegate his authority down to other levels (see later in the chapter). However, Moses' reaction is not that of obedience and gratitude. So at this point, there is no difference between him and the others; Moses was always one of the children of Israel.

(ii)

Put briefly, Moses tries to justify himself before the Lord. His insight into his own inadequacies before the Lord is right—he is not able to shoulder responsibility for the Lord's people. He feels this responsibility very strongly, and feels at the same time helpless before the "anger of the Lord" which was "blazing" at the people for their ingratitude, their lack of trust, their lack of commitment to their calling. We are shown here a typically human reaction to the burden that responsibility often brings. Moses worries and frets like a father does when he feels he cannot cope with the needs of his family and household—yet he does not turn to the true Father in the right spirit, even though Israel's Father is just waiting to be asked to give the gifts necessary. Forgetting his own great confident claim of Num. 10:29, Moses actually accuses the Lord of willing harm to him: "Why hast thou dealt ill with thy servant?'' See how like us Moses is! He accused the Lord of willing harm against the whole of the people before the Exodus too (Exod. 5:22). The Lord showed him then by the Exodus just how wrong he was; and he is shortly to show him again by another miracle.

How many of us forget to turn situations over to the Lord in trust and expectation, instead waiting until they become a burden and then suspecting the Lord of unfairness or not being truly understanding of our situation! He wants to be Father and Lord of all situations, even of those which he has entrusted to our care.

Of course it was the Lord and not Moses who *conceived* Israel, as Moses himself once reminded him (Exod. 33:12–13) and he, not Moses, who *carried* Israel. Compare the beautiful picture given in Isa. 40:11 of the Lord acting as a nurse or a mother might, carrying Israel in his arms. Let us, then, as Moses had to, learn to recognize God as the One to shoulder responsibility, and make sure we give everything daily to him and ask to be shown what his will is.

Jesus is the one who stands between men and God, between sin and holiness, between inability and ability, between curse and blessing, between death and life. Jesus is the only one to accept the commission to represent all of humanity and all of God. He will shoulder all our responsibilities under God, as the prophet saw: ''For to us a child is born, to us a son is given; and the government will be upon his shoulder, and his name will be called 'Wonderful Counsellor, Mighty God, Everlasting Father, Prince of Peace'" (Isa. 9:6).

MOSES CONFESSES II

Numbers 11:10–15 (*cont'd*)

(iii)

Moses' plea for swift merciful death deserves attention. It is not a proof-text of euthenasia in the context, and must not be used as such. Rather than fail in what he understood to be God's task for him, he preferred to die. And acknowledging that not only the task but his life itself comes from the Lord, he asks the Lord to express his love for him by sparing him the failure. Note, he does not ask to be relieved of the task, such was his conviction of the Lord's total and unchangeable claim on him.

Moses the man and Moses the leader of God's people are one and the same, so he asks to be killed so that another may take his place and fulfil God's task. What parallels are there for this in the Old Testament? In Job 3 the sufferer bitterly regrets that he was born at all, and asks in retrospect for death: "Why did I not die at birth...?" (Job 3:11). A little later he makes a plea "that it would please God to crush me, that he would let loose his hand and cut me off" (Job 6:9). Why? Because he would rather have that than have the world believe him to have been unfaithful to God, to have been a sinner and a hypocrite, he who had once been a guide for others.

In 1 Kings 19:4 the prophet Elijah "asked that he might die". Why? Because he had run for his life away from the corrupt power of Queen Jezebel, Ahab's domineering wife. He might have expected persecution after taking a stand for the Lord, yet instead of remaining faithful and going on with his witness to the power of the Lord, he took to his heels. In remorse, rather than live with the failure of his ministry, as he saw it, he asked for death. A fascinating example is also found in Jon. 4:3, where the prophet begs the Lord to take his life "for it is better for me to die than to live". Why? Because God had succeeded in getting Jonah to tell the deadly enemies in Nineveh the good news of the Lord's power and love, and of their need to change their minds and ways. And because rather than see these people find forgiveness for all their wickedness to Israel, he would prefer to die. It went against everything he believed about the Lord and his commitment to Israel, his special people.

(iv)

Moses' request for death in Exod. 32:32 is a different case, since there he asks to die rather than live without his people who deserved to be destroyed for ingratitude to the Lord in building a golden idol so soon after their redemption from Egypt. It is also different in that Moses there first asked that the Lord would forgive them all, thus sparing Moses such loneliness, only suggesting his own death if that should fail.

Many sermons have been preached on all these cases, and articles written on what they have in common. For all the differences between them, one thing stands out. In each case the men misunderstood their responsibilities and privileges under God, and so, rather than experience shame or reproach, they wished for death. Simon Peter misunderstood the plan of God for Jesus, which led to his severe censure (Matt. 16:13–23). There are few tasks as vital as listening to God, getting the message right.

Finally, note must be made of Moses' designation of himself as the Lord's "servant" (v. 11). It would be tempting to try to sum up Moses as God's great lawgiver, or prophet, or judge, or statesman, yet when God himself spoke of Moses to his successor, Joshua, he said: "Moses my servant is dead" (Josh. 1:2). The fact that Moses was God's servant is stressed five times in that opening chapter (1:1, 2, 7, 13, 15), and the New Testament sums up his life and ministry by saying: "Now Moses was faithful in all God's house as a servant" (Heb. 3:5). That is what God wants from us, to be faithful in our service, whatever it be, great or small. If Moses was so like us, then it means that also we can be like him. Maybe not to lead God's people, maybe not to lead anything at all, but to be servants of God, faithful to do whatever asked of us.

In Jesus we can be servants of the Lord, at rest in his promised land. Even Moses, the great servant, was disobedient, and only saw the Promised Land from a distance. He too only got to serve the Lord in the Promised Land when he was with Jesus (Matt. 17:1–3).

A CHARISMATIC MOVEMENT

Numbers 11:16–25

[16]And the Lord said to Moses, "Gather for me seventy men of the elders of Israel, whom you know to be the elders of the people and

officers over them; and bring them to the tent of meeting, and let them take their stand there with you. [17]And I will come down and talk with you there; and I will take some of the spirit which is upon you and put it upon them; and they shall bear the burden of the people with you, that you may not bear it yourself alone. [18]And say to the people, 'Consecrate yourselves for tomorrow, and you shall eat meat; for you have wept in the hearing of the Lord, saying, "Who will give us meat to eat? For it was well with us in Egypt." Therefore the Lord will give you meat, and you shall eat.[19] You shall not eat one day, or two days, or five days, or ten days, or twenty days,[20] but a whole month, until it comes out at your nostrils and becomes loathsome to you, because you have rejected the Lord who is among you, and have wept before him, saying, "Why did we come forth out of Egypt?" ' " [21]But Moses said, "The people among whom I am number six hundred thousand on foot; and thou hast said, 'I will give them meat, that they may eat a whole month!' [22]Shall flocks and herds be slaughtered for them, to suffice them? Or shall all the fish of the sea be gathered together for them, to suffice them?" [23]And the Lord said to Moses, "Is the Lord's hand shortened? Now you shall see whether my word will come true for you or not."

[24]So Moses went out and told the people the words of the Lord; and he gathered seventy men of the elders of the people, and placed them round about the tent. [25]Then the Lord came down in the cloud and spoke to him, and took some of the spirit that was upon him and put it upon the seventy elders; and when the spirit rested upon them, they prophesied. But they did so no more.

(i)

The Lord's answer to Moses' plea is to direct him to select seventy of the elders of the people and gather them together at the tent of meeting. Who were these men? Obviously they were already called by God to positions of authority in the camp, not called out fresh for this service. It is probably best to see them as camp "overseers". Or were they, as some prefer, "secretaries" or "scribes"? In which case it is perhaps right to translate "minor officials". Either way, they suggest a certain structure and system of authority among the people to look after their daily needs. Similar perhaps to the role of the "seven men of good repute" in Acts 6:1–6. Jesus sent out "seventy others" to minister in the towns and villages, charged with his authority to preach and serve (Luke 10:1–10), probably consciously thinking of this incident.

These men, then, have been prepared by God for this coming task. The Lord says he "will come down" to talk with Moses about this new situation, and carry out the necessary work. This is one of only ten verses where God says he will "come down" to manifest himself on earth, which suggests that what is happening here is an important stage in the life of the community. The ordaining of elders is of fundamental importance for God's people, and is extraordinarily exciting in the spiritual life of any congregation if God is behind it.

Moses asked the Lord to relieve him of the burden in one way, but the Lord does it in another. He raises up more men to serve with him. Even when the Lord undertakes to do something for us, he often, if not invariably, does it using other people. God loves to use people, and his people should not only be open and ready to be used, but also open and ready to see God using others, or to hear him speak through others. What is more, the Lord says he "will take some of the spirit" which is upon Moses to put on them at their anointing. In other words, no more pouring out of God's Spirit is necessary; there is enough of God's Spirit there to do what is required. All that is needed is a redistribution of the authority. The root-meaning of the verb is "to join with, share", and here it means to separate off something from a large block for use in other places, which is a form of sharing. It is not competition but communion. Here is a word for the Church, surely. We need to learn the mistake of a totally professional ministry or clergy. Churches can only grow as pastors and lay people share the ministries and the gifts, encouraging ministry in everyone.

(ii)

Also note that the Spirit is "put upon" people by God. Such a movement does not come from within the people concerned; it is not subjective, and merely subjective criteria for saying one is full of the Spirit is not evidence of it. This is the Old Testament insight, and another famous example can be found in 2 Kings 2:15, where the succession of prophet by prophet is greeted by the cry: "The spirit of Elijah rests on Elisha". The Spirit of God is almost tangible or visible, so real is it and powerful. And of course the New Testament finally shows how the Holy Spirit is indeed a Person, not controllable or ownable by any. He moves with the total freedom of God (John 3:8).

Moses is still doubting the power of the Lord to do as he wills. So he says to the Lord, with great stress on the pronoun, "and *you* have said...". All is put, somewhat disbelievingly, onto the Lord, where in fact it belongs. And the Lord asks, rhetorically, is he not able to do it? The implication is that, of course, the Lord can do it. What he has said will happen, his "word will come true" (Isa. 55:11).

The stage is set, and Moses gathers the elders. The Lord descends in the cloud that is there as their guide and the guarantee of his presence with them. Note that God only speaks to Moses, so he is still the specially chosen one (see Num. 12:8). It was a case of Moses' share of the Spirit being shared out, not of any unwillingness of God to give more, and also it shows that Moses was in a sense one of God's "mediators". He spoke to Moses, and Moses passed the message on; he also took the Spirit from Moses to pass on. Under the influence of this Spirit, the seventy "prophesied". This verb connotes the frenzied ecstatic behaviour and speech of those under the control of another's will—the Lord's or not as the case would have it. It is used of Saul, e.g. in 1 Sam. 10:11 and 19:23; and the results could be fairly unconventional if the passage 2 Kings 9:4–11 is to be understood properly, since the prophet is there said to be a "mad fellow".

More positively, however, when the Spirit descended on people he could give various gifts and authoritative ministries: (a) *craftmanship of the highest calibre* (Exod. 31:3); (b) *military skills* (Judg. 6:34; 11:29; 13:25); (c) *prophetic declaration* (here; Isa. 61:1); (d) *interpretation of dreams* (Gen. 41:38). The coming of the Spirit, in other words, empowers one to do what the Lord has in mind. These men were empowered to pray in and *imagine-in* the miracle of God.

If we let God have his way with us, and wait for him to put his Spirit upon us, then whatever gift we receive will enable God to use us in his service.

ELDAD AND MEDAD: JOSHUA AND MOSES

Numbers 11:26–30

26Now two men remained in the camp, one named Eldad, and the other named Medad, and the spirit rested upon them; they were among those registered, but they had not gone out to the tent, and so they prophesied in the camp. 27And a young man ran and told Moses, "Eldad and Medad are prophesying in the camp." 28And Joshua the son of Nun, the minister of Moses, one of his chosen men, said, "My lord Moses, forbid them." 29But Moses said to him, "Are you jealous for my sake? Would that all the Lord's people were prophets, that the Lord would put his spirit upon them!" 30And Moses and the elders of Israel returned to the camp.

(i)

In the middle of all this activity and change, and also in the middle of the camp, were two men who figure in this, one of the most celebrated passages of the Old Testament. For reasons not given, they were not part of the party who went out of the camp to the tent with Moses and Aaron at the Lord's command. Who were they? "Eldad", whose name means *God has loved* or the like, and "Medad", whose name has something to do with either the same root "to be loved" or the root "to cast lots".

Joshua is described as one of Moses' "chosen men", an honour indeed. He is also called "the minister of Moses". The same term is used to describe him as Moses' "minister" in Josh. 1:1, and the Old Testament is at pains to show that there could have been no more worthy successor to Moses than Joshua. In modern Hebrew the term or its associated verb are used of public service in commerce, business, etc., but in classical Hebrew they meant service in the sanctuary to the Lord's people. They are common enough in the book of Numbers (1:50; 3:6, 31; 4:12; 8:26; here;

18:2). But to be a "chosen man" is quite special. Joshua would accompany Moses everywhere.

(ii)

And so to v. 29, one of the outstanding Old Testament verses. Moses wishes that *all* the Israelites were "prophets", not just he himself and the seventy men called by God shortly before. Prophets often expressed themselves ecstatically, extravagantly; but the prophetic call wasn't to a constant dervish-like state. Prophets were expected to read the signs of the times and give spiritual and moral and political direction, even specific directions occasionally. Sometimes they foretold events, though this involved more of an insight into God's character and plans than of a pure ability to predict the future—and we have to remember that such a person could always be a false prophet (Deut. 13:1–5). In the end, the best description of a prophet is that he or she is someone who speaks for God, directly, immediately, faithfully. This is seen clearly in the classic prophetic calls in Isa. 6:8–9; Jer. 1:7; Ezek. 2:3–4; 3:10–11; Amos 7:14–15; Hag. 1:13. Most dramatically of all it is seen in the call of Moses and then his brother Aaron to be Moses' spokesman before Pharaoh. It is put boldly that Aaron will just repeat Moses' words, as Moses in fact just repeats God's words: "and he shall be a mouth for you, and you shall be to him as God" (Exod. 4:10–16; see also Exod. 7:1).

So Moses says in effect that he would like *all* of the people of Israel to be open to the Lord to receive cleanly and clearly any messages from him, and to be obedient to him to pass them on as they received them (compare 1 Cor. 11:23). Thus they would truly be a "light to the nations" (Isa. 42:6). This is the Lord's purpose with his people, and all who follow Jesus Christ are expected to listen and to pass on. Some are still called to the public office of prophethood in the Church, but also, all believers are prophets, both men and women. Long before the coming of Jesus, Moses wanted this. He reprimands Joshua for his alarm, even though he was probably trying to protect Moses' position and authority.

What is not altogether clear is whether Joshua was repri-
manded for being "jealous" or "zealous". It is an awkward word.
In Num. 25:11, for example, the AV has the latter, and the RSV
has the former. And the various other English versions differ
here too. The Hebrew root means "to get worked up", and so can
convey either of the two English attitudes in context. Probably
here it means that Moses does not want Joshua to defend his
position at the expense of God's freedom to choose and use
whoever he wants. Too many leaders in society and even within
the family of the Church are protective of their status. Nothing
stops a community from growing quite so much as a leader who
tries to keep all responsibility, all expertise, all knowledge, all
vision to himself. Leaders must be constantly seeking to help the
Lord create out of their community a "royal priesthood, a holy
nation" who will all minister to each other and to the world.

TOO MUCH OF A GOOD THING?

Numbers 11:31–35

31 And there went forth a wind from the Lord, and it brought quails
from the sea, and let them fall beside the camp, about a day's journey
on this side and a day's journey on the other side, round about the
camp, and about two cubits above the face of the earth. 32 And the
people rose all that day, and all night, and all the next day, and
gathered the quails; he who gathered least gathered ten homers; and
they spread them out for themselves all around the camp. 33 While the
meat was yet between their teeth, before it was consumed, the anger of
the Lord was kindled against the people, and the Lord smote the
people with a very great plague. 34 Therefore the name of that place
was called Kibroth-hattaavah, because there they buried the people
who had the craving. 35 From Kibroth-hattaavah the people journeyed
to Hazeroth; and they remained at Hazeroth.

(i)

In the Old Testament there are several agencies associated with
the Lord's carrying out of his will. One such is "the wind", and
often he sends a strong wind to save his people or to teach them a

lesson (Gen. 8:1; Exod. 10:13, 19; 14:21; Pss. 104:4; 148:8; Jon.1:4). Here it is the wind that marks the beginning of God's miracle by bringing meat out of nowhere. This is of course the mark of God's creativity and activity, distinguishing him from all others, in that he and he alone creates out of nothing at the perfect time and place. So really even the very wind is part of the miracle, it being "a wind from the Lord". As often, God uses natural objects or events to show his control and care. The miracle of God's deeds is that they are the right deeds at the right time in the right place. And the miracle of God's prophetic gifts is that they are the right words at the right time in the right place. This can mean an amazing prediction of far future events or a profound analysis of current political events; it can mean a virgin birth or an influx of sea birds into the wilderness.

The birds are "quails", and the Biblical term is still the word used in modern Egypt. They fly in large numbers across the eastern Mediterranean shores in the spring, returning southwards in early autumn, and on both flights the bedouin and fishermen net them fairly easily. For the people of Israel the miracle is that God says he will bring meat, and brings it—massive quantities of it. They came "a day's journey" all around the camp, and it has been suggested that this was an idiom equivalent to our phrase "a stone's throw". Most of the English versions suggest by their translations that they lay about three feet deep on the ground, but it is possible that the text means they flew about three feet off the ground only, and so were easily caught.

Good meat. Moist also. God provided well. In vv. 18–23 a month is given as the period of consumption, and here it is said that there was still more to be eaten when the judgement came. The phrase "before it was consumed" should be translated for clearer sense "before it ran out". The people gathered them all in immediately and each had at least "ten homers", which is about 100 bushels. In the words of one commentator, this is frankly "gluttonous". According to the text, they "spread them out", presumably to dry out in the sun and bleach (compare Jer. 8:2).

(ii)

So why did some die? The commentators argue back and forth about the effects of gross gluttony, with the old Century Bible saying it was a simple case of "eating to excess". But the text says it was "a very great plague". Speculation abounds on whether they ate the meat raw in their greed and contracted something, or whether it was infested with some disease or parasite, etc., but it remains speculation. Some believe the problem was an unbalanced diet in the wilderness leading to deficiencies in the body and a lowered resistance to diseases of the desert, of which they would be ignorant anyway. Whatever the explanation, their "craving" (v. 4) led to their death. This term "craving" can be used positively (e.g. Ps. 10:17; Isa. 26:8) or negatively (e.g. Ps. 10:3; here), and means an all-consuming passion for something. In this case it had to do with the old life of slavery in Egypt. The poetic justice is that the Lord punished them by the fulfilling of their short-sighted desires.

Something of this in the spiritual realm is conveyed by Jesus in his judgement of religious hypocrites for whom public recognition of their piety is as important as the piety itself. He says that to be "rewarded" by God we must do everything quietly and unseen. To do otherwise is to fail to be "rewarded", yet Jesus says that such people "have their reward" (Matt. 6:1–18, especially vv. 2, 5, 16). What does this mean? It means their short-sighted desires are fulfilled, i.e. to be seen and respected. And yet, though they receive what they want, their spirits are killed. No communication is made with God, no search for God is underway, and so death follows.

The place where the incident happened is given an appropriate name ("Graves of craving"), and the people move on to a place whose name (Hazeroth) is connected with a word meaning a settled home or area where roots are put down. The impression is that lessons were learned and a healing process had begun. This is the only time the verb "journeyed" is used of the camp setting out, it being the same verb as that used in v. 31 for the wind being sent by the Lord. He moved both wind and people according to his will, and to accomplish what he wanted. But alas! the time of learning and healing was to be a long one.

RELIGIOUS JEALOUSY

Numbers 12:1–16

¹Miriam and Aaron spoke against Moses because of the Cushite woman whom he had married, for he had married a Cushite woman; ²and they said, "Has the Lord indeed spoken only through Moses? Has he not spoken through us also?" And the Lord heard it. ³Now the man Moses was very meek, more than all men that were on the face of the earth. ⁴And suddenly the Lord said to Moses and to Aaron and Miriam, "Come out, you three, to the tent of meeting." And the three of them came out. ⁵And the Lord came down in a pillar of cloud, and stood at the door of the tent, and called Aaron and Miriam; and they both came forward. ⁶And he said, "Hear my words: If there is a prophet among you, I the Lord make myself known to him in a vision, I speak with him in a dream. ⁷Not so with my servant Moses; he is entrusted with all my house. ⁸With him I speak mouth to mouth, clearly, and not in dark speech; and he beholds the form of the Lord. Why then were you not afraid to speak against my servant Moses?"

⁹And the anger of the Lord was kindled against them, and he departed; ¹⁰and when the cloud removed from over the tent, behold, Miriam was leprous, as white as snow. And Aaron turned towards Miriam, and behold, she was leprous. ¹¹And Aaron said to Moses, "Oh, my Lord, do not punish us because we have done foolishly and have sinned. ¹²Let her not be as one dead, of whom the flesh is half consumed when he comes out of his mother's womb." ¹³And Moses cried to the Lord, "Heal her, O God, I beseech thee." ¹⁴But the Lord said to Moses, "If her father had but spit in her face, should she not be shamed seven days? Let her be shut up outside the camp seven days, and after that she may be brought in again." ¹⁵So Miriam was shut up outside the camp seven days; and the people did not set out on the march till Miriam was brought in again. ¹⁶After that the people set out from Hazeroth, and encamped in the wilderness of Paran.

(i)

In this chapter the cause for the Lord's intervention is given immediately: "Miriam and Aaron spoke against Moses". What is more, the reason for this is also given immediately: "because of the Cushite woman whom he had married". What was so awful about that? There are strong traditions that the Cushites came from what is otherwise known as Ethiopia. Could it then be that she was not a follower of the Lord, and therefore this angered them? Others believe that Moses caused anger by marrying again after he married Zipporah (Exod. 2:16–21). However, the Jewish traditions try to equate this "Cushite woman" with Zipporah to keep Moses a monogamist. In Hab. 3:7 the places "Cushan" and "Midian" are paralleled, suggesting that they were different names for the same area, or for the same people. So Zipporah's father, the "priest of Midian", might well be equally correctly termed a Cushite.

But if it was Zipporah, why the fuss? Did she exert too much influence on Moses in their opinion? She is never mentioned. Did she allow her father too much influence? In the light of 10:29–32, it is possible that they were jealous of this, but then one would expect it to be mentioned in v. 2 instead of an attack on Moses' own relationship with God. It is a mystery why they were angry. Some Jewish commentators make reference to Exod. 18:2ff., where the phrase "sent her away" could be a euphemism for "divorced". This divorce is therefore seen as the cause for anger. Conjecture allows that perhaps they had spoken against this and he had not listened. The challenge is extremely severe.

In comparison with Joshua's misplaced loyalty in 11:28, protecting Moses' uniqueness, here is a misplaced disloyalty, questioning Moses' uniqueness. After the challenge come the words, "And the Lord heard it. Now the man Moses was very meek . . .". God himself takes up the cause of his servant, and the only time Moses speaks in this episode is when he prays for the healing of the one who challenged him. God will always honour his servants, and in the face of trouble or opposition, if we are surely working for the Lord, then the only truly faithful response is to leave judgement to the Lord, and bless the oppressors. Jesus teaches: "Love your enemies, and pray for those who persecute you" (Matt. 5:44).

(ii)

The description of Moses as "very meek" is important for understanding what God prizes in mankind. It does not mean a whimpering, spineless, uncommitted weakling. Moses never was. The term seems to have a history, with four stages:

(a) *poor, needy* (e.g. Deut. 15:11)
(b) *powerless, without influence* (e.g. Amos 2:7)
(c) *oppressed by the powerful* (e.g. Ps. 10:17)
(d) *therefore, those who rely solely on God in life* (e.g. here; Ps. 37:11; Zeph. 2:3; Matt. 5:5).

Such was Moses, and such will inherit the earth. If the Lord had not heard the challenge, then Moses would have been in trouble. But he did hear; he did call them out of the camp to deal with the situation; he did "come down" in the cloud; and he did speak. More beautiful irony meets the reader here. In parallel with the Lord's fulfilment/judgement noted in 11:31–35, the Lord here fulfils the desire of Miriam and Aaron by speaking to them *not* in dreams or visions, but directly, as to Moses—and yet his message is a judgement on them!

Others see in dreams (Job 4:16) or visions (Ps. 17:15), or hear God in "dark speech", a word meaning a "riddle" (Judg. 14:12; 1 Kings 10:1). In other words, God protects himself by not giving all of himself in his revelations to the not-holy world. But with Moses it was different. It was "mouth to mouth", because Moses' "mouth" had been specially consecrated by the Lord at his call (Exod. 4:12, 15ff.; compare Isa. 6:7; Jer. 1:9). Elsewhere the phrase used is "face to face" (Exod. 33:11; Deut. 34:10). This is a great tribute to Moses. Equally wonderful is the statement that he sees the "form" of the Lord.

At the very least, Moses is hereby designated as unique among the Lord's servants. The day will come when, perfected in the Lord, we too will see the form of the Lord. Paul says it for us: "For now we see in a mirror dimly, but then face to face" (1 Cor. 13:12).

(iii)

The Lord asks a question of Miriam and Aaron which therefore becomes rhetorical: In the face of all this, how could you dare challenge Moses? Still angry, he leaves in the cloud, and then Miriam is seen to be fully "leprous" and "white as snow". Only again in Isa. 1:18 is the latter phrase found. The metaphor in the East is usually used, however, not to symbolize purity, but wet substances, easily broken down. Snaith suggests therefore that it is here used for open, ulcerated wounds, a picture that fits the description "flesh . . . half consumed".

Why was Aaron not similarly punished? Interestingly enough, Miriam is mentioned first at the start of the chapter, a convention quite against the norm, and furthermore the verb there for "spoke" is in the third person feminine. Either she took the lead and he followed, with an uncertainty among the scribes as to whether therefore to include him or not, or more likely, since only she was punished, two separate stories have somehow got mixed up, and Aaron does not really belong here at all. Miriam was a prophetess who played a larger part in Israel's growth than Scripture reveals (see Exod. 15:20; Mic. 6:4). For her lapse she was banished from the camp for seven days—a public shaming to balance her private confrontation. Spitting in someone's face was a way of shaming him or her, when the person's guilt was not enough to warrant excommunication.

That she did not suffer more was due to the intercession of Moses. Aaron begs Moses, whom he had previously challenged, to pray for Miriam, and he does. Note that Job also prayed for his "friends" (Job 42:10). Moses' intercession is effective. It contains only seven words in English, and only five in Hebrew (including the word "please" twice). The lesson is there for us all to learn—prayer works.

THE SPIES: MISSION AND REPORT I

Numbers 13:1–33

[1]The Lord said to Moses, [2]"Send men to spy out the land of Canaan, which I give to the people of Israel; from each tribe of their fathers shall you send a man, every one a leader among them." [3]So Moses sent them from the wilderness of Paran, according to the command of the Lord, all of them men who were heads of the people of Israel. [4]And these were their names: From the tribe of Reuben, Shammu-a the son of Zaccur; [5]from the tribe of Simeon, Shaphat the son of Hori; [6]from the tribe of Judah, Caleb the son of Jephunneh; [7]from the tribe of

Issachar, Igal the son of Joseph; [8]from the tribe of Ephraim, Hoshea the son of Nun; [9]from the tribe of Benjamin, Palti the son of Raphu; [10]from the tribe of Zebulun, Gaddiel the son of Sodi; [11]from the tribe of Joseph (that is the tribe of Manasseh), Gaddi the son of Susi; [12]from the tribe of Dan, Ammiel the son of Gemalli; [13]from the tribe of Asher, Sethur the son of Michael; [14]from the tribe of Naphtali, Nahbi the son of Vophsi; [15]from the tribe of Gad, Geuel the son of Machi. [16] These were the names of the men whom Moses sent to spy out the land. And Moses called Hoshea the son of Nun Joshua.

[17]Moses sent them to spy out the land of Canaan, and said to them, "Go up into the Negeb yonder, and go up into the hill country, [18]and see what the land is, and whether the people who dwell in it are strong or weak, whether they are few or many, [19]and whether the land that they dwell in is good or bad, and whether the cities that they dwell in are camps or strongholds, [20]and whether the land is rich or poor, and whether there is wood in it or not. Be of good courage, and bring some of the fruit of the land." Now the time was the season of the first ripe grapes.

[21]So they went up and spied out the land from the wilderness of Zin to Rehob, near the entrance of Hamath. [22]They went up into the Negeb, and came to Hebron; and Ahiman, Sheshai, and Talmai, the descendants of Anak, were there. (Hebron was built seven years before Zoan in Egypt.) [23]And they came to the Valley of Eshcol, and cut down from there a branch with a single cluster of grapes, and they carried it on a pole between two of them; they brought also some pomegranates and figs. [24]That place was called the Valley of Eshcol, because of the cluster which the men of Israel cut down from there.

[25]At the end of forty days they returned from spying out the land. [26]And they came to Moses and Aaron and to all the congregation of the people of Israel in the wilderness of Paran, at Kadesh; they brought back word to them and to all the congregation, and showed them the fruit of the land. [27]And they told him, " We came to the land to which you sent us; it flows with milk and honey, and this is its fruit. [28]Yet the people who dwell in the land are strong, and the cities are fortified and very large; and besides, we saw the descendants of Anak there. [29]The Amalekites dwell in the land of the Negeb; the Hittites, the Jebusites, and the Amorites dwell in the hill country; and the Canaanites dwell by the sea, and along the Jordan."

³⁰But Caleb quieted the people before Moses, and said, "Let us go up at once, and occupy it; for we are able to overcome it." ³¹Then the men who had gone up with him said, "We are not able to go up against the people; for they are stronger than we." ³²So they brought to the people of Israel an evil report of the land which they had spied out, saying, "The land, through which we have gone, to spy it out, is a land that devours its inhabitants; and all the people that we saw in it are men of great stature. ³³And there we saw the Nephilim (the sons of Anak, who come from the Nephilim); and we seemed to ourselves like grasshoppers, and so we seemed to them."

(i)

An intriguing section, this. God sends out men as spies, to reconnoitre and assess the land, and to report back to the whole camp. Many readers are puzzled as to why he should do that. Why be surreptitious? Why not tell them directly? Well, there is a sad misunderstanding here. The Hebrew really does not talk about "spies" or "spying", as we can see in e.g. the NEB's translation of the verb by "to explore" or the Jerusalem Bible's translation by "to make a reconnaissance". The fact is that God is inviting the tribes to see for themselves via representatives who are considered responsible, how wonderful the land is that God has prepared for them.

As to the men themselves, only Joshua and Caleb are mentioned again, though many of the names seemed common enough. The meanings are interesting, as always, and may be translated thus: "Shammua"—*he has listened*; "Zaccur"—*mindful*; "Shaphat"—*he has judged*; "Hori"—*cavern*; "Caleb"—*dog*; "Jephunneh"—*he has turned*; "Igal"—*he has redeemed*; "Nun"—*fish*; "Palti"—*my deliverance*; "Raphu"—*healed*; "Gaddiel"—*God is my fortune*; "Sodi"—*counsel of the Lord*(?); "Gaddi"—*my fortune*; "Gemalli"—*camel owner*; "Sethur"—*hidden*; "Nahbi"—*timid*; "Vophsi"—an obscure and unknown term; "Geuel"—*majesty of God*(?); "Machi"—*reduced*; "Ammiel"—*God is my kinsman*. In v. 16 we are given the information that Joshua got his name at this time. Moses, who first met the Lord in his revelation of his new personal name (Exod. 6:3), changed Joshua's name from "Hoshea"—*deliverance*, to "Joshua"—*the Lord is deliverance*.

(ii)

They are sent into "the Negeb", which is the hard dry country south of Judea. It is now increasingly irrigated, but the word means "parched". It is often used very broadly to denote the south of the country, which led to the AV mistranslation "southward", though they were moving north. By this time expectations might well have been low. An additional test of faith is now held out tantalizingly before the people like a cluster of grapes before a parched man: to take God at his word despite seeming chances of finding him to be unfaithful. (A challenge put out to all of us from time to time by the Lord!) Almost ironically the men are encouraged to take heart and "bring some of the fruit of the land". It was late July. In their first forty days of exploring they spent August in an area about twenty miles southwest of the Dead Sea, not the "Wilderness of Sin", but of "Zin".

The most important place they visited was Hebron, an ancient site twenty miles south of Jerusalem. The three matriarchs, Sarah, Rebecca and Leah were all buried there. Later David ruled from there for seven years (2 Sam. 5:1–5). Its name means a "confederacy", having been called earlier the "village of four" (Gen. 23:2; Josh. 14:15). Here they met the "descendants of Anak". Who were they? The word means "neck". Comparison with v. 33 suggests to some that they were giants with very long necks; others suggest that they wore necklaces to symbolize a warrior people (compare the use of facial paint by American Indian tribes), or possibly a form of armour on the upper chest and neck. According to 2 Sam. 21:18 ff. four descendants survived to be killed by David's warriors. More will be said of this later.

The men pass on to the "Valley of Eshcol" where they gather a single cluster of grapes to take back to the camp. Eshcol itself means "cluster", and probably was named after the fruitfulness of the area. Then there is the emotional return to camp at Kadesh, about thirty miles south of Beersheba. This was a most important centre for the tribes before their final settlement in Canaan, and the name itself means "sanctuary".

THE SPIES: MISSION AND REPORT II

Numbers 13:1–33 (*cont'd*)

(iii)

The report starts well, with a claim that they have been in a land of "milk and honey". This phrase was used by the Greeks for the food of the gods, and, in a text from about 2,000 B.C., the Egyptian Tale of Sinuhe uses it to describe Northern Galilee. But it is overwhelmingly used by the Israelites of the general area of Canaan. It could be wild-bee honey or date honey, but either way the two substances were moist and sweet and in plentiful supply— symbols of peace and plenty. Not what might be expected from an area called "parched"!

Then comes v. 28 with its awful first word: "Yet". The diffi- culties and the risks follow. The Amalekites were powerful nomads from the deserts south of the Negeb. Saul later tried to destroy them once and for all (1 Sam. 15), but a remnant survived till wiped out finally by 500 Simeonites in Hezekiah's reign (1 Chron. 4:42–43). The Hittites were a strong nation of Asia Minor, but some had settled in Canaan (see Josh. 1:4; Ezek. 16:3). The Jebusites were the original settlers of Jebus (Jerusalem), and retained possession of it till David took it for his capital (2 Sam. 5:5–9). The Amorites came to Canaan from Mesopotamia, and their law codes in particular were a mark in the history of civilization. The enemies Og and Sihon were Amor- ite kings (Num. 21:13, 21). Formidable odds indeed! Yet only Caleb realized the potential of Israel under God and almost casually says: "We are well able to overcome it". That is faith based on knowing the power of the Living God!

(iv)

The doubters say that they are not a match for the opposition, and say the land itself is not worth the trouble. It "devours its inhabitants", meaning either that it is so fruitful that it is constantly warred over, or more likely that it does not produce enough to support those who live there. They conclude by saying that above all they are no match for the Nephilim. Some have linked this word with the Hebrew verb "to fall" and suggest they are descendants of the offspring of the unnatural unions, the "fallen" unions, of Gen. 6:1–4. It is commonly used to designate "giants", alluding to some origin not totally or naturally human. Allusion may be also made to this in Ezek. 32:27, where the "fallen" warriors were exceptionally capable. Here they are linked with the "sons of Anak" of v. 28. In Deut. 3:11 Og is said to have been a giant, and further references and cross-references can be found in Deut. 2:10ff.; 2:20ff.; Gen. 14:5; Josh. 11:21–22. It is possible that Goliath belonged to one of these peoples (2 Sam. 21:16–22; 1 Chron. 20:4–8). In comparison the Israelites felt like "grasshoppers". That is fear based on forgetting the power of the Living God!

Faith and doubt are always in a struggle in our lives. Love and fear both move us and influence us. But when decisions have to be made, then faith must act on its recollection of God's goodness, and love must put its trust in the Lord. Even when odds are awful and pressures are great, our faltering steps must be steps of faith. We need to focus on the power of God, not on the power of the opposition.

DISCOURAGED AND REBELLIOUS

Numbers 14:1–10a

[1]Then all the congregation raised a loud cry; and the people wept that night. [2]And all the people of Israel murmured against Moses and Aaron; the whole congregation said to them, "Would that we had died in the land of Egypt! Or would that we had died in this wilderness! [3]Why does the Lord bring us into this land, to fall by the sword? Our wives and our little ones will become a prey; would it not be better for us to go back to Egypt?"

⁴And they said to one another, "Let us choose a captain, and go back to Egypt." ⁵Then Moses and Aaron fell on their faces before all the assembly of the congregation of the people of Israel. ⁶And Joshua the son of Nun and Caleb the son of Jephunneh, who were among those who had spied out the land, rent their clothes, ⁷ and said to all the congregation of the people of Israel, "The land, which we passed through to spy it out, is an exceedingly good land. ⁸If the Lord delights in us, he will bring us into this land and give it to us, a land which flows with milk and honey. ⁹Only, do not rebel against the Lord; and do not fear the people of the land, for they are bread for us; their protection is removed from them,and the Lord is with us; do not fear them." ¹⁰But all the congregation said to stone them with stones.

(i)

More complaints come from the people as they are disheartened by the news of the scouts. These are just like the moanings at Baal-zephon (Exod. 14), in the wilderness of Sin (Exod. 16), and at Rephidim (Exod. 17). They see each stage as worse than the stage before it, and wish they had died long ago rather than suffer these challenges. Many times the temptation comes to just give up rather than face life's challenges or responsibilities. There is no doubt that freedom has its responsibilities and makes demands on the person given it. The people panic and prefer not to face the future with God. Note the three phrases used to stress that this was the mood of the vast majority: "all the congregation . . . all the people . . . the whole congregation". And note also the three verbs used: "raised a loud cry . . . wept . . . murmured", to show the heaviness of the camp, the depression, the panic. How easily fear spreads! It is the same among God's people today. But one day all will be different, when we are with the Lord in the Promised Land where "perfect love casts out fear" (1 John 4:18).

To go "back to Egypt" (v. 3) is the ultimate curse, being a return to the bondage of slavery and ignorance of the Lord (Hos. 11:5). The Lord himself promises total freedom from this (Deut. 17:16). Thus the glory of the prophecy in Isa. 19:16-25 is that the threat will be removed. What an awful thing it is then to hear from the people themselves that they would prefer to turn on the Lord and the future in favour of their slavery and the past! They even go so far as to try to find a new "captain" to take them back. This is not the will of the Lord, who alone is their "Head" and who wills them to go on. Moses and Aaron fall to the ground in helplessness and desperate intercession. Joshua and Caleb are so upset at this widespread acceptance of the pessimism and defeatism of the other scouts that they tear their clothes, a common sign of grief at bereavement (2 Sam. 1:11–12; 3:31ff.). They insist that all will be well if they please the Lord by seeking him.

(ii)

Then comes the great encouragement. Joshua and Caleb assure the people that the enemies' "protection" has been "removed from them", but the actual term used is "shadow". They have been left exposed and vulnerable to the ferocity of the sun, as it were. In Isa. 32:1–2 there is a lovely picture given of the coming King and his princes who will be like rocks giving shade to the raw, exhausted people. So the metaphor is a powerful one, and by using it, they here tell the people that there is no protection from any other source, human or divine, for the Lord has exposed them (compare Deut. 32:38) and has become Israel's "cover" or protection. The enemies will be as easy to conquer as bread is to eat. So not only are the Israelites not edible grasshoppers to the giants of the land, but in fact the opposite is true—the giants are small to the Lord, and will be like easy meat to the Israelites.

The depth of the tragedy of Israel's fear is shown clearly enough in the desperate reaction to the voices of hope and faith that we have in v. 10*a*. Something terribly drastic and powerful was needed to remedy this situation. The next section leads us to the Lord's response.

MOSES INTERCEDES

Numbers 14:10*b*–39

Then the glory of the Lord appeared at the tent of meeting to all the people of Israel. ¹¹And the Lord said to Moses, "How long will this people despise me? And how long will they not believe in me, in spite of all the signs which I have wrought among them? ¹²I will strike them with the pestilence and disinherit them, and I will make of you a nation greater and mightier than they."

¹³But Moses said to the Lord, "Then the Egyptians will hear of it, for thou didst bring up this people in thy might from among them, ¹⁴and they will tell the inhabitants of this land. They have heard that thou, O Lord, art in the midst of this people; for thou, O Lord, art seen face to face, and thy cloud stands over them and thou goest before them, in a pillar of cloud by day and in a pillar of fire by night. ¹⁵Now if thou dost kill this people as one man, then the nations who have heard thy fame will say, ¹⁶'Because the Lord was not able to bring this people into the land which he swore to give to them, therefore he has slain them in the wilderness.' ¹⁷And now, I pray thee, let the power of the Lord be great as thou hast promised, saying, ¹⁸'The Lord is slow to anger, and abounding in steadfast love, forgiving iniquity and transgression, but he will by no means clear the guilty, visiting the iniquity of fathers upon children, upon the third and upon the fourth generation.' ¹⁹Pardon the iniquity of this people, I pray thee, according to the greatness of thy steadfast love, and according as thou hast forgiven this people, from Egypt even until now."

²⁰Then the Lord said, "I have pardoned, according to your word; ²¹but truly, as I live, and as all the earth shall be filled with the glory of the Lord, ²²none of the men who have seen my glory and my signs which I wrought in Egypt and in the wilderness, and yet have put me to the proof these ten times and have not hearkened to my voice, ²³shall see the land which I swore to give to their fathers; and none of those who despised me shall see it. ²⁴But my servant Caleb, because he has a different spirit and has followed me fully, I will bring into the land into which he went, and his descendants shall possess it. ²⁵Now, since the Amalekites and the Canaanites dwell in the valleys, turn tomorrow and set out for the wilderness by the way to the Red Sea."

²⁶And the Lord said to Moses and to Aaron, ²⁷"How long shall this wicked congregation murmur against me? I have heard the murmurings of the people of Israel, which they murmur against me. ²⁸Say to them, 'As I live,' says the Lord, 'what you have said in my hearing I will do to you: ²⁹your dead bodies shall fall in this wilderness; and of all your number, numbered from twenty years old and upward, who have murmured against me, ³⁰not one shall come into the land where I swore that I would make you dwell, except Caleb the son of Jephunneh and Joshua the son of Nun. ³¹But your little ones, who you said would

become a prey, I will bring in, and they shall know the land which you have despised. ³²But as for you, your dead bodies shall fall in this wilderness. ³³And your children shall be shepherds in the wilderness forty years, and shall suffer for your faithlessness, until the last of your dead bodies lies in the wilderness. ³⁴According to the number of the days in which you spied out the land, forty days, for every day a year, you shall bear your iniquity, forty years, and you shall know my displeasure.' ³⁵I, the Lord, have spoken; surely this will I do to all this wicked congregation that are gathered together against me: in this wilderness they shall come to a full end, and there they shall die."

³⁶And the men whom Moses sent to spy out the land, and who returned and made all the congregation to murmur against him by bringing up an evil report against the land, ³⁷the men who brought up an evil report of the land, died by plague before the Lord. ³⁸But Joshua the son of Nun and Caleb the son of Jephunneh remained alive, of those men who went to spy out the land.

³⁹And Moses told these words to all the people of Israel, and the people mourned greatly.

(i)

God asks how long the people can go on not believing in him. This verb "to believe" means basically "to trust in, rely on", so God is not seeking any intellectual assent to his existence ("The fool says in his heart, 'There is no God' ", Ps. 14:1), but trust in him and his promises. After all, God had given enough of himself, shown enough of his character and will in many "signs", the Exodus from Egypt above all. How could they not see and believe? The Lord decides to punish them with a "pestilence" and by disinheriting them. This of course is a dreadful punishment, cut off from the Promised Land for ever. Just as Israel was nothing before the world, so a new Israel through Moses will be tiny, but will grow to be the Lord's people, the true inheritors of the promise to Abraham (Gen. 12:1ff.).

And as Abraham prayed for the people of Sodom, so Moses prays for Israel as she is then. Moses urges the Lord not to destroy them, and surprisingly enough, does so for the Lord's sake, not the people's. There is the secret of intercession in a nutshell. Only in Israel is it claimed that the Lord is known "face to face" (literally "eye to eye"), i.e. intimately. So everyone is watching, he says, to see if the Lord lives up to his "fame", or if he is unable to fulfil his promises. It was after hearing about the power of the Lord that the prostitute Rahab was led to help his men (Josh. 2:8ff.; compare Isa. 66:18–21; Hab. 3:2). Moses prays that the Lord will show his power to keep his promises in spite of—not the enemies—but those to whom the promises are given. How often it is we, the Lord's own people, who hinder the Lord's display of his glory and power! Only by seeking God's glory will he answer our prayers for the world.

(ii)

So to the great confession of God's character (v. 18). It is a shorter version of the Lord's declaration of himself found in Exod. 34:6–7 after the incident of the golden calf and the shattering of the two tablets of stone. It is found quoted again in Joel 2:13 as an encouragement to Israel to repent before the final judgement, and in Jon. 4:2, indeed, as a reason for Jonah's reluctance to preach the good news of the Lord to the people of Nineveh. In other words, it is used in times of crisis to assert the essential goodness of God.

He is "slow to anger", which is stressed in all the traditions, and full of "steadfast love". This last term occurs some 250 times in the Old Testament, and is the word in modern Hebrew for "grace". It expresses mercy and lovingkindness, of course, but is essentially about God's *faithfulness* and *constancy* within the covenant relationship despite Israel's lack of response. Perhaps the single best word in English is *devotion*.

The verb "to forgive" means "to lift, to carry away", and the word for "iniquity" can also mean the *consequence* of sin, so it could mean "taking away the punishment" or "bearing away the guilt", as well as the sin itself. Then there is the term "transgression", which means personal rebellion. God can and does forgive even this, such is his devotion to us. However, if there are sins deserving of death, then he will punish, i.e. he cannot be taken for granted. But even then he shows his grace in that after four generations the sins will be forgotten. He will not eliminate the entire line of the sinner. At heart he is gracious, but he is not to be played with. Moses urges the Lord to pardon them "as thou hast forgiven this people, from Egypt even until now". What a marvellous play on words there is here, because this word "to forgive" (lit. "to bear up") is that used in Exod. 19:4 where God speaks of "how I bore you on eagle's wings and brought you to myself" (compare Deut. 32:11). The Lord is strong enough to redeem and strong enough to forgive.

He pardons all but the rebels, so the new Israel is going to be a pruned and reformed group, not a totally new group. The phrase "put . . . to the proof" can mean nothing more than the neutral "to test", or it can mean "to tempt". When used of God to men it indicates how he *tests* the endurance of our faith (as he tested Job through Satan), and when used of men to God it indicates the *presumption* that would test God's faithfulness (as Job did God's). Jesus was *tested* in this way by the devil's temptations (Matt. 4:1), and he taught his disciples to ask to be spared such a test (Matt. 6:13). Some believe that the phrase "these ten times" is just an idiom for "repeatedly" (compare Gen. 31:41). Some believe it refers to the ten scouts who each disbelieved in God. The Rabbis held that there were ten actual occasions (Exod. 14:11; Ps. 106:7; Exod. 15:23; 17:2; 16:20, 27; 16:3; Num. 11:4; Exod. 32; Num. 13:25–14:10). At any rate it was a stubborn refusal to surrender to God's grace, by all except Caleb, who had "a different spirit". He will receive his inheritance in the land of promise. Meanwhile the people must now change course and approach Canaan from the east.

The Lord is nagged constantly by the people, a fact brought out in v. 27 by the repetitions of the verb. The Lord speaks strongly. Here is the great "Thus says the Lord" formula rarely found outside the prophetic books. It is found again in this book in the oracles of Balaam. The Lord swears by his own life that he will act as he has said he will, and refers to the time when he pledged himself to give the land to the people. The irony is that the defenceless and unknowing would settle and be strong and live in the land. Under the influence of Num. 32:13 Jewish traditions interpret "shepherds" (v. 33) to mean "wanderers", as do some of the ancient versions. Certainly the verse lays down the punishment of forty years of drifting, not exploring, in the wilderness. They would experience the "displeasure" of the Lord, in bitter contrast to what Caleb and Joshua desired (v. 8). This is an exceptionally strong word, and perhaps the best modern term would be "alienation". The commentary on this whole section of Numbers in Ps. 95:7b–11 reinforces the intensity of the pain the Lord felt at this lack of trust. God hates sin. The people learned a lesson (v. 39), but as so often, it was too costly and too late.

HORMAH: ISRAEL'S DEFEAT

Numbers 14:40–45

40 And they rose early in the morning, and went up to the heights of the hill country, saying, "See, we are here, we will go up to the place which the Lord has promised; for we have sinned." 41 But Moses said, "Why now are you transgressing the command of the Lord, for that will not succeed? 42 Do not go up lest you be struck down before your enemies, for the Lord is not among you. 43 For there the Amalekites and the Canaanites are before you, and you shall fall by the sword; because you have turned back from following the Lord, the Lord will not be with you." 44 But they presumed to go up to the heights of the hill country, although neither the ark of the covenant of the Lord, nor Moses, departed out of the camp. 45 Then the Amalekites and the Canaanites who dwelt in that hill country came down, and defeated them and pursued them, even to Hormah.

With mistaken zeal the people decide to go on and conquer without checking with the Lord if this is his will or not. In fact, in v. 25 he had told them to go on by a different route, but they forgot that in their desire to please and do now what they should have been prepared to do before. Moses vainly tries to warn them. They set off for war without the Lord's blessing. Moses did not go with them, and neither did the ark.

Their sin moved from that of fear and lack of faith (2 Tim. 1:7) to over-confidence and presumption. They "presumed to go up". This word is rare and difficult to define precisely, but there seem to be two possible roots. The one means "to be reckless", and perhaps that is best here. The other seems to mean "to swell" since its nouns mean "mound" or "tumour" (2 Kings 5:24; Deut. 28:27). The verb occurs in Hab. 2:4 where the sense of being puffed up would suit, and so some believe that the sense here is that they acted with self-confidence and went out puffed up in themselves without seeking the Lord's immediate will. At any rate they took the Lord for granted. There is no doubt that the Lord's plan was for them to take that land, but not then or there. There is a lesson for us to learn here. Knowing the Lord's vision in a work is necessary, but so is constant walking in his will. We cannot tell him what to do.

In 21:1–3 we are given an account of the ultimate capture of Hormah. So the Lord had the plan and the timing, and worked it all out his way. On this occasion, we are told, the inhabitants of the area "pursued them". This is not the best translation possible, since the verb means "to crush by beating", and indeed the Greek version has "cut them in pieces". The Jewish scholar Rashi renders "pounded them, blow upon blow". The name of the place itself means "destruction", and comes from a word that suggests complete, humiliating defeat. Originally it was an important Canaanite royal city (Josh. 12:14). In the *Lord's* timing it became an Israelite city, but in the the Israelites' timing it remained a Canaanite city. The lesson is clear.

OFFERINGS: MEAT AND DRINK

Numbers 15:1–16

[1]The Lord said to Moses, [2]"Say to the people of Israel, When you come into the land you are to inhabit, which I give you, [3]and you offer to the Lord from the herd or from the flock an offering by fire or a burnt offering or a sacrifice, to fulfil a vow or as a freewill offering or at your appointed feasts, to make a pleasing odour to the Lord, [4]then he who brings his offering shall offer to the Lord a cereal offering of a tenth of an ephah of fine flour, mixed with a fourth of a hin of oil; [5]and wine for the drink offering, a fourth of a hin, you shall prepare with the burnt offering, or for the sacrifice, for each lamb. [6]Or for a ram, you shall

prepare for a cereal offering two tenths of an ephah of fine flour mixed
with a third of a hin of oil; [7]and for the drink offering you shall offer a
third of a hin of wine, a pleasing odour to the Lord. [8]And when you
prepare a bull for a burnt offering, or for a sacrifice, to fulfil a vow, or
for peace offerings to the Lord, [9]then one shall offer with the bull a
cereal offering of three tenths of an ephah of fine flour, mixed with half
a hin of oil, [10]and you shall offer for the drink offering half a hin of
wine, as an offering by fire, a pleasing odour to the Lord.

[11]"Thus it shall be done for each bull or ram, or for each of the male
lambs or the kids. [12]According to the number that you prepare, so
shall you do with every one according to their number. [13]All who are
native shall do these things in this way, in offering an offering by fire, a
pleasing odour to the Lord. [14]And if a stranger is sojourning with you,
or any one is among you throughout your generations, and he wishes to
offer an offering by fire, a pleasing odour to the Lord, he shall do as
you do. [15]For the assembly, there shall be one statute for you and for
the stranger who sojourns with you, a perpetual statute throughout
your generations; as you are, so shall the sojourner be before the Lord.
[16]One law and one ordinance shall be for you and for the stranger who
sojourns with you."

(i)

Here come some of the regulations for the appropriate offerings
to be made to the Lord. The chief concern is about the proper
amounts of flour, oil and wine to be offered with the animal
sacrifices. In Ezek. 46:5–7, 11, 14, there is a different value scale
given, and there are other scales too, reflecting other groups and
values (Lev. 6:14ff.; 23:17). The exact amounts deemed necessary must have varied in the various periods of the people's
history. What needs to be noted though is that in every group or
period the tradition was that such an offering was a sacred meal.
When the people were nomadic or semi-nomadic, the natural
sacrifice would be flesh. Later, when they settled to agriculture in
Canaan, the common means of sacrifice for the community became corn, oil, wine (Deut. 7:13; Jer. 31:12). So here the Lord
tells them that these rules are for the future, when they are
farmers: "When you come into the land . . ." (vv. 2, 18). Also to
be noted is the fact that the amounts increase with the size of the

animal that the people can afford to sacrifice (vv. 4–5, 6–7, 8–9). The principle is that they give as they are able to give, along the lines set out clearly in Lev. 5:7–13 and in Ezek. 46:11, "as much as one is able to give". To give to God less than we are able to give is to insult him and to be a worthless servant (see Matt. 25:14–30).

There are three situations given here which demand such offerings of a meal to the Lord: "to fulfil a vow or as a freewill offering or at . . . appointed feasts" (v. 4). But the purpose is the same for all of them: "to make a pleasing odour to the Lord". This term is found over forty times in the Old Testament, and about half of these are in the book of Numbers, with six in this chapter alone. The language is what is called anthropomorphic, i.e. God is portrayed in vividly human terms, having a meal prepared for him and enjoying the savoury smell of the food. This picture was common in the cultures surrounding Israel, and the Israelites were still children of their time. It is embarrassing to modern thought to come across these passages when the fundamental truth is that "God is spirit", and that those who worship him must worship "in spirit and truth" (John 4:24); yet the fact of them must be faced. Attempts by modern commentators to allegorize these historical facts into "spiritual facts" are to be avoided since they deny the very grounding of our faith in history. Of course we can and do sift out the *principles* involved behind the beliefs of any given period, but always without doing damage to the way our faith has developed.

(ii)

Three terms are used in vv. 15–16 to describe the basis of Israel's constitution as the people of God. The basic relationship was one of covenant, i.e. promise and pledge, grace and commitment, but there was a constitutional element too. The three terms are: (a) *law*, (b) *ordinance*, (c) *statute*. The first is the Hebrew "Torah" and comes from a root meaning "to throw, to project" and is therefore very inaccurately translated "law", as if it were a cold unmoving legal concept. A far better translation might be "revelation", i.e. a teaching aimed at the people by God. But a good translation would certainly be "direction", conveying not only the sense of authority and truth, but also of progress towards the goal of realizing the truth in life. The second term is from a root which means establishing justice, vindicating, making a final ruling, or the like. An ordinance is a final ruling, so perhaps a good translation would be "authoritative ruling". It is the third term that comes closest to the meaning of our "laws of the realm". The root-meaning is "to engrave" and indicates an absolute principle or rule. The maintenance of Israel's relationship with her Lord thus involved obeying commands which were to be seen as the final and binding rulings in God's directing of them to be the people he wanted them to be.

What is more, these commands are also binding on the "stranger who sojourns" with Israel. This translation is not strictly accurate, as in fact this type of person was not a "stranger" in the sense of a drifter or a journeyer who chanced to meet Israel and exchange greetings. The root means "to settle", and the term was a technical one for someone who, although foreign by birth to Israel, came to live with them as one of them. The appropriate translation is "proselyte". The RSV makes us think almost of a tourist, whereas these people were residents. Such a person is almost an Israelite. The basic rationale is that Israel was once a "sojourner" in Egypt until she was delivered by God (Exod. 22:21; Deut. 5:14–15), and so should welcome those seeking the Lord from wherever they come. Even later Israel saw herself as sojourning in the Lord's land: "Hear my prayer, O Lord, and give ear to my cry; hold not thy peace at my tears! For I am thy passing guest, a sojourner, like all my fathers" (Ps. 39:12; compare Ps. 119:19; Lev. 25:23). So what right could she have to refuse people entry with her into the ways of the Lord?

There was, then, a precedent for Israel's revelation, direction in life, to be shared with non-Israelites, but only if they joined the camp and "became" Israelites as far as it was possible. The Gospel is that God's direction is for *all* people who accept Jesus as the full revelation of God. No accident of birth can hinder us from knowing the Lord because: "There is neither Jew nor Greek, there is neither slave nor free, there is neither male nor female;

for you are all one in Christ Jesus" (Gal. 3:28). We are all joined to him, and in him become like him.

There is a further principle hinted at in this passage. The New Testament puts it like this: ". . . for here we have no continuing city, but we seek the city which is to come" (Heb. 13:14).

OFFERINGS: CAKE

Numbers 15:17–21

[17]The Lord said to Moses, [18]"Say to the people of Israel, When you come into the land to which I bring you [19]and when you eat of the food of the land, you shall present an offering to the Lord. [20]Of the first of your coarse meal you shall present a cake as an offering; as an offering from the threshing floor, so shall you present it. [21]Of the first of your coarse meal you shall give to the Lord an offering throughout your generations.

This short section is not without some interest for the modern reader. Once again the text looks forward to a time still in the future when the people will be settled in Canaan. This "offering" is called a "heave-offering" in some translations, which hardly serves to clarify its meaning. The word denotes a part "lifted off" from a larger whole. Some suggest a good translation would be "contribution", but a fine and clear phrase would be "selected portion". What is this portion then? It is a truism to state that we must give to the Lord, but to know what to give is worth searching for. The important point is that the people must give from "the first" of the produce. Some have tried to argue that this refers to the first part of every meal prepared, but the overall impression one gets when taking other references into account is that it refers to the first-fruits of the harvest. Such was the desire to please God, however, that the traditions in the Talmud say that the first thing to do in preparing to bake is to set aside God's portion.

This particular symbol of all the harvest is due to God since all of it is a gift from him. It was to be prepared as "a cake", i.e. a loaf. This was the usual bread for the Temple in later years, called the "shew-bread", and was not burned but given to all the priesthood to eat. Special breads at festivals are common enough. The special bread for Sabbath is still called by the same name used here in the Hebrew. And in Christian custom Harvest Thanksgiving is often symbolized by the offering of foods to God around the Lord's Table, for instance when a local baker prepares a special loaf designed as a wheatsheaf.

To mark celebrations with special customs, foods, etc., is quite natural, but it is only spiritual and acceptable if we keep the Lord and our call to glorify his name at the centre of all we do. In offering up to God, we are really only returning to him what is his by right. Perhaps now would be a good time for the reader to re-assess how much he is giving up to God from his time, energy, talents and money.

SINS, UN-PREMEDITATED AND PREMEDITATED

Numbers 15:22–31

22"But if you err, and do not observe all these commandments which the Lord has spoken to Moses, 23all that the Lord has commanded you by Moses, from the day that the Lord gave commandment, and onward throughout your generations, 24then if it was done unwittingly without the knowledge of the congregation, all the congregation shall offer one young bull for a burnt offering, a pleasing odour to the Lord, with its cereal offering and its drink offering, according to the ordinance, and one male goat for a sin offering. 25And the priest shall make atonement for all the congregation of the people of Israel, and they shall be forgiven; because it was an error, and they have brought their offering, an offering by fire to the Lord, and their sin offering before the Lord, for their error. 26And all the congregation of the people of Israel shall be forgiven, and the stranger who sojourns among them, because the whole population was involved in the error.

27"If one person sins unwittingly, he shall offer a female goat a year old for a sin offering. 28And the priest shall make atonement before the Lord for the person who commits an error, when he sins unwittingly, to make atonement for him; and he shall be forgiven. 29You shall have one law for him who does anything unwittingly, for him who is native among the people of Israel, and for the stranger who sojourns among them. [30]But the person who does anything with a high hand, whether he is native or a sojourner, reviles the Lord, and that person shall be cut off from among his people. [31]Because he has despised the word of the Lord, and has broken his commandment, that person shall be utterly cut off; his iniquity shall be upon him."

(i)

This section deals with those who "do not observe" commandments like the ones just given. It falls into three parts: (a) *unintentional sin by or involving the whole community* (vv. 22–26); (b) *unintentional sin by a single individual* (vv. 27–29); (c) *intentional sin by an individual* (vv. 30–31). The distinction between intentional and unintentional sins is significant. There is no human legalism here, but a real appreciation of the ambiguities and the weaknesses of life.

The unintentional sins are those done "without the knowledge of the congregation", or literally, "away from the eyes of the congregation", and done "unwittingly", or literally, "by wandering off", or "by mistake". In these cases there is a relevant offering, and the priest ministers the atoning sacrifice for the Lord. The result for the people is the wonderful one that "they shall be forgiven". But the offering, the sacrifice, is still necessary, even for such sins. God's holiness cannot be in any way compromised. It must also be made clear that the forgiveness is not because of any inherent cause and effect relationship between the priest's actions or words and the fact of forgiveness. The ground of the forgiveness is the free grace of God (see 14:18), and the sacrifice is God's ordained means to remove the barrier to the action of God's grace. Professor Davidson puts it well:

> None of the prophets, not even Ezekiel, refers to sacrifice as the means to atonement for the sins of the people; God forgives of his grace and mercy alone.

(ii)

According to this priestly vision of sacrifice, however, there is no forgiveness for intentional or conscious sinning against the Lord's revealed ways. The phrase "with a high hand" means defiantly or arrogantly. In Exod. 14:8 it is used of the escaping Israelites who left Egypt triumphantly and proudly; but here it signifies that other sort of pride that is listed, rightly, as one of the seven Deadly Sins. In contrast, the Hebrew word for "to worship" God means "to throw oneself down prostrate".

Those who do not worship, but defy the Lord, are said to "revile" him. This is not a common term at all, is very strong, and is only found here in the Pentateuch. It is the pure self-centredness of man before God, and is punished by being "cut off" from the people. Another very strong word, found again in the Pentateuch only in Gen. 25:34 of Esau despising his birthright, is that such a person has "despised" the "word of the Lord". These two terms indicate someone who has cut himself off from any healthy relationship with the Lord or his people, and so is unable to make a freewill offering to put things right. He is therefore truly "cut off from among his people".

Is this state of spirit perhaps that called the "unforgivable sin"? Jesus said: ". . . whoever speaks against the Holy Spirit will not be forgiven" (Matt. 12:32) in the context of an encounter with certain Pharisees who saw Jesus perform miracles yet said he was evil. They rejected the evidence of God's holy love so much that they could not recognize it when they met it.

THE SABBATH BREAKER

Numbers 15:32–36

[32]While the people of Israel were in the wilderness, they found a man gathering sticks on the sabbath day. [33]And those who found him gathering sticks brought him to Moses and Aaron, and to all the congregation. [34]They put him in custody, because it had not been made plain what should be done to him. [35]And the Lord said to Moses, "The man shall be put to death; all the congregation shall stone him with stones outside the camp." [36]And all the congregation brought him outside the camp, and stoned him to death with stones, as the Lord commanded Moses.

An example of an intentional sin is now included to illustrate how it should be dealt with. A similar passage is Lev. 24:10–23 where a man is found guilty of blasphemy, i.e. breaking the third of the Ten Commandments. Here the man desecrates the Sabbath by working on it, and therefore breaks the fourth of the Ten Commandments.

The Lord's will is sought and the means of execution is to be stoning the offender to death. Such execution avoids any letting of blood and therefore any blood-guilt. There are eleven offences punishable by stoning according to the Old Testament: idolatry (Deut. 17:2–7); encouragement of idolatry (Deut. 13:6–10); child sacrifice (Lev. 20:2–5); prophecy in the name of another god (Deut. 13:1–5); divination (Lev. 20:27); blasphemy (Lev. 24:15–16); breaking the Sabbath (here); murder by an ox (Exod. 21:28–29); adultery (Deut. 22:22ff.); rebellion by a son (Deut. 21:18ff.); violation of God's ban on plunder devoted to him (Josh. 7:25).

In the New Testament it occurs a few times. Jesus refers to Israel's stoning of the prophets sent to restore her to God, once in a parable (Matt. 21:35) and once in a moment of painful meditation (Matt. 23:37). Such cases of stoning were of course quite illegal. In John 10:31 we see how the leaders wanted to stone Jesus for what they believed to be blasphemy, and in Acts 14:5 the crowd tried to stone Paul and Barnabas for what amounted to blasphemy too. But the most celebrated occasion is that recorded by some ancient manuscripts as John 7:53–8:11, where a woman interrupted in the act of adultery is brought to Jesus to get his verdict on whether or not she should be punished as the Lord directed Moses here in Numbers. Jesus gives the famous and wonderful reply that only the sinless should stone her, and they all leave. Two things about that passage must be said in trying to find Jesus' opinion of this section in Numbers. He does not deny the validity of the punishment. But he directs our attention towards the forgiveness and reformation of the offender, fulfilling the "law" by going beyond it.

As Christians, then, we cannot possibly approve of a death penalty for breaking the Sabbath; but we must try to understand the reasoning behind it. To the Old Testament it is a question of vindicating God's lordship over life. The stoning is done "outside the camp" so as not to profane it with death, and so as to symbolize the offender's exclusion from the people. He is well and truly "cut off from among his people" (v. 30). The only way for an Israelite to stop being an Israelite, to lose his right to belong to the camp, to be condemned by the Lord in this way, is by wilful rejection of the Lord. And the only way one of Jesus' followers can be separated from him (Matt. 12:31–32) is by a similar rejection. Nothing else can do it (Rom. 8:38–39). Even as we abhor this law, we do well to ponder its motivation.

TASSELS

Numbers 15:37–41

> [37]The Lord said to Moses, [38]"Speak to the people of Israel, and bid them to make tassels on the corners of their garments throughout their generations, and to put upon the tassel of each corner a cord of blue; [39]and it shall be to you a tassel to look upon and remember all the commandments of the Lord, to do them, not to follow after your own heart and your own eyes, which you are inclined to go after wantonly. [40]So you shall remember and do all my commandments, and be holy to your God. [41]I am the Lord your God, who brought you out of the land of Egypt, to be your God: I am the Lord your God."

(i)

The chapter closes with the command to wear certain clothing as an aid to devotion. The oldest text in the Old Testament on this matter of "tassels" is Deut. 22:12, which is bare in its description. Here there is more explanation. But first of all what were they? Was the piece of clothing in question one with a continuous fringe or one with four tassels at the corners? The different English translations reflect both interpretations. The Greek version has "edges", which lies behind the use of "hem" in certain translations of Matt. 9:20. Ezek. 8:3, however, has "lock" (of hair) for the same Hebrew word; and the Deut. 22:12 passage uses a word for something twisted round itself, as in the decoration on the pillars described in 1 Kings 7:17, suggesting perhaps four hanging pieces of work. On the other hand, the word translated "corners" simply means something which stands out from a main piece, so it could refer equally well to a continuous hem. It is impossible to be certain. The Rabbinic tradition has come down in favour of four separate tassels. The "cord of blue" is interpreted as being symbolic of the sea (the dye was from a sea mollusc), the sea as symbolic of the sky, in terms of its vastness and colour, and the sky as symbolic of the glory of God, in terms of its being in the direction of and part of his heaven.

The tassels are visual reminders of the presence and commands of the Lord. Obedience to God is the mark of a holy people, and in v. 40 the point of it all is succinctly underlined, that Israel will constantly be reminded of God's commands, do them, and so "be holy to . . . God". Presumably that is why this passage comes here after the differentiation between intentional and unintentional sins, and immediately after the case of deliberate sinning—to show how a simple visual device can help one remember the Lord and so help prevent any unintentional sins. Modern orthodox Jews of course still wear the tassels.

According to Jewish tradition the tassels are to be made from three threads, with five knots to each. Why? The Rabbis believed that they could count 613 commandments given by God in the Torah. The numerical value of the letters of the Hebrew word for "tassels" is 600. Yet v. 40 says these are an aid to doing "all" of the Lord's commandments. So they obtained the other thirteen by means of the threads and knots.

(ii)

There is irony in v. 39 where sin is defined as the inclination "to follow after your own heart". The verb means literally "to turn about". It is the same one used of the scouts sent out to explore the Promised Land. God is saying to the people that the only place he wants them to explore, the only place he wants them to consider as their home, is his Promised Land, not their self-seeking hearts. To go forward not backward; to trust not retreat; to give sovereignty to God not assume it for themselves.

There is no doubt that Jesus obeyed the command given in this passage, since in Matt. 9:20 and Matt. 14:36 people are shown to have been healed by touching simply the "fringe of his garment", or as some have it, the "hem of his garment". This is not the bottom of his long robe trailing in the dust (as many preachers interpret it), but is the very Greek word used of the "tassels" in the Greek translation of this passage. Jesus' tassels were believed to be especially powerful, symbolic not only of his devotion to God, but also of God's devotion to him. His would be a simple and ordinary garment, as we gather from his condemnation of the showy devotion of certain Jews who wore very long tassels as a kind of quantitative demonstration of the quality of their devotion. They were not reminding others of *God* but of *themselves*. It is far too easy to let our obedience to God and our devotion to him become known and noticed. The left hand really should not know what the right hand is doing (Matt. 6:3).

(iii)

Finally comes the sovereign claim of God. Twice we have the phrase "I am the Lord your God". On several occasions when the Lord is giving commands and demanding certain behaviour, he puts at the close of them all this statement (e.g. Lev. 19:36–37; 22:32–33; 26:13). It is the summing up of all the laws and the goal of them all—to know the Lord as God and to know that God is our *Lord*. Most famously it is found at the beginning of the Ten Commandments (Exod. 20:2–17). It is the source of all the laws and the prerequisite of seeking to obey them, and the only chance of keeping them—to know the Lord God as Redeemer. Before the Lord came to his people at Sinai, where this book picks up the story, he came to them at the Red Sea. Before they knew the Lord to be the transcendent Creator or the bountiful Sustainer they knew him to be the potent Redeemer. That is why they listened to him at Sinai. In theological jargon, God's indicative precedes his imperative. In simpler English, before God tells his children what to do he enables them to do it and shows them how much he cares for them.

THE GREAT REBELLION I

Numbers 16:1–35

[1]Now Korah the son of Izhar, son of Kohath, son of Levi, and Dathan and Abiram the sons of Eliab, and On the son of Peleth, sons of Reuben, [2]took men; and they rose up before Moses, with a number of the people of Israel, two hundred and fifty leaders of the congregation, chosen from the assembly, well-known men; [3]and they assembled themselves together against Moses and against Aaron, and said to them, "You have gone too far! For all the congregation are holy, every one of them, and the Lord is among them; why then do you exalt yourselves above the assembly of the Lord?" [4]When Moses heard it, he fell on his face; [5]and he said to Korah and all his company, "In the morning the Lord will show who is his, and who is holy, and will cause him to come near to him; him whom he will choose he will cause to come near to him. [6]Do this: take censers, Korah and all his company; [7]put fire in them and put incense upon them before the Lord tomorrow, and the man whom the Lord chooses shall be the holy one. You have gone too far, sons of Levi!" [8]And Moses said to Korah, "Hear now, you sons of Levi: [9]is it too small a thing for you that the God of Israel has separated you from the congregation of Israel, to bring you near to himself, to do service in the tabernacle of the Lord, and to stand before the congregation to minister to them; [10]and that he has brought you near him, and all your brethren the sons of Levi with you? And would you seek the priesthood also? [11]Therefore it is against the Lord that you and all your company have gathered together; what is Aaron that you murmur against him?"

[12]And Moses sent to call Dathan and Abiram the sons of Eliab; and they said, "We will not come up. [13]Is it a small thing that you have brought us up out of a land flowing with milk and honey, to kill us in the wilderness, that you must also make yourself a prince over us? [14]Moreover you have not brought us into a land flowing with milk and honey, nor given us inheritance of fields and vineyards. Will you put out the eyes of these men? We will not come up."

[15]And Moses was very angry, and said to the Lord, "Do not respect their offering. I have not taken one ass from them, and I have not harmed one of them." [16]And Moses said to Korah, "Be present, you and all your company, before the Lord, you and they, and Aaron, tomorrow; [17]and let every one of you take his censer, and put incense upon it, and every one of you bring before the Lord his censer, two

hundred and fifty censers; you also, and Aaron, each his censer." 18So every man took his censer, and they put fire in them and laid incense upon them, and they stood at the entrance of the tent of meeting with Moses and Aaron. 19Then Korah assembled all the congregation against them at the entrance of the tent of meeting. And the glory of the Lord appeared to all the congregation.

20And the Lord said to Moses and to Aaron, 21"Separate yourselves from among this congregation, that I may consume them in a moment." 22And they fell on their faces, and said, "O God, the God of the spirits of all flesh, shall one man sin, and wilt thou be angry with all the congregation?" 23And the Lord said to Moses, 24"Say to the congregation, Get away from about the dwelling of Korah, Dathan, and Abiram."

25Then Moses rose and went to Dathan and Abiram; and the elders of Israel followed him. 26And he said to the congregation, "Depart, I pray you, from the tents of these wicked men, and touch nothing of theirs, lest you be swept away with all their sins." 27So they got away from about the dwelling of Korah, Dathan, and Abiram; and Dathan and Abiram came out and stood at the door of their tents, together with their wives, their sons, and their little ones. 28And Moses said, "Hereby you shall know that the Lord has sent me to do all these works, and that it has not been of my own accord. 29If these men die the common death of all men, or if they are visited by the fate of all men, then the Lord has not sent me. 30But if the Lord creates something new, and the ground opens its mouth, and swallows them up, with all that belongs to them, and they go down alive into Sheol, then you shall know that these men have despised the Lord."

31And as he finished speaking all these words, the ground under them split asunder; 32and the earth opened its mouth and swallowed them up, with their households and all the men that belonged to Korah and all their goods. 33So they and all that belonged to them went down alive into Sheol; and the earth closed over them, and they perished from the midst of the assembly. 34And all Israel that were round about them fled at their cry; for they said, "Lest the earth swallow us up!" 35And fire came forth from the Lord, and consumed the two hundred and fifty men offering the incense.

(i)

A careful reading of this chapter shows a certain lack of cohesion, which is probably the result of the weaving together of two sources. The first is from priestly circles about a revolt by Korah and some Levites against the authority of Aaron. This tradition alone is known in Num. 27:3. The second is from other circles, and is about a revolt by two Reubenites Dathan and Abiram against the authority of Moses' leadership. This tradition alone is known by Deut. 11:6 and Ps. 106:16ff.

The cause of the two rebellions probably was plain envy and self-seeking. At one point (see Gen. 49:3–4) the Reubenites had been a powerful tribe, but had fallen away. The Kohathites (Korah's family) were Levites of course, and maybe at the very start were priests, but later their duties were restricted to the music of the sanctuary, as seen in the headings of Pss. 42–49, 84, 85, 87, 88. So perhaps we have behind this chapter memories of the power struggles that go on in all communities, even those of God's people.

In this commentary, however, we will not make too much of the two traditions, but content ourselves with taking the lessons as they come.

(ii)

The men that Korah took were not the "rabble" of 11:4, but the "leaders . . . chosen . . . well-known". They would act with thought and purpose, and v. 15 shows they had brought an offering to the Lord. They clearly thought that they were showing their true humility before God before going on to make sincere—though mistaken—complaint to Moses and Aaron. There is a neat pun in the text, since the word for "leaders" comes from the same root as the word used for "to exalt oneself" in the charge they bring (v. 3). It was, of course, they who were exalting themselves. Further irony is seen in the description of them as "well-known", literally "men of name". Outcasts, or in modern slang, "nobodies", are "men without name" (Job 30:8), but to be famous means to have a name among people (Gen. 6:4; 1 Chron. 5:24). Their desire for a name led them away from the Lord, so that to this day they have a name as enemies of God.

Their accusation is that Moses and Aaron "have gone too far". They speak eloquently, and their statement that "all the congregation are holy" is of course true (see Exod. 19:6): but they have failed to see that God chose Moses and Aaron for special roles within the community. No pastor, nor prophet, nor evangelist is holier than any other local believer, but they have God-given roles within the local congregation and the wider Church. Both truths have to be recognized. How many of the heresies and rebellions in the history of the Church have arisen through emphasizing one truth at the expense of the other?

(iii)

Moses' reaction was not one of intercession this time. Instead he threw himself down helpless before the Lord, and left the matter to him. It was a wise decision. Not only would the Lord "show who is his" (v. 5) (compare 2 Tim. 2:19: "The Lord knows who are his"). But in this case the challenge was coming from others of God's anointed people (v. 8). This was not a laity versus clergy dispute but a clergy versus clergy dispute, as is made clear when Moses turned their own words back on them (compare v. 7 with v. 3). It was a dispute about the authority of the priesthood.

And yet what was really at stake was whether all the people were willing to accept the authority of God. As v. 11 asks: "What is Aaron . . .?" To criticize him was really to criticize God. A parallel passage in Exod. 16:2–8 ends with the categorical statement: "Your murmurings are not against us but against the Lord". Moses says much the same here in vv. 28ff., and events prove him right.

St. Paul puts the lesson for Christians in this way: "Let every person be subject to the governing authorities. For there is no authority except from God . . ." (Rom. 13:1–2). We remember too that when Pilate confronted Jesus with crucifixion by asking why he didn't fear his power over him, Jesus said: "You would have no power over me unless it had been given you from above" (John 19:11). There is food for thought here.

THE GREAT REBELLION II

Numbers 16:1–35 (*cont'd*)

(iv)

Moses asks Dathan and Abiram to come and settle the matter together, but they send a contemptuous reply, even implying (see v. 15) that Moses and Aaron were feathering their own nests (compare 1 Sam. 12:1–3). They accuse them of attempting to lord it over the people, and of exploiting their present desperate situation for their own ends. Indeed it is the fault of Moses and Aaron that they are in this situation at all. Did they not make them leave "a land flowing with milk and honey" (v. 13)?

Here is an exceptional verse. This phrase "milk and honey", symbolizing vast numbers of fat cattle and vast areas of luscious fruit dripping with juice, is used eighteen times for the land of Israel. It is a phrase learned in Sunday Schools for the Promised Land. Yet here it is used of Egypt, the place of bondage. Is this simply wilful perversion of the truth? Probably not. When Joseph first went down to Egypt, in the days of the well-disposed Pharaoh, he invited all his family to come "and I will give you the best of the land of Egypt, and you shall eat the fat of the land" (Gen. 45:16–20). They were settled in the fruitful land of Goshen, and were put in charge of the cattle (Gen. 47:6). Even during the plagues this land stayed fruitful and fertile. It is to this paradise that the men refer. Yet how wrong they were! Blind to the Lord's provision and his ordained Promised Land, they hankered after the best that the world could offer.

They go on to accuse Moses and Aaron of wanting to kill the people and compare them to vultures pecking at dead bodies (v. 14: compare Prov. 30:17). Moses responds by challenging everyone to appear with censers of incense at the sanctuary to let the Lord speak. They duly assemble and "the glory of the Lord appeared to all the congregation" (v. 19). The "glory of the Lord" often appears in Scripture before severe judgement. It is mentioned in 14:10 and later in this chapter at v. 42. The term for "glory" originally meant, and still does in modern Hebrew, "weight". It can be used physically or metaphorically, e.g. of wealth (Isa. 61:6), of armed strength (Isa. 8:7), of royalty (Esth. 1:4), of reputation (Job 29:20), or of spirituality (Ps. 8:5). It was particularly associated with Jerusalem and the Temple. It speaks of the awe-ful and numinous atmosphere of certain places or environments "heavy" with the presence of God. In the Gospels it is used significantly with respect to Jesus at his birth, i.e. his first coming (Luke 2:29ff.), at his transfiguration (Luke 9:32), and at his second coming (Matt. 25:31). He is to the Christian the place where God's presence is most intensely present in the world, and he proclaims the judgement and salvation of God. Jesus always seeks his Father's glory as the Father seeks his (John 8:50ff.). Paul teaches that the Church is the "glory of Christ" as she reflects his glory (2 Cor. 8:23).

With the present passage in mind, we could say that to glorify God is to let God be God and choose as he wills. But even if we do not, he nevertheless comes to us in his glory and we have to meet him on his terms in spite of ourselves.

(v)

God decides to punish all except Moses and Aaron, and this time Moses and Aaron intercede for their opponents. They pray to the Lord as "the God of the spirits of all flesh" (v. 22), a designation found again only in Num. 27:16. God is seen as the God of *all* people.

As a result of this intercession God determines to punish only the guilty households, and tells the congregation to clear away from the "dwelling" of Korah, Dathan and Abiram. The people follow Moses at the last moment and are spared. Moses proceeds to claim that imminent events will prove that the Lord has been behind everything, not his own desires and intentions. Death comes to us all, he says; it is "visited" by a common destiny set by God. But the death the rebels will die will be something special.

The Hebrew of v. 30 is literally that God will "create a creation". This verb (*bara*) is used in the Old Testament only of God's divine activity. It occurs as the second word of the Bible of God creating the cosmos out of chaos. It is also used of his creation of his chosen people (Isa. 43:1, 7, 15). Again it is used of the Lord's miraculous creation of clean hearts in his people (Ps. 51:10). It becomes the word for God's new creation of a new world (Isa. 48:6). Often it is used of something unusual or unpredictable (e.g. Jer. 31:22). So Moses says that if an unexpected death occurs then it will be evidence of the Lord being behind it and also behind the whole pilgrimage. Thereupon the earth's surface cracks wide open and the rebels disappear into the bowels of the earth, down into the "underworld", or "Sheol" as the Old Testament has it. God shows with a vengeance who are his and who are not (v. 5). Not only are these families destroyed, but they go "alive", i.e. fully conscious, into the place where the Lord most definitely is not. They could not be further away from the Lord.

(vi)

There is no evidence that the Israelites ever believed in complete extinction following physical death. But the "life" after death in which they believed is only vaguely and forebodingly hinted at. There is no clear doctrine in the Old Testament, but it certainly does not picture a place of torturous torment. That idea developed later. A dimension existed after death, and certain clues are to be found as to its nature. These may be listed as follows: (a) oblivion (Ps. 88:12); (b) inability to experience God's presence (Ps. 88:5); (c) inability to praise God (Isa. 38:18; Pss. 6:5; 30:9; 115:17); (d) location beneath the earth (here; Job 26:5; Jon. 2:6); (e) weariness (Job 3:17); (f) attenuation (Ps. 88:4); (g) thirst (Isa. 5:13); (h) awful silence (Pss. 94:17; 115:17); (i) darkness (Job 10:21–22). It is referred to as "the Pit" (Job 33:18; Ps. 28:1) and as "Abaddon" (Job 26:6), but the real name for it in Israel was "Sheol". To this terrible place the households went.

To this same terrible place Jesus went. As the Apostles' Creed puts it: "He descended into hell" (compare 1 Pet. 4:6). We know more fully than the Old Testament. Nothing can separate the Christian from the love of Christ—not even death (Rom. 8:37ff.). Those who trust the Lord have a glorious life ahead, since he has conquered death and the grave! The story of the great rebellion does not show us the Old Testament at its best but, read in the light of the New, it has some very valuable lessons to teach.

AARON'S PRIESTHOOD VINDICATED!

Numbers 16:36–50

36Then the Lord said to Moses, 37"Tell Eleazar the son of Aaron the priest to take up the censers out of the blaze; then scatter the fire far and wide. For they are holy, 38the censers of these men who have sinned at the cost of their lives; so let them be made into hammered plates as a covering for the altar, for they offered them before the Lord; therefore they are holy. Thus they shall be a sign to the people of Israel." 39So Eleazar the priest took the bronze censers, which those who were burned had offered; and they were hammered out as a covering for the altar, 40to be a reminder to the people of Israel, so that no one who is not a priest, who is not of the descendants of Aaron, should draw near to burn incense before the Lord, lest he become as Korah and as his company—as the Lord said to Eleazar through Moses.

41But on the morrow all the congregation of the people of Israel murmured against Moses and against Aaron, saying, "You have killed the people of the Lord." 42And when the congregation had assembled against Moses and against Aaron, they turned toward the tent of meeting; and behold, the cloud covered it, and the glory of the Lord appeared. 43And Moses and Aaron came to the front of the tent of meeting, 44and the Lord said to Moses, 45"Get away from the midst of this congregation, that I may consume them in a moment." And they fell on their faces. 46And Moses said to Aaron, "Take your censer, and put fire therein from off the altar, and lay incense on it, and carry it quickly to the congregation, and make atonement for them; for wrath has gone forth from the Lord, the plague has begun." 47So Aaron took it as Moses said, and ran into the midst of the assembly; and behold, the plague had already begun among the people; and he put on the incense, and made atonement for the people. 48And he stood between the dead and the living; and the plague was stopped. 49Now those who died by the plague were fourteen thousand seven hundred, besides those who died in the affair of Korah. 50And Aaron returned to Moses at the entrance of the tent of meeting, when the plague was stopped.

The clear purpose of this section is to support and seal the prerogative of the Aaronic priesthood.

The "censers" or shallow shovels for carrying coals back and forth to the altar, which had belonged to Korah and his company, are disposed of. Eleazar is called to oversee the turning of them into plates to cover the altar, presumably because Aaron, as High Priest, cannot have any contact with the dead or with their property (Lev. 21:10–11). Eleazar is Aaron's son and later succeeds him as High Priest (Num. 20:22–29). His act as a surrogate of the High Priest is called "a sign to the people of Israel" and is a warning to anyone "who is not a priest" not to try to be a priest and behave as a priest. This whole period had been intense for all the people and had been trying of the Lord's patience, and yet, almost unbelievably, the next day all the people were dissenting again. They accused Moses and Aaron very forcibly, with an emphatic stress, saying: "You have killed the people of the Lord".

Again, however, the "glory of the Lord" appears in judgement and vindication (v. 42). Moses and Aaron approach the tent of meeting and are told by the Lord to take shelter while he destroys the people. They fall down helpless, but Moses is inspired to act. The Lord is furious with the people and his "wrath" is shown in the outbreak of a "plague". There are four terms for "plague" altogether, and the book of Numbers uses three of the four terms, which may indicate variants of one disease or separate diseases (11:33; 14:37; 16:46f.). But whatever it was, a dreaded fast-spreading killer invaded the camp.

Moses commissions Aaron to "make atonement" for the sins of the people. Interestingly, no blood is required for the atonement, just hot coals from the altar and incense! The usual rule is that blood is needed (see Lev. 17:11), but not always, as can be seen here and in Exod. 30:15 where half a shekel is enough. It is not known what Aaron actually did, but he ran into the middle of the camp, where the plague was already rampant, and "made atonement for the people". Here was vindication of Aaron and his line. He risked contact with the dead and, the text dramatically and strikingly has it, "he stood between the dead and the living" (v. 48).

Jesus came to us supremely as the High Priest who stands between us and death. To respond to him and accept him as Lord of life is to enter the land of the living. In the Creed we assert our belief in Jesus' coming again to judge "the quick and the dead", i.e. the living and the dead (see 1 Thess. 4:15–17); and he will be feared for "the wrath of the Lamb" (Rev. 6:16). This is not a losing of temper nor a selfish frustration, but the Lord's steady, deliberate, predictable insistence on resisting, attacking, and overcoming evil. It was then in the wilderness, and will be in the last of all judgements, the Lord's *love* that judges. His will is that none should be so condemned, so this same Jesus stands between us and death that we may live: "I am the way, and the truth, and the life; no one comes to the Father but by me" (John 14:6).

AARON'S ROD

Numbers 17:1–13

[1]The Lord said to Moses, [2]"Speak to the people of Israel, and get from them rods, one for each fathers' house, from all their leaders according to their fathers' houses, twelve rods. Write each man's name upon his rod, [3]and write Aaron's name upon the rod of Levi. For there shall be one rod for the head of each fathers' house. [4]Then you shall deposit them in the tent of meeting before the testimony, where I meet with you. [5]And the rod of the man whom I choose shall sprout; thus I will make to cease from me the murmurings of the people of Israel, which they murmur against you." [6]Moses spoke to the people of Israel; and all their leaders gave him rods, one for each leader, according to their fathers' houses, twelve rods; and the rod of Aaron was among their rods. [7]And Moses deposited the rods before the Lord in the tent of the testimony.

[8]And on the morrow Moses went into the tent of the testimony; and behold, the rod of Aaron for the house of Levi had sprouted and put forth buds, and produced blossoms, and it bore ripe almonds. [9]Then Moses brought out all the rods from before the Lord to all the people of Israel; and they looked, and each man took his rod. [10]And the Lord said to Moses, "Put back the rod of Aaron before the testimony, to be kept as a sign for the rebels, that you may make an end of their

murmurings against me, lest they die." ¹¹Thus did Moses; as the Lord commanded him, so he did.

¹²And the people of Israel said to Moses, "Behold, we perish, we are undone, we are all undone. ¹³Every one who comes near, who comes near to the tabernacle of the Lord, shall die. Are we all to perish?"

In this chapter we have the celebrated story of how Aaron's rod, a piece of dead wood, blossomed into life. Each tribe had its rod, but that of Levi, his tribe, was special. There is a play on words throughout the chapter, since the Hebrew for "rod" and for "tribe" is the same.

The rods, all dead and manhandled, are laid in the tent of meeting for the Lord to do something with them. He will cause one of them to "sprout" as his sign that that tribe is chosen. This verb means "to blossom" when used of buds on trees or of flowers, but it also serves as a metaphor for the restored Israel coming to full and beautiful life (Hos. 14:6; Isa. 27:6; 66:14), and as a metaphor for the life of the truly righteous being full of prosperity (Pss. 92:13; 72:7; Prov. 11:28). In v. 8 we see that not only is Aaron's rod chosen, and not only do living "buds" appear miraculously, but also "blossoms" and "ripe almonds". It is a total vindication of Aaron, and speaks of the joy of the Lord in so vindicating him with an excess of fruit over what was necessary. The almond tree is the first to blossom in Israel, in the early spring, and is known proverbially for this (see Jer. 1:11). This miraculous rod is never referred to again, but according to Jewish tradition it was kept faithfully until King Josiah hid it for safety with the dish containing the manna (Exod. 16:33) and the one containing the water for sprinkling (Num. 19:19). When the Messiah comes, they believe, he will restore it to the people of Israel.

The rod served, then, as a reminder and symbol, like the pot of manna. Primarily it was kept for the benefit of "the rebels". There had been several dissents and rebellions before this, but here a unique phrase is used. The Hebrew says "sons of rebellion", which means people wholly given over to rebellion and identified with it. Similar phrases are "people of rebellion" (Isa.

30:9) and "house of rebellion" (Ezek. 2:5), but none is as strong as this. It stands in contrast to the term for the Israelites, the "sons of Israel", which means the "sons of wrestling with God". True faith involves a real and sometimes blunt honesty with ourselves and with God, and often a struggling with his will for us, but it has nothing in common with rebellion against him or stepping out of his rule into self-rule. There must come a time in all our struggling with God when like Job we surrender to him, or we run the risk of entering the arena of rebellion and leaving the arena of faith.

The people react passionately to this vindication of Aaron. Many commentators see this as a kind of melodramatic self-pity rather than genuine repentance. But perhaps the people rightly discerned the Lord's wrath. Or perhaps the right way to understand the final two verses is to read them together with the next chapter. This deals with the duties and levies of the Levites and would thereby be given a suitably awesome context.

DUTIES AND DUES OF PRIESTS AND LEVITES

Numbers 18:1–32

[1]So the Lord said to Aaron, "You and your sons and your fathers' house with you shall bear iniquity in connection with the sanctuary; and you and your sons with you shall bear iniquity in connection with your priesthood. [2]And with you bring your brethren also, the tribe of Levi, the tribe of your father, that they may join you, and minister to you while you and your sons with you are before the tent of the testimony. [3]They shall attend you and attend to all duties of the tent; but shall not come near to the vessels of the sanctuary or to the altar, lest they, and you, die. [4]They shall join you, and attend to the tent of meeting, for all the service of the tent; and no one else shall come near you. [5]And you shall attend to the duties of the sanctuary and the duties of the altar, that there be wrath no more upon the people of Israel. [6]And behold, I have taken your brethren the Levites from among the people of Israel; they are a gift to you, given to the Lord, to do the service of the tent of meeting. [7]And you and your sons with you shall attend to your priesthood for all that concerns the altar and that is

within the veil; and you shall serve. I give your priesthood as a gift, and any one else who comes near shall be put to death."

8Then the Lord said to Aaron, "And behold, I have given you whatever is kept of the offerings made to me, all the consecrated things of the people of Israel; I have given them to you as a portion, and to your sons as a perpetual due. 9This shall be yours of the most holy things, reserved from the fire; every offering of theirs, every cereal offering of theirs and every sin offering of theirs and every guilt offering of theirs, which they render to me, shall be most holy to you and to your sons. 10In a most holy place shall you eat of it; every male may eat of it; it is holy to you. 11This also is yours, the offering of their gift, all the wave offerings of the people of Israel; I have given them to you, and to your sons and daughters with you, as a perpetual due; every one who is clean in your house may eat of it. 12All the best of the oil, and all the best of the wine and of the grain, the first fruits of what they give to the Lord, I give to you. 13The first ripe fruits of all that is in their land, which they bring to the Lord, shall be yours; every one who is clean in your house may eat of it. 14Every devoted thing in Israel shall be yours. 15Everything that opens the womb of all flesh, whether man or beast, which they offer to the Lord, shall be yours; nevertheless the first-born of man you shall redeem, and the firstling of unclean beasts you shall redeem. 16And their redemption price (at a month old you shall redeem them) you shall fix at five shekels in silver, according to the shekel of the sanctuary, which is twenty gerahs. 17But the firstling of a cow, or the firstling of a sheep, or the firstling of a goat, you shall not redeem; they are holy. You shall sprinkle their blood upon the altar, and shall burn their fat as an offering by fire, a pleasing odour to the Lord; 18but their flesh shall be yours, as the breast that is waved and as the right thigh are yours. 19All the holy offerings which the people of Israel present to the Lord I give to you, and to your sons and daughters with you, as a perpetual due; it is a covenant of salt for ever before the Lord for you and for your offspring with you." 20And the Lord said to Aaron, "You shall have no inheritance in their land, neither shall you have any portion among them; I am your portion and your inheritance among the people of Israel.

21"To the Levites I have given every tithe in Israel for an inheritance, in return for their service which they serve, their service in the tent of meeting. 22And henceforth the people of Israel shall not come near the tent of meeting, lest they bear sin and die. 23But the Levites shall do the service of the tent of meeting, and they shall bear their iniquity; it shall be a perpetual statute throughout your generations; and among the people of Israel they shall have no inheritance. [24]For the tithe of the people of Israel, which they present as an offering to the Lord, I have given to the Levites for an inheritance; therefore I have said of them that they shall have no inheritance among the people of Israel."

[25]And the Lord said to Moses, [26]"Moreover you shall say to the Levites, 'When you take from the people of Israel the tithe which I have given you from them for your inheritance, then you shall present an offering from it to the Lord, a tithe of the tithe. [27]And your offering shall be reckoned to you as though it were the grain of the threshing floor, and as the fullness of the wine press. [28]So shall you also present an offering to the Lord from all your tithes, which you receive from the people of Israel; and from it you shall give the Lord's offering to Aaron the priest. [29]Out of all the gifts to you, you shall present every offering due to the Lord, from all the best of them, giving the hallowed part from them.' [30]Therefore you shall say to them, 'When you have offered from it the best of it, then the rest shall be reckoned to the Levites as produce of the threshing floor, and as produce of the wine press; [31]and you may eat it in any place, you and your households; for it is your reward in return for your service in the tent of meeting. [32]And you shall bear no sin by reason of it, when you have offered the best of it. And you shall not profane the holy things of the people of Israel, lest you die.'"

(i)

This chapter falls quite naturally into four sections. The first section is vv. 1–7 on the various duties of the Levites. The sanctuary was seen to be, so to speak, "charged" with a spiritual force, and the priests were, to continue the metaphor, "conductors" of this force to the people. What is more, the priests had to "earth" the dangerous side of it (see v. 5*b*). In this sense they "bear iniquity" for the people. They have to make atonement for their own sins (Lev. 16:6) and for unwitting defilement of the sanctuary (Lev. 16:16), and thus ward off all the risks involved.

In v. 6 it is stressed how the Levites' service is as necessary to God's plans as that of the priests. They are "a gift" to the priests, but only to be "given to the Lord". The words translated "gift" are literally "a service of a gift". Such is the priesthood as understood here, with any other facing a death penalty for presuming to take this gift for himself.

(ii)

The second section is vv. 8–20 on the priests' levies or dues. There is similar provision for the support of the priesthood in Deut. 18:1–8; Lev. 6:16ff.; Ezek. 44:28ff. The priests are to get for their daily bread that which is "kept" from the people's offerings. A better translation would be "reserved" (see v. 9). It has to be noted that only some of the offerings were available to them "as a portion". They were not free to help themselves to whatever they wanted. What was burned on the altar was, of course, God's. Of the rest certain things were "holy" and could be shared by the priests' families, and certain were "most holy"; these could not go out of the Holy Place or be eaten by any but the priests (compare Lev. 6:16, 24).

The priests' portion also included the "first-fruits", brought in thanksgiving by the people at harvest, and what are in v. 14 called "devoted" things. This word has to do with the "separation" of objects from regular or profane use to a special or holy use. It is the same word found in Arabic as "hareem" that is, the place set apart for the husband's use. Anything so "devoted" to the Lord could not be returned to secular use (Lev. 27:28). It is this idea that lies behind the horrific practice of putting Canaanite cities to the "ban", as it called, for daring to oppose the God of Israel. See 21:2–3, where Israel made such a vow against Hormah and as a result had to destroy it utterly with all its inhabitants. Here, however, it is things like the first-fruits just mentioned and the first-born that are meant, unless it were the first-born of men or of unclean animals, which had to be redeemed by payment of a specified sum of money (which presumably went to the priests too). Clean animals, that is, those that could be killed for sacrifice, were not exempt.

These provisions for the priesthood are called a "perpetual due" and a "covenant of salt". This is obviously an idiom for an irrevocable bond. Salt is invaluable in the Middle East, and so the vision of the fertile land in Ezek. 47:1–12 contains explicit reference to salt-water swamps. It was used on burnt-offerings to please the Lord (Lev. 2:13; Ezek. 43:24). Salt was a preservative against decay and so became a symbol for that which will never decay. In fact there was an idiom "to eat a man's salt", which meant to create an unbreakable bond of fellowship between people, and the Arabic word for "a treaty" comes straight from the verb "to salt" something. So such a covenant or agreement would be utterly binding. With this background it is possible to understand better the sayings of Jesus in Mark 9:49–50.

The second section closes with the beautiful words of v. 20. Like the Levites (Deut. 10:9) the priests had no "portion" with other Israelites, but the Lord was their portion, and what was his was theirs. They did not live as others, from the results of agricultural or pastoral work, but from Israel's offerings to the Lord.

(iii)

The third section is vv. 21–24 on the Levites' general tithe. Tithing was common enough throughout the ancient Near East, and was certainly practised in Israel. In early times the tithe of every third year was given over to the Levites and the disadvantaged (Deut. 14:28–29). A later situation is reflected in this passage, where every year's tithe goes to the Levites, with no mention of the underprivileged. Are these references the background to Matt. 23:23 and Luke 11:42, where Jesus accuses the Pharisees of over-zealousness with regard to the content of the tithe, and under-zealousness with regard to the principles that had originally been enshrined in it?

The final section is vv. 25–32 on the priests' special tithe from the Levites. The Levites are to choose the finest tenth of the tenth given to them and give this to the priests. Their own tithe (and presumably the priests') are referred to as a "reward" for "service". A better translation would be: "it is your due". God's ministers need not be ashamed that they are maintained by God's people, but they should remember that their "due" comes from the people's offerings to God.

THE RED HEIFER

Numbers 19:1–22

[1]Now the Lord said to Moses and to Aaron, [2]"This is the statute of the law which the Lord has commanded: Tell the people of Israel to bring you a red heifer without defect, in which there is no blemish, and upon which a yoke has never come. [3]And you shall give her to Eleazar the priest, and she shall be taken outside the camp and slaughtered before him; [4]and Eleazar the priest shall take some of her blood with his finger, and sprinkle some of her blood toward the front of the tent of meeting seven times. [5]And the heifer shall be burned in his sight; her skin, her flesh, and her blood, with her dung, shall be burned; [6]and the priest shall take cedarwood and hyssop and scarlet stuff, and cast them into the midst of the burning of the heifer. [7]Then the priest shall wash his clothes and bathe his body in water, and afterwards he shall come into the camp; and the priest shall be unclean until evening. [8]He who burns the heifer shall wash his clothes in water and bathe his body in water, and shall be unclean until evening. [9]And a man who is clean shall gather up the ashes of the heifer, and deposit them outside the camp in a clean place; and they shall be kept for the congregation of the people of Israel for the water for impurity, for the removal of sin. [10]And he who gathers the ashes of the heifer shall wash his clothes, and be unclean until evening. And this shall be to the people of Israel, and to the stranger who sojourns among them, a perpetual statute.

[11]"He who touches the dead body of any person shall be unclean seven days; [12]he shall cleanse himself with the water on the third day and on the seventh day, and so be clean; but if he does not cleanse himself on the third day and on the seventh day, he will not become clean. [13]Whoever touches a dead person, the body of any man who has died, and does not cleanse himself, defiles the tabernacle of the Lord, and that person shall be cut off from Israel; because the water for impurity was not thrown upon him, he shall be unclean; his uncleanliness is still on him.

[14]"This is the law when a man dies in a tent: every one who comes into the tent, and every one who is in the tent, shall be unclean seven days. [15]And every open vessel, which has no cover fastened upon it, is unclean. [16]Whoever in the open field touches one who is slain with a sword, or a dead body, or a bone of a man, or a grave, shall be unclean seven days. [17]For the unclean they shall take some ashes of the burnt

sin offering, and running water shall be added in a vessel; [18]then a clean person shall take hyssop, and dip it in the water, and sprinkle it upon the tent, and upon all the furnishings, and upon the persons who were there, and upon him who touched the bone, or the slain, or the dead, or the grave; [19]and the clean person shall sprinkle upon the unclean on the third day and on the seventh day; thus on the seventh day he shall cleanse him, and he shall wash his clothes and bathe himself in water, and at evening he shall be clean.

[20]"But the man who is unclean and does not cleanse himself, that person shall be cut off from the midst of the assembly, since he has defiled the sanctuary of the Lord; because the water for impurity has not been thrown upon him, he is unclean. [21]And it shall be a perpetual statute for them. He who sprinkles the water for impurity shall wash his clothes; and he who touches the water for impurity shall be unclean until evening. [22]And whatever the unclean person touches shall be unclean; and any one who touches it shall be unclean until evening."

(i)

The Rabbis saw this as the most enigmatic rite in the Old Testament, some going so far as to say that even the wise Solomon gave up trying to understand it properly. The problem for them was that "it cleanses the defiled, and defiles the clean". The idea that dead bodies were a source of defilement was ancient and widespread, and there were several rites to remove this defilement, but this one is quite unique. Most Jewish and Christian interpreters have treated the passage allegorically. The Rabbinic tradition, for instance, is that the High Priest went with the heifer to the Mount of Olives for the sacrifice, i.e. east of the Temple; that because of this the walls on the east of the city were built lower so that he could see right into the sanctuary through the Gate of Nicanor from the spot where the blood was sprinkled.

The Hebrew word indicates any female cow of between two and five years of age (compare 1 Sam. 6:7). It is possible that this rite was set up to contrast that of Exod. 32 where the people made a "golden calf" which was burned and whose ashes were mixed with water and drunk. Whereas there the *people* defiled the Lord, here *he* makes a way for cleansing the people. The cow then has to be perfect in form and the Lord has to have been its one and only master. It is "red", perhaps to symbolize the importance of its blood, and to further symbolize the use of the fire as a purifying agent (compare Num. 31:23). Its importance is sealed by the calling of the rite by the unusual phrase "statute of the law", i.e. a deliberate and specific decree from God.

The cow was to be slaughtered, of course, and because the High Priest could not have contact with anything unclean, the next in authority, Eleazar, was sent to organize this. But much more importantly, it is to be noted that this is the *only* case where the slaughter took place "outside the camp". It cannot therefore have been seen as a sacrifice, but it was a sacred act of some sort. Flesh was sometimes taken outside the camp to be burned, but only after the sacrifice for sin was made (Lev. 4:11–12, 21; 8:17; 9:11; 16:27; Heb. 13:11) and for other reasons than those given here. So why was this done? We simply do not know. But further evidence of the act's sacredness is the dedicatory sprinkling of the blood to the Lord (literally "toward the front of the tent of meeting") seven times. Another aspect of the act whose meaning is not known is that the "blood" was then "burned". Why? This is only found here. Even the "skin" of animals was only exceptionally burned (Lev. 4:11, 20), and the blood was kept to be thrown against the altar or sprinkled appropriately.

(ii)

As the whole animal is burning, the priest adds to the agents three other items: (a) *cedarwood*, possibly as a symbol of might and imperishability, since that wood is so hard and long-living (see Ps. 29:5; Isa. 2:13); or possibly of splendour (see Song of S. 1:17; Jer. 22:14); (b) *hyssop*, which is a cleansing and purifying agent (see Exod. 12:22; Lev. 14:4, 6; Ps. 51:7); and (c) *scarlet stuff* which was made from cloths dyed in a substance distilled mainly from certain insects. The colour suggests blood and fire, both of which were purifying agents. The Tabernacle cloths (Exod. 25:4) and the priests' clothes (Exod. 28:5ff.) were scarlet. At Qumran the warrior priests wore scarlet, and there is, of course, the telling image of Jesus in a scarlet robe (Matt. 27:28). John tells in his Gospel that "hyssop" was offered to Jesus on the cross too (John

19:29), recalling its redemptive imagery, probably with Exodus 12 in mind. The only other case of these three items being used together is in Lev. 14 where, however, they are bound together to be used as a sprinkler. Here they are merely burned. This is, then, clearly a terribly potent rite, storing up immense spiritual power.

Such is the potential energy that the priest is rendered "taboo" by it and is unclean for the rest of that day. Holiness and uncleanness were alike seen as contagious (see the amazing statement in Ezek. 44:19), and so the priest had to wash thoroughly. The word used for washing his clothes is also used for washing oneself from sin in Ps. 51:2 and Jer. 2:22. By Jesus' day the common phrase was that contact with holiness "defiles the hands", irrespective of intention or moral character. Even reading from a scroll of the Scriptures made one unclean, and readers had to wash thoroughly. Jesus had some hard words to say of such ideas: "what comes out of ... the heart ... defiles a man" (Matt. 15:10–20), not eating with "unwashed hands" or any external action; but Israel was at this time not yet ready for this profound insight.

(iii)

The "ashes" from this sacrifice were to be stored in a "clean place", as would be expected. But another unique thing is required, namely that this place be "outside the camp". Why? Ashes could be caught up easily by breezes and blown about, so perhaps it was an extra safeguard for the camp, to ensure none would fan out over it. They were mixed with the "water for impurity", i.e. for removing impurity. Even this phrase is rare, occurring again only in Num. 31:23. The whole was to be used for cleansing from the terrible defilement of coming into contact with a corpse. Anyone refusing to be cleansed in this way was removed from fellowship with Israel altogether. The phrase "from the midst of the assembly" in v. 20 is another unique one, and stresses the point.

A selection of circumstances leading to uncleanness is given, and a description of how to order the remedy. It was in fact to help avoid cases like that of v. 16 that the tradition arose of painting all graves white so that they could be noticed and kept at a safe distance. Jesus refers to this custom to point out to certain Pharisees that their show of purity only served to attract attention to all that was unclean in them (see Matt. 23:27 and compare Paul in Acts 23:3).

(iv)

So a recap of the chapter. What is clear is that the symbols are designed to combat death. The redness of the cow and the material represent blood, and the *life* is in the blood (Gen. 9:4; Lev. 17:11); the cedar is known for its longevity; the "running water" (v. 17) is called literally in the Hebrew "living water". Jesus offers us all this total and wonderful antidote to death in his own blood (John 6:52–59), and offers us also the beautiful "water of life" (Rev. 21:6). He is the one without blemish of any sort, and the only one who never came under the yoke of sin. He is the one who offered himself as a sacrifice outside the city of God, made all the more perfect by the fact that he did so not under compulsion but in trustful and free obedience.

MOSES SINS

Numbers 20:1–13

¹And the people of Israel, the whole congregation, came into the wilderness of Zin in the first month, and the people stayed in Kadesh; and Miriam died there, and was buried there.

²Now there was no water for the congregation; and they assembled themselves together against Moses and against Aaron. ³And the people contended with Moses, and said, "Would that we had died when our brethren died before the Lord! ⁴Why have you brought the assembly of the Lord into this wilderness, that we should die here, both we and our cattle? ⁵And why have you made us come up out of Egypt, to bring us to this evil place? It is no place for grain, or figs, or vines, or pomegranates; and there is no water to drink." ⁶Then Moses and Aaron went from the presence of the assembly to the door of the tent of meeting, and fell on their faces. And the glory of the Lord appeared to them, ⁷and the Lord said to Moses, ⁸"Take the rod, and assemble

the congregation, you and Aaron your brother, and tell the rock before their eyes to yield its water; so you shall bring water out of the rock for them; so you shall give drink to the congregation and their cattle." ⁹And Moses took the rod from before the Lord, as he commanded him.

¹⁰And Moses and Aaron gathered the assembly together before the rock, and he said to them, "Hear now, you rebels; shall we bring forth water for you out of this rock?" ¹¹And Moses lifted up his hand and struck the rock with his rod twice; and water came forth abundantly, and the congregation drank, and their cattle. ¹²And the Lord said to Moses and Aaron, "Because you did not believe in me, to sanctify me in the eyes of the people of Israel, therefore you shall not bring this assembly into the land which I have given them." ¹³These are the waters of Meribah, where the people of Israel contended with the Lord, and he showed himself holy among them.

(i)

After the wandering in the wilderness of Paran, prior to reaching the Promised Land (Num. 13:3; 14:32), the people move on to Kadesh through the wilderness of Zin (Num. 13:21). Here they resort to complaint again, and in fact this episode is a parallel to that recounted in Exod. 17:1–7. It is further referred to in Ps. 95:7–11. Kadesh was a highly significant place in their sojourn, as shall be seen. Also important to note by way of introduction is that in this one section we see how none of Moses' family, not himself, nor his brother Aaron, nor his sister Miriam, in fact went with the Israelites into the Promised Land. It is a sad passage in Jewish tradition.

A death actually reported in this first verse is that of Miriam, although neither place nor manner is told. The affair is very matter-of-fact, perhaps reflecting a coldness towards her after her challenge of Moses' authority (12:1–15), though she was accorded honour later (Mic. 6:4) because of her role at the Exodus (Exod. 15).

Those still alive had wished for death again rather than have to arrive at another testing ground and find it not as they would like, i.e. without "water". Again they speak against Moses and Aaron. They have neither courage nor trust to face the future. It often happens with us that the future seems frightening or insecure, and we wish it would disappear. Here the people melodramatically wish for death rather than face a testing tomorrow (compare 14:2; Exod. 16:3). We are called to take up crosses daily to follow the Lord.

Their sizing up of the situation (v. 5) wasn't quite accurate. Some things they did not have, but what they did have was the Lord, and freedom to worship and follow him. That is sweet food indeed (see Deut. 8:3 where a similar occasion calls out the Lord's provision and the lesson that "man does not live by bread alone, but by everything that proceeds out of the mouth of the Lord"). In Exod. 19:4 the Lord does not say he has brought them to the wilderness, but to himself. Here it was the same, but their self-centredness held sway. Moses and Aaron again intercede, and the "glory of the Lord" again appears.

Moses is told by the Lord to take "the rod", further defined in v. 9 as being "before the Lord", probably therefore that of 17:10. Be that as it may, it became a great symbol of popular piety, as did the "rock" from which the water came. There were two main traditions that evolved: (a) the water followed them to Canaan; (b) the rock followed them to Canaan. Lest the reader smile too readily, Paul knew and used the latter idea in 1 Cor. 10:4, comparing the rock to Christ.

(ii)

Somewhere in the few verses must come the sin of Moses and Aaron, but alas it is not self-evident. Jewish tradition has it that the reason was not written down so as to protect their honour from mockery. It is sufficient to know that they sinned (like everyone) and the Lord punished them. Judaism does teach that the greater the person the stricter the standard of judgement, and so whatever it was that happened, Moses and Aaron obviously failed the Lord seriously. Verse 10 is the crucial one: either the "rebels" were the people or they were the two leaders.

Here are the options: (a) *the people are rebellious* and somehow this reflects on lack of leadership (see Deut. 1:37); (b) *Moses and Aaron are doubtful* of the miracle happening; (c) *Moses*

struck the rock with the rod when told only to speak to it, and
therefore showed doubt, or anger, or arrogance in adding to
God's command; (d) *Moses acted altogether out of bitterness* and
so failed to see things God's way, acting reluctantly (compare
Jonah). The latter has become a favourite interpretation, and
there is support for it in Ps. 106:32–33.

In the text what is said is that they failed to "sanctify" the Lord
before the people. The importance of this, of bringing glory and
honour to God's gracious holy character, is brought out in the
lovely prophecy of Isa. 29:22–24. To "sanctify" God is, then, to
praise him for being God, not man, and to let him be seen as God.
The word has the idea of being separate and means to show God
as being wholly other from us yet ready and willing to commit
himself to us.

The final verse explains why the city whose name commemor-
ates the idea of sanctifying the Lord (Kadesh means "holy") was
given the additional name Meribah or "contention"; see also
27:14. In spite of them all he "showed himself holy among them".
A better translation would be "vindicated himself as holy".
How? By the miracle of producing the water in spite of lack of
faith that he could. Let us praise God that his working is not
dependent on us!

NOW LET US PASS!

Numbers 20:14–21

¹⁴Moses sent messengers from Kadesh to the king of Edom, "Thus
says your brother Israel: You know all the adversity that has befallen
us: ¹⁵how our fathers went down to Egypt, and we dwelt in Egypt a
long time; and the Egyptians dealt harshly with us and our fathers;
¹⁶and when we cried to the Lord, he heard our voice, and sent an angel
and brought us forth out of Egypt; and here we are in Kadesh, a city on
the edge of your territory. ¹⁷Now let us pass through your land. We will
not pass through field or vineyard, neither will we drink water from a
well; we will go along the King's Highway, we will not turn aside to the
right hand or to the left, until we have passed through your territory."
¹⁸But Edom said to him, "You shall not pass through, lest I come out

with the sword against you." ¹⁹And the people of Israel said to him, "We will go up by the highway; and if we drink of your water, I and my cattle, then I will pay for it; let me only pass through on foot, nothing more." ²⁰But he said, "You shall not pass through." And Edom came out against them with many men, and with a strong force. ²¹Thus Edom refused to give Israel passage through his territory; so Israel turned away from him.

The people are about to move into the region of Edom and Moab, the third geographical area mentioned in the Introduction.

It is difficult to pinpoint the route taken by the Israelites at this stage. But at the start Israel tried to rouse Edom's sympathy, so that she could cross that nation's land. Moses sent "messengers" on a fairly informal basis, assuming that permission would be given with pleasure. He refers to Israel as Edom's "brother", a relationship recalled to Edom's shame in Amos 1:11 and in Obad. 10, 12. The story of Jacob and Esau in Genesis also reflects the close blood ties that existed between the two peoples. So Moses expects comfort and assistance.

In v. 16 Moses refers to the angel sent by the Lord to guide the people out of Egypt. See Exod. 23:20 for the lovely words of this promise: "Behold, I send an angel before you, to guard you on the way and to bring you to the place which I have prepared". See also *Additional Note 5*.

Moses pledges that there will be no plundering of the land, but they merely wish to "pass through". If they are not allowed to they must take a long detour, so he stresses that their intentions are peaceful and in fact undertakes to pay for any water they may need to drink. The route that Moses wished to use was an established trade route for the commercial caravans, and for diplomatic travel, so it had royal protection, hence its name, the King's Highway. This road is again mentioned in Num. 21:22, and ran from Damascus to the Gulf of Aqaba along the east of Canaan. It met other roads crossing it and was peppered with fortresses (Gen. 14). After a typical history of security and destruction, reflecting war and peace in the area, Emperor Trajan rebuilt it around A.D. 106 and called it Trajan's Road. There is a road in modern Jordan based on it.

For some reason the Edomite king refused to allow them safe swift passage. Moreover, he came out with a show of strength against them. Israel withdrew. The Lord had not told them to fight and for once they did not take an initiative. It is a necessary thing in life to learn when to do battle and when not to.

AARON DIES

Numbers 20:22–29

²²And they journeyed from Kadesh, and the people of Israel, the whole congregation, came to Mount Hor. ²³And the Lord said to Moses and Aaron at Mount Hor, on the border of the land of Edom, ²⁴"Aaron shall be gathered to his people; for he shall not enter the land which I have given to the people of Israel, because you rebelled against my command at the waters of Meribah. ²⁵Take Aaron and Eleazar his son, and bring them up to Mount Hor; ²⁶and strip Aaron of his garments, and put them upon Eleazar his son; and Aaron shall be gathered to his people, and shall die there." ²⁷Moses did as the Lord commanded; and they went up Mount Hor in the sight of all the congregation. ²⁸And Moses stripped Aaron of his garments, and put them upon Eleazar his son; and Aaron died there on the top of the mountain. Then Moses and Eleazar came down from the mountain. ²⁹And when all the congregation saw that Aaron was dead, all the house of Israel wept for Aaron thirty days.

Several sites have been more or less plausibly suggested for Mount Hor, but certainty is impossible. What is known is that Aaron died there, and was presumably buried by Moses and Eleazar. The Hebrew idiom has it that he was "gathered to his people". The last word has a plural form and denotes the closest kinsfolk. It is a warm phrase like the parallel ones of "being gathered to one's fathers" or "sleeping with one's fathers" (e.g. Judg. 2:10; 1 Kings 1:21; 14:31). However, Aaron's death was still in part a punishment for not fully obeying the Lord's "command" (literally "mouth") in the incident recounted in 20:1–13 (see especially v. 12).

Aaron's death is as puzzlingly matter-of-fact in its telling as was that of Miriam (20:1). Not much is said of the basic facts at all, and it took an editor (33:38–39) to record his age as 123 years, and the time of his death as the first of the fifth month, forty years after the Exodus. We are told here that his robes of office were removed from him and given symbolically to his eldest son Eleazar who became High Priest after his father. The making of these robes is described in Exod. 39:1–31, and the ceremony of robing Aaron is recorded in Lev. 8:7–9. The robes symbolized the essential ministry of the High Priest as a mediator: the coloured robes, the gold, the gems standing for the glory of God's presence, and the breastplate with the names of the twelve tribes standing for Israel. The only time he could take off these robes of office was when entering the "holy place" on the Day of Atonement (Lev. 16:4, 23).

So great was the loss that the people mourned for thirty days, the same honour accorded to Moses (Deut. 34:8). In Jewish tradition Aaron is remembered especially as a great peacemaker. Rabbi Hillel, one of Jesus' greatest predecessors, said that his followers had to be each "a disciple of Aaron, loving peace and pursuing peace, loving his fellow-men and bringing them near the Torah". Such was the reputation of Aaron as a peacemaker that the Rabbis argued that he was missed more than even Moses. What is the basis of this? When Moses died, the text reads: "And *the people of Israel* wept for Moses" (Deut. 34:8). But when Aaron died, the text reads: "*all the house of Israel* wept for Aaron".

Jesus had marvellous words to say about making peace: "Blessed are the peacemakers, for they shall be called the sons of God" (Matt. 5:9). Not those who love peace, no matter how much they do; not those who keep the peace, no matter how tolerant they are; not even those who pray for peace, no matter how sincere they may be; but those, like Jesus, who set out to *make* peace, to be active in reconciling people. Such people are truly acting as God's children, and will know his fatherly love and blessings. And to such children is the promise that they will never die.

HORMAH: ISRAEL'S VICTORY

Numbers 21:1-3

> [1]When the Canaanite, the king of Arad, who dwelt in the Negeb, heard that Israel was coming by the way of Atharim, he fought against Israel, and took some of them captive. [2]And Israel vowed a vow to the Lord, and said, "If thou wilt indeed give this people into my hand, then I will utterly destroy their cities." [3]And the Lord hearkened to the voice of Israel, and gave over the Canaanites; and they utterly destroyed them and their cities; so the name of the place was called Hormah.

The king of Arad fought the Israelites and even captured some. It is not said whether Israel chose to fight, unlike against Edom (20:21), or whether he surprised them on the march and made off with captives. However it was, it happened "by the way of Atharim". Theories as to the meaning of this are many. It could mean the way of certain well-known palm trees, or the way taken by the scouts earlier on, or the way of an established caravan route or tracks. This last suggestion is perhaps the best, fitting with the desire of the Israelites to make a swift passage through these lands on the easiest routes (see 20:17; 21:22).

The people—note that Moses is not mentioned—turn to the Lord for vindication. They pledge themselves to surrender everything up to him if he fights for them and gives them victory over the king's forces. The RSV's "utterly destroy" is related to the Hebrew word for "destruction" which became the name of the place. The Lord accepts their vow, and under him they fight and win, and in fact they do destroy everything.

There are several dimensions to an analysis of Israel's wars. If the Lord initiates a war then it is his war, and so a "holy war". Such are called the Lord's wars (e.g. 1 Sam. 25:28) and in them Israel is known as the Lord's army (e.g. 1 Sam. 17:45). The context is usually the conquest of Canaan. Such holy wars are attributed to two reasons: (a) fulfilment of promises to the patriarchs (Gen. 15:18-21; Exod. 3:8, 17, etc); (b) judgement on the pagan Canaanites (Gen. 15:16; Deut. 9:4; etc.). But one

cannot simply say that Israel's wars are synonymous with the
Lord's wars, for Israel often acted presumptuously and self-
confidently (e.g. Num. 13-14). Even when she won, we today are
sometimes distressed—and rightly so—by the triumphant manner in which she assumed that the Lord was always on her side
and by the lack of pity which—as here—she showed to her
enemies.

The significance of all this for those who follow the Lord Jesus
Christ is clear and sound. We may not *assume* that all our spiritual
and mundane battles are also the Lord's, for we may have acted
presumptuously or selfishly. However, if we are on the Lord's
side, and are wearing the armour he has provided (Eph.
6:10–17), then the very powers of Hell itself shall not destroy us,
for it will be the Lord that they are fighting (Matt. 16:18). In the
words of the hymn:

> Fierce may be the conflict,
> Strong may be the foe,
> But the King's own army
> None can overthrow.
> Round his standard ranging,
> Victory is secure,
> For his truth unchanging
> Makes the triumph sure.

THE PILGRIMS REBEL!

Numbers 21:4–9

[4]From Mount Hor they set out by the way to the Red Sea, to go around
the land of Edom; and the people became impatient on the way. [5]And
the people spoke against God and against Moses, "Why have you
brought us up out of Egypt to die in the wilderness? For there is no
food and no water, and we loathe this worthless food." [6]Then the Lord
sent fiery serpents among the people, and they bit the people, so that
many people of Israel died. [7]And the people came to Moses, and said,
"We have sinned, for we have spoken against the Lord and against
you; pray to the Lord, that he take away the serpents from us." So
Moses prayed for the people. [8]And the Lord said to Moses, "Make a

fiery serpent, and set it on a pole; and every one who is bitten, when he sees it, shall live." ⁹So Moses made a bronze serpent, and set it on a pole; and if a serpent bit any man, he would look at the bronze serpent and live.

According to Jewish tradition this was the last and the worst of Israel's apostasies in the wilderness. The plague of serpents was a most terrible curse from the Lord. The Hebrew idiom is that the people's "soul was shortened". Having a "short spirit" means being impatient, unable to keep one's temper in check, unable to keep one's self-discipline (compare Judg. 16:16). It is the opposite of being "long-suffering": "He who is slow to anger has great understanding, but he who has a hasty temper exalts folly" (Prov. 14:29). This same gracious gift of God is to be found in Paul's list of the fruits of the Spirit (Gal. 5:22–23). Having a "short soul", indeed, really means more than being impatient, it means being thoroughly discouraged. The people were depressed and cheerless.

They had been rejected by the kings of Edom and Arad, and had lost their High Priest, Aaron. So they bitterly complained *again* to Moses, but the text makes it clear that in so doing they were "speaking against God". They complained that there was no daily provision of food and water, only "worthless food" and the food they called this was the manna, a gift from God! Such a blatant contempt for God's gift and purpose for them evoked his great anger. The punishment took the form of deadly "fiery serpents", so-called not from their physical appearance but from the burning sensation of their venom in the body. Most interesting is that the word for "serpents" is *seraphim*—the very word of Isa. 6 for the creatures around the Lord's throne. In that passage they are angelic servants of the Lord, yet here they are also his servants; there they praise and glorify him in adoration, here they glorify him by vindicating him in judgement. Perhaps then the seraphim here are to be seen as heavenly beings, not earthly reptiles? This fits better with the idea of them as messengers, and suits texts such as Ps. 104:1–4. But this time they are messengers of death, and the people quickly acknowledge their fault and confess to the Lord and Moses (compare 12:11), who intercedes for them.

God provides an unexpected antidote to the serpents, not by means of a serum based on their venom, but by means of an artificial serpent set up high on a "pole", which need be only looked at for recovery and presumably immunity thereafter.

It is not said that the Israelites kept this serpent and took it with them, but in 2 Kings 18:4 part of the much-needed reformative work of King Hezekiah was to destroy a "bronze serpent that Moses had made" and which was being used in pagan worship. It is likely, therefore, that the Israelites did keep it and that later on it degenerated to a pagan symbol under the influence of the various cults that held sway in Israel for so long, many of which may themselves have involved the worship of serpent gods.

But the Lord alone is the Healer. And this passage shows just that. The serpents brought death and the Lord brought the cure. Why didn't he just rid them of the serpents? Because this way he showed that only he was the Healing God, and was in fact also Lord of the serpents. The prophet Hosea encourages the people to return to the Lord "for he has torn, that he may heal us; he has stricken, and he will bind us up" (6:1). Even more directly God himself asserts to the people after the Exodus: "I am the Lord, your healer" (Exod. 15:26).

The New Testament knows of this episode too. In 1 Cor. 10:9 Paul refers to the judgement and the deaths, but in John 3:14 we find Jesus focusing on the antidote, and telling us that he is the antidote to our death-orientated sinful lives. As the Lord used the form of a serpent to counter the effects of the serpents, so the New Testament teaches that the counter to the effects of sin and death is found in Jesus who was made sin for us.

But it is to the Old Testament expression of God's Gospel that we turn in conclusion. In this passage we see a simple call to look and live, in other words a call to look in faith and trust so that the Lord can show himself to be worthy of that trust and bring life. The prophet issues a similar invitation:

> Turn to me and be saved,
> all the ends of the earth!
>   (Isa. 45:22)

THE MARCH FROM ARABAH

Numbers 21:10–20

¹⁰And the people of Israel set out, and encamped in Oboth. ¹¹And they set out from Oboth, and encamped at Iye-abarim, in the wilderness which is opposite Moab, toward the sunrise. ¹²From there they set out, and encamped in the Valley of Zered. ¹³From there they set out, and encamped on the other side of the Arnon, which is in the wilderness, that extends from the boundary of the Amorites; for the Arnon is the boundary of Moab, between Moab and the Amorites. ¹⁴Wherefore it is said in the Book of the Wars of the Lord,

> "Waheb in Suphah,
> and the valleys of the Arnon,
> ¹⁵and the slope of the valleys
> that extends to the seat of Ar,
> and leans to the border of Moab."

¹⁶And from there they continued to Beer; that is the well of which the Lord said to Moses, "Gather the people together, and I will give them water." ¹⁷Then Israel sang this song:

> "Spring up, O well!—Sing to it!—
> ¹⁸the well which the princes dug,
> which the nobles of the people delved,
> with the sceptre and with their staves."

And from the wilderness they went on to Mattanah, ¹⁹and from Mattanah to Nahaliel, and from Nahaliel to Bamoth, ²⁰and from Bamoth to the valley lying in the region of Moab by the top of Pisgah which looks down upon the desert.

In this passage there is a reference to an ancient collection called "The Book of the Wars of the Lord", although curiously enough the excerpt is in no way militaristic or martial in tone. (See *Additional Note 6.*) This book was probably an anthology of poetry composed by balladeers about scenes from the days of the settlement in Canaan. The "wars of the Lord" were those fought under him (compare 1 Sam. 18:17; 25:28) against his foes (Judg. 5:31). Such wars were sacred and called for special consecration of the people (Josh. 3:5; Isa. 13:3; Jer. 6:4; 51:27; Joel 3:9; Mic. 3:5), the very idiom in Hebrew for to prepare for war being "to consecrate war". (See further the commentary on 21:1–3.)

The second song quoted here (vv. 17–18) was sung on every third Sabbath according to Rabbinic tradition. In this song the people exhort one another to sing to the well in a sort of prayer or plea that it will continue to supply their needs. On the third Sabbath it was sung as a prayer to the Lord that he would continue to refresh his people even while they were in exile. Jesus has said clearly to us in a conversation that took place around another well that: "Everyone who drinks of this water will thirst again, but whoever drinks of the water that I shall give him will never thirst; the water that I shall give him will become in him a spring of water welling up to eternal life" (John 4:13–14).

VICTORY OVER SIHON AND OG

Numbers 21:21–35

[21]Then Israel sent messengers to Sihon king of the Amorites, saying, [22]"Let me pass through your land; we will not turn aside into field or vineyard; we will not drink the water of a well; we will go by the King's Highway, until we have passed through your territory." [23]But Sihon would not allow Israel to pass through his territory. He gathered all his men together, and went out against Israel to the wilderness, and came to Jahaz, and fought against Israel. [24]And Israel slew him with the edge of the sword, and took possession of his land from the Arnon to the Jabbok, as far as to the Ammonites; for Jazer was the boundary of the Ammonites. [25]And Israel took all these cities, and Israel settled in all the cities of the Amorites, in Heshbon, and in all its villages. [26]For Heshbon was the city of Sihon the king of the Amorites, who had fought against the former king of Moab and taken all his land out of his hand, as far as the Arnon. [27]Therefore the ballad singers say,

"Come to Heshbon, let it be built,
 let the city of Sihon be established.
[28]For fire went forth from Heshbon,

flame from the city of Sihon.

It devoured Ar of Moab,

the lords of the heights of the Arnon.

29Woe to you, O Moab!

You are undone, O people of Chemosh!

He has made his sons fugitives,

and his daughters captives, to an Amorite king, Sihon.

30So their posterity perished from Heshbon, as far as Dibon,

and we laid waste until fire spread to Medeba."

31Thus Israel dwelt in the land of the Amorites. 32And Moses sent to spy out Jazer; and they took its villages, and dispossessed the Amorites that were there. 33Then they turned and went up by the way to Bashan; and Og the king of Bashan came out against them, he and all his people, to battle at Edre-i. 34But the Lord said to Moses, "Do not fear him; for I have given him into your hand, and all his people, and his land; and you shall do to him as you did to Sihon king of the Amorites, who dwelt at Heshbon." 35So they slew him, and his sons, and all his people, until there was not one survivor left to him; and they possessed his land.

(i)

This victory and the one recounted in the next section (vv. 33ff.) became great favourites in Israel. Parallel accounts can be found in Deut. 2:24–37 and Judg. 11:19–22. Sihon was one of the legendary great kings of the area. He came out aggressively against Israel while they were still in the wilderness, refusing passage through his region. Israel's men won the battle, and routed the opposition all the way from the Arnon river to the Jabbok river. The latter river was the natural boundary between the Amorites and the Ammonites, showing that at this time Moab was under Amorite control.

The writer quotes from an ancient poetic source on the subject. It is part of a piece sung by the "bards" of ancient Israel. Such pieces would be committed to memory and eventually transmitted to written documents like the Book of the Wars of the Lord mentioned earlier in the chapter.

The national god of Moab is mentioned in v. 29—"Chemosh". He had a reputation as a most powerful god and is mentioned eight times in five different chapters of the Old Testament. The name seems to have something to do with "fire" and is probably a title as opposed to a personal name. This verse is quoted almost in full in Jer. 48:46 except that there the verbs are all made passive, removing the idea that Chemosh took the lead in delivering his people into Amorite hands. It is interesting that the Moabite Stone, one of the most famous archaeological inscriptions to have been found in the Biblical area, contains a similar sentiment. On this King Mesha says that "Chemosh was angry with his land" and therefore let the Israelite King Omri oppress Moab "many days".

After the quotation is ended the narrative resumes with a reaffirmation that Israel controlled the land between the two rivers, consolidating her position and settling in the country.

(ii)

Og the king of Bashan was one of Israel's most powerful enemies in her folk memory. The defeat of Sihon and Og gave the lie to the fears expressed by Caleb's brothers in 13:28ff. about the great warriors and strong citadels she would confront. See Deut. 3:1ff. for a parallel account of this incident.

The strategic result of the victory over Og was that Israel now controlled the whole territory of Transjordan. She was almost ready to move into Canaan. So proud was she of such victories against overwhelming odds that she celebrated them in the songs of her Temple (Pss. 135:11–12; 136:17–22).

In Deut. 3:11 further information is given about Og. He is called the last of the dreaded "Rephaim". This word has two different references. It is the name, first, of the shades or spirits in Sheol and, second, of fabled peoples in Canaan who had almost died out before Israel began to live there. Obviously it is the second meaning that is relevant here. The Rephaim are compared to the Anakim in Deut. 2:10–11 and 20–21, and belong with them to the giant races of Israel's folk memory. Their massive weapons are recalled in 2 Sam. 21:16, 18, 20, 22.

Israel has now arrived on the plains of Moab opposite Jericho (22:1), where a new and exciting chapter in her adventures is about to begin.

B. THE PEOPLE OF ISRAEL AND THE TRIALS OF ADJUSTMENT

BALAAM AND BALAK: AN INTRODUCTION

The whole section chapters 22–24 concerns the destiny of Israel and yet the principal characters never come into contact with the people, and neither of them are Israelites. The section is obviously separate in character and origin from the rest of the book. It is not a short episode but a story with a long and involved plot, and a good story too; there is a sense of drama and climax, and there are undoubtedly historical figures at the root of all this. But it would seem that (as often) there was more than one tradition. The chapters reflect several sources that have been combined to produce our present text, some of them probably later than Balaam's time. We must take the mixed character of the section into account in assessing its message for us today.

The name Balaam seems to be derived from a root meaning "to swallow, engulf", sometimes used quite simply of the digestive processes, and sometimes metaphorically of the destruction of peoples (e.g. Job 20:15; Exod. 15:12; Num. 16:30ff.) It is not an Israelite name, and some have suggested it is another form of Bela, also called a son of Beor and identified as a king of Edom in Gen. 36:32. Other suggestions have been that he was named after a tribal god, or was nicknamed "swallower of people" because of his profession as a purveyor of curses.

Balaam has suffered, probably unfairly, in Jewish tradition and in Christian tradition too. The Syriac translation has a number of variants calling him a "false prophet". In Deut. 23:4–5 the implication is clearly that Balaam had agreed to curse Israel but was prevented by the Lord (see also Josh. 24:9–10 and Neh. 13:2). Josh. 13:22 has him as a "soothsayer" slain by Israel. There is even a later allusion in Numbers (31:8, 16) blaming him for the terrible apostasy "in the matter of Peor" (25:1–15). Then in the Jewish *Sayings of the Fathers* there is the tradition that he was "blood-thirsty" and "deceitful" with "no place in the world to come". Furthermore, the New Testament reflects only the critical traditions. We do not know the actual background to Rev. 2:14–15, but somehow it was linked to non-Biblical sources on Balaam. 2 Pet. 2:15–16 tells us that Balaam insisted on mercenary payment for acting on behalf of God (compare Jude 11). In spite of his words of blessing he is regarded as a wicked enemy of God's people. So many commentators have tried their best to read between the lines of chapters 22–24 and infer Balaam's weakness or deviousness. I do not think they are right. But let the text speak for itself. The matter will also be considered again when we reach 31:13–24.

BALAK HIRES BALAAM: MOVE ONE

Numbers 22:1–14

[1]Then the people of Israel set out, and encamped in the plains of Moab beyond the Jordan at Jericho. [2]And Balak the son of Zippor saw all that Israel had done to the Amorites. [3]And Moab was in great dread of the people, because they were many; Moab was overcome with fear of the people of Israel. [4]And Moab said to the elders of Midian, "This horde will now lick up all that is round about us, as the ox licks up the grass of the field." So Balak the son of Zippor, who was king of Moab at that time, [5]sent messengers to Balaam the son of Beor at Pethor, which is near the River, in the land of Amaw to call him, saying, "Behold, a people has come out of Egypt; they cover the face of the earth, and they are dwelling opposite me. [6]Come now, curse this people for me, since they are too mighty for me; perhaps I shall be able to defeat them and drive them from the land; for I know that he whom you bless is blessed, and he whom you curse is cursed."

[7]So the elders of Moab and the elders of Midian departed with the fees for divination in their hand; and they came to Balaam, and gave him Balak's message. [8]And he said to them, "Lodge here this night, and I will bring back word to you, as the Lord speaks to me"; so the princes of Moab stayed with Balaam .[9]And God came to Balaam and said, "Who are these men with you?" [10]And Balaam said to God,

"Balak the son of Zippor, king of Moab, has sent to me, saying, [11]'Behold, a people has come out of Egypt, and it covers the face of the earth; now come, curse them for me; perhaps I shall be able to fight against them and drive them out.'" [12]God said to Balaam, "You shall not go with them; you shall not curse the people, for they are blessed." [13]So Balaam rose in the morning, and said to the princes of Balak, "Go to your own land; for the Lord has refused to let me go with you." [14]So the princes of Moab rose and went to Balak, and said, "Balaam refuses to come with us."

(i)

Threatened by Israel's success and now proximity, the king of Moab acted out of "dread" and warned his neighbours that the numerically superior Israelites were pausing only to size up the area as their next sphere of conquest. He sent word to "the elders of Midian" who joined him in his concern and his decision to consult Balaam. Balak's fear was that they would "cover the face of the earth", a phrase used of the plague of locusts in Exod. 10:5, 15.

The messengers headed off to invite Balaam to come serve their master, and travelled to Pethor "which is near the River" (v. 5). The RSV has given a capital letter to this last word since on its own it usually refers to the Great River—the Euphrates. If this is correct, then Pethor may be the city called in the Assyrian annals Pitru, which sat on the Euphrates. However, that was some 400 miles away, a huge distance for Balaam to come on an ass (v. 21). The Vulgate (the Latin translation), sensing the difficulty perhaps, takes the word not as a place called Pethor, but as a participle from the verb "to interpret dreams", thus producing: "Balaam the son of Beor, the soothsayer". There is further uncertainty about "in the land of Amaw", for which the Syriac, Samaritan and Vulgate versions have "in the land of the Ammonites", which is achieved by the slightest of textual changes. But this again looks like substituting a better-known name for a lesser, and is not very convincing. The fact is that we are not at all sure where Balaam lived.

It is interesting that Balak calls Israel simply "a people" which had "come out of Egypt". He makes no mention either of her God, nor of the fact that it was he who delivered Israel from Egypt. Did he know nothing of this or was he not saying, precisely because he did know? At any rate he considered the threat Israel posed dangerous enough to send some distance to a famous seer and to commission him to curse Israel.

Curses were invoked against any who might oppose one in the future (e.g. 2 Sam. 18:32; Dan. 4:15–16) or who were presently engaged in opposition (e.g. Jer. 10:25; Pss. 35:4–8; 79:6–12), and were really an expression of the desire for God (or the gods) to share one's conviction that the enemy needed destroying or harming. Balak is convinced that the very words of the curse will be effective *as* they are spoken, since blessings and curses were in ancient times generally seen as irrevocable when uttered; see Gen. 27:33. So if Balaam cursed Israel he, Balak, would be safe.

(ii)

Confident of this, the delegation sets out with what the RSV calls the "fees for divination". Two things need saying here, the first of which is that "fees" are *not* mentioned in the text, nor are the "rewards" of the AV. The text merely says that they took "the divinations". The second point, however, is that, even if, as many argue, we must understand this to mean "fees", since it makes no sense to take the means of divination to a professional, there is no necessary implication that Balaam was avaricious or evil. The tradition behind 2 Peter and Jude (see the last section) quite ignores the fact that as a professional he was entitled to payment. In 1 Sam. 9:7ff. Saul was at a loss to find payment of some sort for Samuel; in 1 Kings 14:1ff. Jeroboam sent his wife with gifts as payment for the prophet Ahijah; in 2 Kings 8:8ff. some considerable wealth is taken as payment to Elisha on behalf of the king of Syria. The plain fact is that, as the story itself emphasizes, Balaam later on (v. 18) turned down the great wealth he was offered in order to speak the Lord's message.

A more perturbing problem is why Balaam calls his god—and remember he is no Israelite—by the name of Israel's God, i.e. Yahweh or, as it is usually translated, "the Lord". This he does frequently in the discourse (e.g. 22:8, 13). It is odd to find this here, and the switching is odd too between this peculiarly Israelite title and the general term "God", which does not surprise us so much. There are four theories to be found among commentators:

(a) One of the sources or editors behind these chapters had Balaam as a worshipper of the Lord, and therefore a friend of Israel.

(b) Balaam needed to seek not only his own gods, and those of Balak, but also the Lord, to see who was most powerful. Therefore he found out the power of Israel's god and called on his name.

(c) Israel's Lord also chose occasionally to reveal himself to non-Israelites (compare Exod. 18 (Jethro); Isa. 45:1; Job 1:20, etc.), therefore we have a case of real revelation here.

(d) The editor could not conceive of such oracles not being from the Lord, and so he put the name of the Lord on Balaam's lips, though it had not been there originally.

The last explanation is the most satisfactory. But it is really a minor point. Though Balaam might not have known it, it *was* the Lord who inspired him. The end result is that he refused to visit Balak because he realized that Israel enjoyed a blessing which he could not undo with a curse.

BALAK HIRES BALAAM: MOVE TWO

Numbers 22:15–20

[15]Once again Balak sent princes, more in number and more honourable than they. [16]And they came to Balaam and said to him, "Thus says Balak the son of Zippor: 'Let nothing hinder you from coming to me; [17]for I will surely do you great honour, and whatever you say to me I will do; come, curse this people for me.'" [18]But Balaam answered and said to the servants of Balak, "Though Balak were to give me his house full of silver and gold, I could not go beyond the command of the Lord my God, to do less or more. [19]Pray, now, tarry here this night also, that I may know what more the Lord will say to me." [20]And God came to Balaam at night and said to him, "If the men have come to call you, rise, go with them; but only what I bid you, that shall you do."

Balak, perhaps understandably from his point of view, assumes that Balaam's refusal to come reflects a feeling only that the incentives were not powerful enough. So he sends a more prestigious delegation back to Balaam, promising to give him "great honour". This understanding of the situation probably says more about Balak's character than Balaam's. Balaam's future fame, he assumes, is assured if he comes to curse Israel. How ironic that indeed his fame has been universally assured because God sent him to bless Israel!

Balaam's second reply is marvellous, the sort of statement all believers dream of being able to make for the Lord. The idiom "to do less or more" is typically Hebrew and means simply that he could not do anything without first having the "command of the Lord". So saying, he bids the delegation accept his hospitality for the night while he once again seeks what the Lord's will is. Whereas before he was forbidden to go, he is now given permission to accompany them with the proviso that he stick exactly to God's plan. Balaam is to be used as a messenger of the Lord to proclaim his choice of and blessing of Israel before Balak and his allies. It is just like the Lord to take hold of a potentially treacherous situation and use it for his own glory. And here is the beauty of the episode, that it will not be Balaam who is greatly honoured after all, but rather the Living God, the Lord of Israel.

GOD SPEAKS TO BALAAM:
THE ASS AND THE ANGEL

Numbers 22:21–35

21So Balaam rose in the morning, and saddled his ass, and went with the princes of Moab. 22But God's anger was kindled because he went; and the angel of the Lord took his stand in the way as his adversary. Now he was riding on the ass, and his two servants were with him. 23And the ass saw the angel of the Lord standing in the road, with a drawn sword in his hand; and the ass turned aside out of the road, and went into the field; and Balaam struck the ass, to turn her into the road. 24Then the angel of the Lord stood in a narrow path between the vineyards, with a wall on either side. [25]And when the ass saw the angel of the Lord, she pushed against the wall, and pressed Balaam's foot against the wall; so he struck her again. [26]Then the angel of the Lord went ahead, and stood in a narrow place, where there was no way to turn either to the right or to the left. [27]When the ass saw the angel of the Lord, she lay down under Balaam; and Balaam's anger was kindled, and he struck the ass with his staff. [28]Then the Lord opened the mouth of the ass, and she said to Balaam, "What have I done to you, that you have struck me these three times?" [29]And Balaam said to the ass, "Because you have made sport of me. I wish I had a sword in my hand, for then I would kill you." [30]And the ass said to Balaam, "Am I not your ass, upon which you have ridden all your life long to this day? Was I ever accustomed to do so to you?" And he said, "No."

[31]Then the Lord opened the eyes of Balaam, and he saw the angel of the Lord standing in the way, with his drawn sword in his hand; and he bowed his head, and fell on his face. [32]And the angel of the Lord said to him, "Why have you struck your ass these three times? Behold, I have come forth to withstand you, because your way is perverse before me, [33]and the ass saw me, and turned aside before me these three times. If she had not turned aside from me, surely just now I would have slain you and let her live." [34]Then Balaam said to the angel of the Lord, "I have sinned, for I did not know that thou didst stand in the road against me. Now therefore, if it is evil in thy sight, I will go back again." [35]And the angel of the Lord said to Balaam, "Go with the men; but only the word which I bid you, that shall you speak." So Balaam went on with the princes of Balak.

(i)

In the morning Balaam sets out for Moab with his ass. We get perturbed today that an ass should speak, but this passage, as people in Old Testament times would have quickly realized, is not about "ass" at all. It is in fact making the point that the medium of God's message is not important—only the message is. An ass or an angel, it doesn't matter.

It seems strange that, having commanded Balaam to go, God is in v. 22 described as angry with him "because he went". It is possible to translate instead "as he was going", suggesting that something happened on the way, perhaps in Balaam's attitude and desires, to displease God. On the other hand, it is easier to assume that we have evidence here of a second source, which was critical of Balaam, as that behind v. 20 had been more kindly disposed towards him. However it happened, an "angel of the Lord" was sent to be Balaam's "adversary", a strong word appearing later in the name "Satan", God's own adversary. See Job chapters 1–2 where Satan is God's adversary in the heavenly court, whose task it was to bring cases against human beings (it was only after the Old Testament period that Satan developed into another name for the Devil).

(ii)

The ass sees the angel and avoids him, and is beaten for this by Balaam, who sees nothing. This is good drama, preparing the reader for a climax, and may be compared with the story of Elisha and his servant in 2 Kings 6:15–18 and indeed with the story of Paul's conversion in Acts 9:3–7. In these stories, too, there were those who could not or would not see.

A second time the angel appears in a "narrow path", and in trying to squeeze past the ass is again beaten. Then comes the third and final intervention of the angel in a spot even narrower, with no room for the ass to get by. The ass promptly lies down and for a third time is beaten by Balaam. Twice then Balaam was invited to see what the ass saw and recognized; and twice the ass was allowed to spare him confrontation with the sword-wielding angel. But at this point the Lord "opened the mouth" of the ass so that the animal spoke. Interestingly, this is the same expression used of the Lord's commissioning of Ezekiel in 3:27 and 33:22, thus confirming the point made before that God's choice of messenger is not important.

The angel says he has come to oppose Balaam because his way is "perverse". The Hebrew word occurs again in Job 16:11, and seems to have the meaning of "to throw precipitately". The Syriac translators read a different form of the same verb to get the good sense of "because you headed straight for me" (compare NEB). However, some scholars believe another similar word was original, meaning "to be evil". The RSV's "perverse" adopts this reading, which is supported in other ancient versions. Whatever the exact sense, Balaam learned from the angel how the ass which he wanted to kill had saved him from death.

Sadly, we too often go blundering on our way, blind to the warnings of God until he has to use "asses" to stop us. We are reminded again of Paul's words in 1 Cor. 1:27–29:

> But God chose what is foolish in the world to shame the wise, God chose what is weak in the world to shame the strong, God chose what is low and despised in the world . . . so that no human being might boast in the presence of God.

Balaam repents and offers to return home, but the angel speaks for God and commands him to go on. Whereas God in v. 20 commanded him to "do" only what he was told, the angel's message is that he should "speak" only the words he is given. Perhaps the change in emphasis in the command is to suggest that there was a danger of Balaam, being a seer, saying a few words of his own as well as those of the Lord. Therefore the Lord intercepted and corrected him.

BALAAM SPEAKS TO BALAK

Numbers 22:36–40

36When Balak heard that Balaam had come, he went out to meet him at the city of Moab, on the boundary formed by the Arnon, at the extremity of the boundary. 37And Balak said to Balaam, "Did I not send to you to call you? Why did you not come to me? Am I not able to honour you?" 38Balaam said to Balak, "Lo, I have come to you! Have I now any power at all to speak anything? The word that God puts in my mouth, that must I speak." 39Then Balaam went with Balak, and they came to Kiriath-huzoth. 40And Balak sacrificed oxen and sheep, and sent to Balaam and to the princes who were with him.

Balaam's approach must have been watched with great satisfaction by Balak, but also with some frustration. No doubt he felt his pride hurt because his first offer of "honour" had been turned down. At any rate, he did not wait till Balaam arrived at his city, but went out to intercept him en route.

Balak speaks immediately, chiding Balaam for not responding sooner to his invitation. Did Balaam not realize how important he, Balak, was? But Balaam responds marvellously by reminding Balak of the real hierarchy of importance, and that God's will is the most important factor in the whole episode. He answers in accord with the angel's directive given in v. 35, and provides as good a definition of prophecy as could be found. In 23:5 it is plainly stated that "the Lord put a word in Balaam's mouth", again repeated in 23:16. The prophet Micaiah was also once pressured to speak certain words sought by a king, but to speak them in the name of the Lord. His reply was similar: "As the Lord lives, what the Lord says to me, that I will speak" (1 Kings 22:14).

Balak of course was anticipating a curse to be spoken, but it is a matter of speculation whether or not Balaam himself yet knew the truth of the coming blessings. What is worth noting is how the drama is kept tight by Balaam's reply to Balak. He uses the general term "God" when stating his position and not the personal name "the Lord", so that no hint is yet given to Balak that it was the very God of the nation which Balak was seeking to destroy who was behind Balaam and in control of him.

Balak prepared a ceremonial meal involving the slaughtering of animals for sacrifice and a sacrificial feast. This would also be part of the honouring process, showing Balaam off as the commissioned servant of king Balak (compare 1 Sam. 9:22ff.). Balak may even have wished to initiate Balaam into the "sacral community of Moab" by having him eat at the feast with the leaders of the area and so tie him in with Moab's gods. Balaam, however, was now under the Lord. He resisted the implications of the festivities, and said abruptly that he had no power of his own, but could only speak what "God" said to him.

There is tension and irony all through this scene, but there is also an underlying message worth attending to. When temptations press and flattery is around, it is wise to remember Balaam's words: "The word that God puts in my mouth, that [and only that] must I speak."

BALAAM CANNOT CURSE ISRAEL

Numbers 22:41–23:12

⁴¹And on the morrow Balak took Balaam and brought him up to Bamoth-baal; and from there he saw the nearest of the people. ¹And Balaam said to Balak, "Build for me here seven altars, and provide for me here seven bulls and seven rams." ²Balak did as Balaam had said; and Balak and Balaam offered on each altar a bull and a ram. ³And Balaam said to Balak, "Stand beside your burnt offering, and I will go; perhaps the Lord will come to meet me; and whatever he shows me I will tell you." And he went to a bare height. ⁴And God met Balaam; and Balaam said to him, "I have prepared the seven altars, and I have offered upon each altar a bull and a ram." ⁵And the Lord put a word in Balaam's mouth, and said, "Return to Balak, and thus you shall speak." ⁶And he returned to him, and lo, he and all the princes of Moab were standing beside his burnt offering. ⁷And Balaam took up his discourse, and said,

"From Aram Balak has brought me,
   the king of Moab from the eastern mountains:
'Come, curse Jacob for me,
   and come, denounce Israel!'
⁸How can I curse whom God has not cursed?
   How can I denounce whom the Lord has not denounced?
⁹For from the top of the mountains I see him,
   from the hills I behold him;
lo, a people dwelling alone,
   and not reckoning itself among the nations!
¹⁰Who can count the dust of Jacob,
   or number the fourth part of Israel?
Let me die the death of the righteous,
   and let my end be like his!"

¹¹And Balak said to Balaam, "What have you done to me? I took you to curse my enemies, and behold, you have done nothing but bless them." ¹²And he answered, "Must I not take heed to speak what the Lord puts in my mouth?"

(i)

The two men went to "Bamoth-baal" to get a panoramic view of the people who were causing such concern to Balak. From the

RSV we might assume that this was the name of a town or a district. That is not the correct picture at all. The words mean in Hebrew "the high places of Baal", and refer to specially prepared natural sites high up in the hilly country used as centres of worship. From the numinous sense derived from being in such a place a priest or prophet was meant to be in the ripest condition for hearing a divine communication; from such a place, high up and in the clear air, it was possible to have the best view of the movement of stars or clouds or flocks of birds, all of which were used to interpret the will of the gods. To such a place, and with therefore an unambiguous intention, Balak took Balaam.

In order to curse comprehensively Balaam was obviously expected to be able to *see* the people (compare 23:13 and 27), so they got up high to get the necessary perspective on them, and the Hebrew says that Balaam saw the "extremity" of the people. The RSV interprets this as the part closest to him and so translates "the nearest of the people", whereas some versions prefer the opposite extreme and have "the farthest" of the people, meaning *all* of them. It is argued that only by seeing them all could Balaam say what he said in 23:9–10. No doubt he could have been just as impressed by their numbers had he only seen a fraction of them and known that it was just a fraction. But in fact it makes much better sense of 23:13, 27 if it is understood to mean all of them, since Balak on these two later occasions seems to conclude that the size of the opposition had frightened Balaam and takes him to different places where fewer of them are visible in the hope that this will encourage him to curse freely. So vainly and pathetically does the king try to manipulate the prophet.

Balaam begins his preparations by arranging for seven altars to be built, and calls for the same number of bulls and rams for sacrifice. He makes Balak sacrifice at each altar a certain "burnt offering". Although the RSV says both sacrificed, this does not square with vv. 3, 6, 14, 15, 17 and 30, which all imply Balak alone, and sure enough the Greek version only has Balak in v. 2. Balaam actually leaves Balak and heads off into the hills to seek God's will. The plain sense is that he needs to be alone to receive his oracle. This hope that the Lord will "meet" him is also expressed in the language used in Exod. 3:18, 5:3 and Amos 4:12 of the Lord coming and speaking to his people, so it would appear that Balaam too expected an oracle from God. And the Lord came to him and put a word in his mouth, a phrase used, as we saw earlier, particularly in the book of Ezekiel.

(ii)

When Balaam does speak, his "discourse" is given in a lovely poetic form. He begins by claiming his lack of responsibility for the coming words and events—he was "brought" from his home to this place. He has been called to "curse Jacob and denounce Israel", a paralleling of names that is a marked feature of all four oracles (23:10, 21, 23; 24:5, 17). Parallelism itself is a feature of this type of poetry, but the "Jacob/Israel" parallelism is only characteristic of two other prophets: Isa. 40–55 (seventeen times) and Mic. 1–3 (four times). There are three terms here used for "to curse" or similar, stressing the passionate desire of Balak to be rid of Israel.

However, in the spirit of 22:38, Balaam is unable to meet Balak's need. His rhetoric is simple yet profound. Israel is "dwelling alone", as the RSV puts it. She is, and knows herself to be, the special people of the Lord (compare Exod. 19:5; Amos 3:2) and as such is not alone in the sense of lonely, but in the sense of unique.

This people, he continues, is innumerable. "Who can count the dust of Jacob?" is a rhetorical question recalling the promise to Abram: "I will make your descendants as the dust of the earth". Jacob himself also received the same promise (Gen. 28:14) and here Balaam speaks of its fulfilment already. However, the next line of the RSV involves an improbable continuation of this hyperbole. "Fourth part" would be a peculiar variant of "the nearest of the people" in 22:41, even if that translation were correct. By a slight re-reading of the text, some propose a term "crowds" instead of "the fourth part", but the RSV footnote, "dust clouds", is really the best suggestion. It is based on a similar word in another Semitic language.

The oracle ends strangely, with a wish on Balaam's part to die the "death of the righteous", and it is likely that although the words were originally from Balaam they were not originally part of the oracle. Following his oracle he wishes for himself a destiny like that of Israel, such is his conviction of her future security and happiness. The RSV, like most translations, interprets one of the Hebrew words as "end", i.e. "end of life", but if it is accepted that this is not part of the original oracle, then it can be translated as the Greek version does here, and as the RSV does in Jer. 31:17 by "descendants". Balaam wants his descendants to enjoy a future of joy and security like Israel would under God's blessing.

Such is the first oracle. Without being strongly positive at all it clearly sets out the Lord's position vis-à-vis Israel. Balaam again says how he has no responsibility beyond speaking what the Lord tells him to. Balak is intensely frustrated since he realizes that this is in fact a rejection of his wishes and a blessing of Israel in disguise. It is worth noting in closing the irony of Balak who "took" Balaam, whereas it was in reality the Lord who had "taken" him. The struggle between the Lord and Balak becomes more intense yet, but the greatest blessings are also still to come.

BALAAM MUST BLESS ISRAEL

Numbers 23:13–24

13 And Balak said to him, "Come with me to another place, from which you may see them; you shall see only the nearest of them, and shall not see them all; then curse them for me from there." 14 And he took him to the field of Zophim, to the top of Pisgah, and built seven altars, and offered a bull and a ram on each altar. 15 Balaam said to Balak, "Stand here beside your burnt offering, while I meet the Lord yonder." 16 And the Lord met Balaam, and put a word in his mouth, and said, "Return to Balak, and thus shall you speak." 17 And he came to him, and, lo, he was standing beside his burnt offering, and the princes of Moab with him. And Balak said to him, "What has the Lord spoken?" 18 And Balaam took up his discourse, and said,

"Rise, Balak, and hear;
hearken to me, O son of Zippor:

¹⁹God is not man, that he should lie,
  or a son of man, that he should repent.
 Has he said, and will he not do it?
  Or has he spoken, and will he not fulfil it?
²⁰Behold, I received a command to bless;
  he has blessed, and I cannot revoke it.
²¹He has not beheld misfortune in Jacob;
  nor has he seen trouble in Israel.
 The Lord their God is with them,
  and the shout of a king is among them.
²²God brings them out of Egypt;
  they have as it were the horns of the wild ox.
²³For there is no enchantment against Jacob,
  no divination against Israel;
 now it shall be said of Jacob and Israel,
  'What has God wrought!'
²⁴Behold, a people! As a lioness it rises up
  and as a lion it lifts itself;
 it does not lie down till it devours the prey,
  and drinks the blood of the slain.''

(i)

Balak tries again. He is hoping that the "God" behind the first oracle will be inconsistent or capricious, as the gods were believed to be, but he learns that Israel's God is constant and faithful (v. 19). There will be no change, even though Balak takes Balaam to "another place" to see another view of an "extremity" of this people, which might make them seem less formidable. The God of this people does not lie or change his mind.

This word "lie" has a particular shade of meaning in Hebrew, which is best brought out by comparing two texts from the prophets. In Isa. 58:11 it is used for a spring failing to produce the sweet refreshing water that it ought to: Israel would be "like a watered garden, like a spring of water, whose waters fail not". Then in Hab. 2:3 it is used of an oracle that seemed to fail, but did not: "It hastens to the end—it will not lie". The word is really about not fulfilling promises rather than plain telling lies. Balaam is saying that, unlike mankind, God will not fail to keep his promises. He is not a "son of man" either, meaning what the NEB well translates in the frequent occurrences of this phrase in the book of Ezekiel, "mortal man". The word "repent" actually means "to be sorry". Israel's God, however, never acts in ignorance or under impulse and so never needs to be sorry. Compare 1 Sam. 15:29.

(ii)

In v. 21 Balaam speaks of the Lord being with Israel, "and the shout of a king is among them." This is a difficult phrase. Does it mean that the Israelites were heard and perhaps seen joyfully acclaiming the Lord as their King, as in the NEB rendering "acclaimed among them as king"? One of the great mediaeval commentators, Rashi, has another suggestion, linking the word "shout" with a number of other words meaning "companion" or "friend". According to him, Balaam was saying that the kindness or benevolence of their King was resting on them. Presumably this idea lies behind the NEB footnote with its alternative translation: "Royal care is bestowed on them." This gives an equally attractive picture.

Verse 22 opens with a fascinating use of the present participle, in that God is said to be still bringing Israel into freedom. The Exodus is still going on during the settlement period, and to interfere with Israel is to interfere with the redeeming work of the Lord. Israel is said to have the horns of a "wild ox", considered to be untameable (Job 39:9ff.) and dangerous (Ps. 22:21); but here the nuance is probably of power and strength. The AV has "unicorn", a beast now known to be mythical but still believed in 1611 to have existed.

The thought of v. 23 following on from v. 21 is that because God is with his people, there can be no "enchantment" or "divination" against them. The preposition is ambiguous, and could mean, as the NEB takes it, that none of this forbidden activity was allowed "*in* Israel". But that is weak compared with the RSV which has Balaam, himself a professional seer, admitting that no such activity could possibly prevail "*against* Israel", because she had been brought into being by the Lord.

Israel is finally compared to the regal and fearsome "lioness" and "lion", female and male to stress her completeness and so God's total control. The image is used in 24:9 of God himself, but was used often enough of Israel under God (e.g. Gen. 49:9 of the tribe of Judah; Deut. 33:20 of the tribe of Gad). It would be worse than foolish to attempt to attack Israel, since it would be like facing wild lions on one's own.

The oracle is best summed up in the terse words of the second half of v. 23, which the NEB translates intelligently: "Now is the time to say of Jacob and of Israel, 'See what God has wrought' ". In Deut. 32:23–27 the Lord reveals that he only refrained from scattering a sinful Israel irrevocably since that would lead to people denying that he had miraculously redeemed and settled them. In short, they would deny that he had "wrought all this". There is a warning for God's people in this, but also a great hope. Have we the faith to believe that today too the Lord will show the world who is in charge? This very same phrase of v. 23 is used by Habakkuk in 1:5: "Look among the nations, and see; wonder and be astounded. For I am doing a work in your days that you would not believe if told."

BALAAM PROPHESIES

Numbers 23:25–24:9

[25]And Balak said to Balaam, "Neither curse them at all, nor bless them at all." [26]But Balaam answered Balak, "Did I not tell you, 'All that the Lord says, that I must do'?" [27]And Balak said to Balaam, "Come now, I will take you to another place; perhaps it will please God that you may curse them for me from there." [28]So Balak took Balaam to the top of Peor, that overlooks the desert. [29]And Balaam said to Balak, "Build for me here seven altars, and provide for me here seven bulls and seven rams." [30]And Balak did as Balaam had said, and offered a bull and a ram on each altar.

[1]When Balaam saw that it pleased the Lord to bless Israel, he did not go, as at other times, to look for omens, but set his face toward the wilderness. [2]And Balaam lifted up his eyes, and saw Israel encamping tribe by tribe. And the Spirit of God came upon him, [3]and he took up

his discourse, and said,
"The oracle of Balaam the son of Beor,
     the oracle of the man whose eye is opened,
⁴the oracle of him who hears the words of God,
     who sees the vision of the Almighty,
     falling down, but having his eyes uncovered:
⁵how fair are your tents, O Jacob,
     your encampments, O Israel!
⁶Like valleys that stretch afar,
     like gardens beside a river,
  like aloes that the Lord has planted,
     like cedar trees beside the waters.
⁷Water shall flow from his buckets,
     and his seed shall be in many waters,
  his king shall be higher than Agag,
     and his kingdom shall be exalted.
⁸God brings him out of Egypt;
     he has as it were the horns of the wild ox,
  he shall eat up the nations his adversaries,
     and shall break their bones in pieces,
     and pierce them through with his arrows.
⁹He couched, he lay down like a lion,
     and like a lioness; who will rouse him up?
  Blessed be every one who blesses you,
     and cursed be every one who curses you."

(i)

Rather pathetically and comically this section begins with Balak in a panic, begging Balaam at least not to bless Israel if he cannot bring himself to curse them. But Balaam stands firm on his promise to the Lord to speak what he says. Determined to the end, Balak tries another vantage point for a last attempt at a curse. The same sacrificial procedure is ordered and carried out. So the scene is set for the fulfilment or final dashing of Balak's hopes. Balaam is now so convinced of the Lord's will that he even refuses to resort to divination "as at other times". The phrase "as at other times" can mean "as previously" (e.g. 1 Sam. 3:10) or "as customarily" (e.g. 1 Sam. 20:25) , and probably the latter is meant here. So strong was the Lord's dealing with him that he abandoned his usual—and necessary—custom of seeking signs.

Of great historical interest is the fact that one tradition of Syriac manuscripts of the book of Numbers inserts a line before v. 2 which says: "The lesson of the epiphany of our Saviour Jesus." Other traditions have variants of this, showing how this chapter was widely interpreted as being Messianic by the early Church. The Jewish Targums also adopt a Messianic interpretation. In the eyes of both synagogue and Church these next two oracles were prophecies of a coming Messiah.

There is much debate on the condition of Balaam as he spoke. The RSV has the phrase "whose eye is opened", but includes two alternatives in a footnote. All in all five interpretations of a difficult Hebrew word have been seriously offered by scholars, three being found in the RSV. They can be summarized as follows:

(a) *whose eye is open*—the usual interpretation, also found in the Syriac versions. This finds support in the parallel idea of the last line of v. 4. The meaning is either that he was in a fixed kind of trance to see his "vision of the Almighty", or that he had clear vision.

(b) *whose eye is closed*—agreeing with the Vulgate by using a Hebrew root which occurs in this sense in Lam. 3:9. This might mean that he was in a trance-like sleep, or that he was shutting out all distractions in a form of prayer, so that he looked not for the usual portents around him, but for the revelation of the Spirit within him.

(c) *whose eye is perfect*—agreeing probably with the Septuagint and with the Targums by splitting the single adjective into two words to give another root for the adjective. The NEB "clear" seems to adopt this interpretation. The meaning would then be that his vision was accurate and to be trusted.

(d) *whose eye is stern*—from an Arabic root meaning "grim-faced", presumably to stress the serious and weighty matter at hand.

(e) *whose eye is spiteful*—from the same Arabic root in another form meaning "to be vexed". In other words Balaam was loath to bless but had to anyway.

Probably the first translation, as in the RSV, is best. Balaam has had his eyes opened for the first time by God and genuinely begins to prophesy. He goes on further to give his credentials as being in the power of and presence of God. He claims to hear the very "words of God", and he claims to see "the vision of the Almighty". Under this potent influence he confesses to "falling down". What could this mean? It has been suggested that it means: (a) *in a sleep or trance* (compare Gen. 15:12; Job 4:13); (b) *in reverence* (compare Judg. 13:20); (c) *under the force of the Spirit* (compare Isa. 8:11; Ezek. 3:14). Probably the first is intended, meaning in a trance-like state "but" nevertheless with "his eyes uncovered". The idea then is that under the power of God's Spirit he is stripped of all but the revelation of Almighty God.

How glorious if we in Christ's Church could when needed block out all else and see only him and hear only his words!

(ii)

Balaam opens up his "discourse" with a prophetic vision of Israel as a beautiful and impressive people grouped under the Lord. To this day v. 5 is read aloud at the start of the daily morning service in synagogues. There follows what looks like an allusion to the paradisal life of Eden; compare Isa. 1:30; 58:11. Possibly instead of "valleys" we should translate "palm trees". Eastern gardens are in fact largely composed of trees and tall shrubs for shade, rather than pretty flowers.

The text of v. 7 is disturbed and complex. The first line is plainly a simple image of a man with plenty of water in his well and enough to spare, i.e. a picture of plenty. It is interesting, however, that the Greek and Syriac versions and the Targums take it as a Messianic prophecy: "A man shall come out of his seed, and he shall rule over many nations . . .". Not a few scholars prefer the reading in the second line of "nations" for "waters", involving only a slight change of text. An ingenious suggestion has come from Gray, who keeps the Hebrew consonants for "his seed" but reads different vowels to get "his arm". Accepting the reading "nations" his translation thus goes: "and his arm shall be upon many nations", meaning that he will be dominant over his enemies; compare Isa. 30:30; 48:14. The "he" is, of course, Israel, as in v. 8, which then carries on the mood of military and political success. The verb translated "pierce through" really means "to smash in pieces, shatter", and does not fit with talking of "arrows". By again changing the vowels, we get the Hebrew word for "loins", thus producing a translation like the NEB: "and smash their limbs in pieces".

Finally there comes a picture of majesty in peace, as contrasted with the picture of power in war in 23:24 (and in the previous verse). The seal on the prophecy in the last two lines is absolute and authoritative. It echoes and reinforces the promise already given to Jacob/Israel in Isaac's blessing of Gen. 27:29, which in turn echoes and begins to work on the promise given to Abraham by God recorded in Gen. 12:1–3. We may not care for the warlike overtones of this passage, but the promise that God's people will be "blessed" and not "cursed" still stands, as does the insight that the rest of the world will be "blessed" or "cursed" as they react to God's people.

BALAAM PROPHESIES AGAIN I

Numbers 24:10–25

10 And Balak's anger was kindled against Balaam, and he struck his hands together; and Balak said to Balaam, "I called you to curse my enemies, and behold, you have blessed them these three times. 11 Therefore now flee to your place; I said, 'I will certainly honour you,' but the Lord has held you back from honour." 12 And Balaam said to Balak, "Did I not tell your messenger whom you sent to me, 13'If Balak should give me his house full of silver and gold, I would not be able to go beyond the word of the Lord, to do either good or bad of my own will; what the Lord speaks, that will I speak'? 14 And now, behold, I am going to my people; come, I will let you know what this people will do to your people in the latter days." 15 And he took up his discourse, and said,
"The oracle of Balaam the son of Beor,
    the oracle of the man whose eye is opened,

¹⁶the oracle of him who hears the words of God,
>   and knows the knowledge of the Most High,
> who sees the vision of the Almighty,
>   falling down, but having his eyes uncovered:
¹⁷I see him, but not now;
>   I behold him, but not nigh:
> a star shall come forth out of Jacob,
>   and a sceptre shall rise out of Israel;
> it shall crush the forehead of Moab,
>   and break down all the sons of Sheth.
¹⁸Edom shall be disposed,
>   Seir also, his enemies, shall be dispossessed,
>   while Israel does valiantly.
¹⁹By Jacob shall dominion be exercised,
>   and the survivors of cities be destroyed!"
²⁰Then he looked on Amalek and took up his discourse, and said,
> "Amalek was the first of the nations,
>   but in the end he shall come to destruction."
²¹And he looked on the Kenite, and took up his discourse, and said,
> "Enduring is your dwelling place,
>   and your nest is set in the rock;
²²nevertheless Kain shall be wasted.
>   How long shall Asshur take you away captive?"
²³And he took up his discourse, and said,
> "Alas, who shall live when God does this?
²⁴But ships shall come from Kittim
>   and shall afflict Asshur and Eber;
>   and he also shall come to destruction."
²⁵Then Balaam rose, and went back to his place; and Balak also went his way.

(i)

Balaam's second "disclosure" is one of the most interesting and controversial passages in the Old Testament, full of disputed readings. Moreover, the traditional view that vv. 15–24 constitute one whole oracle does not really convince. It is better to divide the text into four separate short oracles, or at the least four partial oracles. These are: (a) vv. 15–19; (b) v. 20; (c) vv. 21–22; (d) vv. 23–24.

Balaam says "I told you so" to Balak, referring back to 22:18, and then prepares to take his leave. Balak had hinted at his intention to punish Balaam by ordering him to "flee" back home. Balaam thereupon coolly says that he is ready to go, but only after yet another, and this time spontaneous, blessing of Israel. Far from fearing him, he risks further infuriating him. Notice the casual and unworried way in which he refers to "my people . . . this people . . . your people" (v. 14). Then, beginning as he did in the third oracle, he prophesies. Balaam is speaking under the commission of God, and therefore speaks as one who "knows the knowledge of the most High". In other words he is granted a revelation so that he knows what God knows about Israel; he is in on God's plans. The prophet Amos expresses the same wonderful privilege rhetorically: "Surely the Lord God does nothing, without revealing his secret to his servants the prophets" (Amos 3:7).

(ii)

Balaam sees someone in the future becoming a great warrior-king. In Hebrew there is no neuter case, since every noun is either masculine or feminine, even if it is an inanimate object. So in terse symbolic passages like the present one it can be a difficult decision whether a pronoun means *he* or *it*. In v. 17 the RSV has decided that the last two lines are neuter, but the *it* is better translated *he* there, as in the first line of the verse. But who is the *he* referred to? Israel? A future leader? The Messiah? All these interpretations have been advanced, but first the whole verse must be examined. The action is not for the immediate future, since this person or personification is "not now . . . not nigh". There is, however, a clue that it will be action by a king, not Israel personified, in that a "star" shall be involved; for star imagery was common for royalty in the ancient East.

"Sceptre" is another royal metaphor (see Ps. 45:6; Amos 1:5, 8). But who is this prince, this warrior? The obvious historical figure to cite would be King David who did defeat the Moabites decisively according to 2 Sam. 8:2, and Seir (a name for Edom) according to 2 Sam. 8:13–14. But how could Balaam know about him, and what interest could this have for Balak? Perhaps Balaam prophesied that a king of Israel would one day arise who would conquer the lands Israel was now passing through, and this general prophecy was touched up later to make it fit more exactly with David.

BALAAM PROPHESIES AGAIN II

Numbers 24:10–25 (*cont'd*)

(iii)

In v. 20 we have a cryptic oracle on "Amalek". There are no verbs at all in the Hebrew, so the tenses have to be supplied in English. In what sense were the Amalekites "first of the nations"? Hardly because they were the most powerful nation in the area, or the oldest. Probably what is meant is that they were the *first to war with Israel*—and this squares with Exod. 17:8–15. This oracle then is a simple prophecy of ultimate destruction for a fierce nomadic people who had taken the opportunity of Israel's weakness in the desert to attack her.

Then in vv. 21–22 comes an oracle on the "Kenites", who as another nomadic race were associated closely with the Amalekites (e.g. 1 Sam. 15:6). However, they were also closely associated with Israel through Moses' father-in-law (see Judg. 4:11). Because of this both Saul and David tried to help them (1 Sam. 15:16; 30:29). Yet they too were destined to vanish from the arena of history for their opposition to Israel. Their settlements were in mountainous terrain, high up in the rocks, readily defensible and relatively safe. This characteristic is also noted of the wider group of the Edomites as a whole in Obad. 3–4 where the phrase "though your nest is set among the stars" parallels the phrase here about the Kenites' "nest" being established "in the rock".

(iv)

Their removal is to come about through "Asshur", a term which

has caused enormous difficulty to interpreters, because Assyria
only comes on the Palestinian scene in the ninth or eighth centuries B.C. The NEB gets rid of Assyria by changing the text:
"How long must you dwell here in my sight?", but this is more of
an evasion than a translation. Then, in vv. 23–24 comes an oracle
against this victor "Asshur" itself and an ally called "Eber", who
will be destroyed by a fleet and army from "Kittim". This is the
most cryptic of all the oracles. Some feel that v. 23 is a later
insertion into an originally whole oracle of vv. 21–24, in other
words, Assyria will reign supreme till God's purpose with her is
over and her own time for punishment comes. Others argue that
the last line of v. 22 should be taken out of the oracle about the
Kenites and transferred to the last oracle. The beginning of this
would then read:

And he took up his discourse, and said,
"How long shall Asshur have you captive?
Alas, who shall live when God appoints him [a time]?"

The final verses thus look ahead to the rise of Assyria's empire, in
which for a time Israel was included, and see this as under God
and his plans. This would square with the Old Testament view
that it is God and God alone who moves the nations (Amos 9:7),
and that in fact he used Assyria to punish Israel before finally
punishing her (Isa. 10:5–11). The implication is, of course, that
this oracle was not originally from Balaam, but was inserted
among his prophecies at a later date.

(v)

Lastly, what (or rather who) were the "Kittim"? The word comes
from a Greek name of a place called Kition in Cyprus, and was at
first used to refer to Cyprus or to the Cypriots. In the Old
Testament it refers more generally to the peoples living not only
in Cyprus but along the northern Mediterranean coast, and to the
invaders who came from these regions, notably the Macedonians
(see 1 Maccabees 1:1). By the time of the Dead Sea Scrolls, the
"Kittim" were any contemporary foreign powers, usually the
Romans. And what of "Eber"? According to Gen. 10:21–25 he

was an ancestor of all the Semitic peoples, and according to Gen. 11:14–26 only an ancestor of the Hebrews, giving them their name. In the present context, however, it should most probably be taken to refer to not a distinct people but (as the word can mean) "the region beyond", in this case the land beyond the Euphrates river, in fact another name for Assyria. This makes sense then of the singular "he" in the next line, with its forecast that Assyria will in its turn fall to another people sent by God as his plan goes on unfolding, this people to come from the islands and coasts of the North Mediterranean.

These very complex texts, probably not all from the mouth of Balaam (though they all forecast the doom of Israel's emenies) have caused endless difficulties to scholars. Readers who wish to know more about them may consult one of the larger commentaries on Numbers. We have also noted how frequently they have been interpreted as prophecies of the Messiah, by the Jews first and then by the Christians. Not many of us would take such interpretations seriously nowadays, but the interested reader can consult *Additional Note* 7, where I give some examples from Jewish and Christian writings.

APOSTASY AT PEOR

Numbers 25:1–5

¹While Israel dwelt in Shittim the people began to play the harlot with the daughters of Moab. ²These invited the people to the sacrifices of their gods, and the people ate, and bowed down to their gods. ³So Israel yoked himself to Baal of Peor. And the anger of the Lord was kindled against Israel; ⁴and the Lord said to Moses, "Take all the chiefs of the people, and hang them in the sun before the Lord, that the fierce anger of the Lord may turn away from Israel." ⁵And Moses said to the judges of Israel, "Every one of you slay his men who have yoked themselves to Baal of Peor."

(i)

The people of Israel have arrived at a spot called Shittim, where they settled for some time. According to Num. 33:49 it was the last stopping-place of the people before they crossed into Canaan and, in keeping with this, Joshua is said to have sent out spies from there to reconnoitre Jericho (Josh. 2:1). The term means "acacia trees" or "meadow of acacia trees", and must have been an attractive spot to camp. But it became too comfortable and led to unholy tendencies which resulted in sexual promiscuity with young women from the enemy tribe of Moab. This period became infamous and is even referred to in the New Testament (Rev. 2:14; compare 2 Pet. 2:15).

What happened as a result of this promiscuity—not, as some have said, causing it—was that the people were invited to enjoy the culture and religious life of their neighbours. It was the well-known snowball pattern of sin. Many Israelites attended sacrificial feasts to Moab's gods and, to all intents and purposes, honoured these gods. It was an open flouting of the first of the Ten Commandments: "You shall have no other gods before/besides me" (Exod. 20:3).

A similar problem presented itself to the early Church, when Paul had to deal with Christians who were "eating food offered to idols" (1 Cor. 8). He also spoke categorically in saying: "Do you not know that he who joins himself to a prostitute becomes one with her?" (1 Cor. 6:16). For this reason, although "God so loved the world that he gave his only Son" (John 3:16), we are commanded, "Do not love the world or the things in the world. If any one loves the world, love for the Father is not in him" (1 John 2:15). To love the world with a view to participation in its pleasures and purposes is to walk away from God, but to love the world with a view to its redemption from its pleasures and purposes is to walk with God.

(ii)

The punishment of representatives, the "chiefs of the people", was unusual and the manner seems to have been unusually cruel too. The RSV translation, "hang them in the sun", is in fact fairly bland. The verb used does not mean "to hang". The Septuagint translates "expose" them, perhaps meaning leave them tied in the sun to fry in its merciless heat; another Greek translation (Aquila) has "impale" them; the Vulgate renders "hang them on gibbets". The great Jewish commentator, Rashi, has "hang", saying that they were first stoned, as befits idolatry, and then displayed to prevent further idolatry. However, there is a parallel Arabic word which means to "fall down", and we may have here a causative form meaning that the chiefs were to be "flung down", i.e. over a cliff. Compare 2 Chron. 25:12; Luke 4:29. The probable meaning, then, is that they were thrown off a cliff and left unburied to be bleached by the sun.

After Jesus was rejected by the synagogue authorities in Nazareth for declaring himself to be the Lord's own anointed Messiah, they actually tried to be rid of him in this way (Luke 4:29). It is an awful irony that the One who cares for us more than we can ever imagine and who can bring us into full communion with the true God, should have been threatened with an end befitting those who sought to lead Israel away to false gods.

PHINEHAS' ENTHUSIASM

Numbers 25:6–18

⁶And behold, one of the people of Israel came and brought a Midianite woman to his family, in the sight of Moses and in the sight of the whole congregation of the people of Israel, while they were weeping at the door of the tent of meeting. ⁷When Phinehas the son of Eleazar, son of Aaron the priest, saw it, he rose and left the congregation, and took a spear in his hand ⁸and went after the man of Israel into the inner room, and pierced both of them, the man of Israel and the woman, through her body. Thus the plague was stayed from the people of Israel. ⁹Nevertheless those that died by the plague were twenty-four thousand.

¹⁰And the Lord said to Moses, ¹¹"Phinehas the son of Eleazar, son of Aaron the priest, has turned back my wrath from the people of Israel, in that he was jealous with my jealousy among them, so that I did not consume the people of Israel in my jealousy. ¹²Therefore say, 'Behold, I give to him my covenant of peace; ¹³and it shall be to him, and to his descendants after him, the covenant of a perpetual priest-

hood, because he was jealous for his God, and made atonement for the people of Israel.' "

14The name of the slain man of Israel, who was slain with the Midianite woman, was Zimri the son of Salu, head of a fathers' house belonging to the Simeonites. 15And the name of the Midianite woman who was slain was Cozbi the daughter of Zur, who was the head of the people of a fathers' house in Midian.

16And the Lord said to Moses, 17"Harass the Midianites, and smite them; 18for they have harassed you with their wiles, with which they beguiled you in the matter of Peor, and in the matter of Cozbi, the daughter of the prince of Midian, their sister, who was slain on the day of the plague on account of Peor."

There are some features of the story which seem to have been omitted, because in v. 6 there is an abrupt change from general sinning with Moabite women to a particular illicit union between a "man of Israel" and a Midianite woman. Once v. 9 is reached, it becomes obvious that a "plague" had broken out in the camp, where of course it would spread with frightening speed. Verse 8 suggests that this act took place in the wake of the previous ones while the people were still weeping in shame. The High Priest, Eleazar, was unable to deal with the situation, but his son, Phinehas (an Egyptian name, probably meaning "negro") was able and willing. His zeal for the Lord on this occasion became legendary, and he was held up as a great hero among those who opposed foreign conquerors many centuries afterwards (see Ecclesiasticus 45:23–24; 1 Maccabees 2:26). But his name appears on other occasions too. At one point Moses sends him out with a task force to deal with the Midianites, and Phinehas seems there to be a sort of warrior-priest since he takes "the vessels of the sanctuary and the trumpets for the alarm" (Num. 31:6). In Josh. 22:9–34 the ten western tribes (i.e. west of the river Jordan) prepare for war with the two eastern tribes which are suspected of idolatry. The delegation to discover the facts is led by Phinehas, this time a diplomat-priest, but with the warrior in him not forgotten. Still later, there was a time when the tribe of Benjamin offended the other tribes and Phinehas headed the commission of enquiry (Judg. 20:27–28).

His devotion to the Lord is seen here in his rather savage intrusion into the bed-chamber of the man's tent to spear both him and the women in the act of sexual sin. Obviously the sinning stopped, but the plague had already claimed "twenty-four thousand" victims. Estimates must have varied on the exact number, and presumably different traditions grew up around these estimates, for in 1 Cor. 10:8 the figure given is "twenty-three thousand".

The Lord commends him highly to Moses for this action (see 2 Kings 10:16 for a similar case of "zeal for the Lord"). Phinehas, we are told, showed God's own jealousy or zeal. As in many another Old Testament passage, Israel's violent behaviour is not at all to our liking, especially when God's approval is claimed for it.

In acknowledgement of his loyalty, the Lord gives Phinehas a "covenant of peace" (see Isa. 54:10; Mal. 2:4–5). This is a much more attractive phrase. As C. S. Lewis puts it, we are to be like "little Christs" if we are to call ourselves his disciples. We must pray that in the midst of the glaring injustices of our world, in the midst of the growing gaps between all sorts of "haves and have-nots", in the midst of a growing secularism and pluralism, in the midst even of the presence of sin in the Church, God will be able to make us zealous with his zeal, but as his Son showed it forth, not as Phinehas did. Then indeed we may experience his "covenant of peace" in our lives.

THE SECOND COUNT

Numbers 26:1–65

[1]After the plague the Lord said to Moses and to Eleazar the son of Aaron, the priest, [2]"Take a census of all the congregation of the people of Israel, from twenty years old and upward, by their fathers' houses, all in Israel who are able to go forth to war." [3]And Moses and Eleazar the priest spoke with them in the plains of Moab by the Jordan at Jericho, saying, [4]"Take a census of the people, from twenty years old and upward," as the Lord commanded Moses. The people of Israel, who came forth out of the land of Egypt, were:

⁵Reuben, the first-born of Israel; the sons of Reuben: of Hanoch, the family of the Hanochites; of Pallu, the family of the Palluites; ⁶of Hezron, the family of the Hezronites; of Carmi, the family of the Carmites. ⁷These are the families of the Reubenites; and their number was forty-three thousand seven hundred and thirty. ⁸And the sons of Pallu: Eliab. ⁹The sons of Eliab: Nemu-el, Dathan, and Abiram. These are the Dathan and Abiram, chosen from the congregation, who contended against Moses and Aaron in the company of Korah, when they contended against the Lord, ¹⁰and the earth opened its mouth and swallowed them up together with Korah, when that company died, when the fire devoured two hundred and fifty men; and they became a warning. ¹¹Notwithstanding, the sons of Korah did not die.

¹²The sons of Simeon according to their families: of Nemu-el, the family of the Nemuelites; of Jamin, the family of the Jaminites; of Jachin, the family of the Jachinites; ¹³of Zerah, the family of the Zerahites; of Shaul, the family of the Shaulites. ¹⁴These are the families of the Simeonites, twenty-two thousand two hundred.

¹⁵The sons of Gad according to their families: of Zephon, the family of the Zephonites; of Haggi, the family of the Haggites; of Shuni, the family of the Shunites; ¹⁶of Ozni, the family of the Oznites; of Eri, the family of the Erites; ¹⁷of Arod, the family of the Arodites; of Areli, the family of the Arelites. ¹⁸These are the families of the sons of Gad according to their number, forty thousand five hundred.

¹⁹The sons of Judah were Er and Onan; and Er and Onan died in the land of Canaan. ²⁰And the sons of Judah according to their families were: of Shelah, the family of the Shelanites; of Perez, the family of the Perezites; of Zerah, the family of the Zerahites. ²¹And the sons of Perez were: of Hezron, the family of the Hezronites; of Hamul, the family of the Hamulites. ²²These are the families of Judah according to their number, seventy-six thousand five hundred.

²³The sons of Issachar according to their families: of Tola, the family of the Tolaites; of Puvah, the family of the Punites; ²⁴of Jashub, the family of the Jashubites; of Shimron, the family of the Shimronites. ²⁵These are the families of Issachar according to their number, sixty-four thousand three hundred.

²⁶The sons of Zebulun, according to their families: of Sered, the family of the Seredites; of Elon, the family of the Elonites; of Jahleel, the family of the Jahleelites. ²⁷These are the families of the Zebulunites according to their number, sixty thousand five hundred.

²⁸The sons of Joseph according to their families: Manasseh and Ephraim. ²⁹The sons of Manasseh: of Machir, the family of the Machirites; and Machir was the father of Gilead; of Gilead, the family of the Gileadites. ³⁰These are the sons of Gilead: of Iezer, the family of the Iezerites; of Helek, the family of the Helekites; ³¹and of Asri-el, the family of the Asrielites; and of Shechem, the family of the Shechemites; ³²and of Shemida, the family of the Shemidaites; and of Hepher, the family of the Hepherites. ³³Now Zelophehad the son of Hepher had no sons, but daughters: and the names of the daughters of Zelophehad were Mahlah, Noah, Hoglah, Milcah, and Tirzah. ³⁴These are the families of Manasseh; and their number was fifty-two thousand seven hundred.

³⁵These are the sons of Ephraim according to their families: of Shuthelah, the family of the Shuthelahites; of Becher, the family of the Becherites; of Tahan, the family of the Tahanites. ³⁶And these are the sons of Shuthelah: of Eran, the family of the Eranites. ³⁷These are the families of the sons of Ephraim according to their number, thirty-two thousand five hundred. These are the sons of Joseph according to their families.

³⁸The sons of Benjamin according to their families: of Bela, the family of the Bela-ites; of Ashbel, the family of the Ashbelites; of Ahiram, the family of the Ahiramites; ³⁹of Shephupham, the family of the Shuphamites; of Hupham, the family of the Huphamites. ⁴⁰And the sons of Bela were Ard and Naaman: of Ard, the family of the Ardites; of Naaman, the family of the Naamites. ⁴¹These are the sons of Benjamin according to their families; and their number was forty-five thousand six hundred.

⁴²These are the sons of Dan according to their families: of Shuham, the family of the Shuhamites. These are the families of Dan according to their families. ⁴³All the families of the Shuhamites, according to their number, were sixty-four thousand four hundred.

⁴⁴The sons of Asher according to their families: of Imnah, the family of the Imnites; of Ishvi, the family of the Ishvites; of Beriah, the family of the Beriites. ⁴⁵Of the sons of Beriah: of Heber, the family of the Heberites; of Malchi-el, the family of the Malchi-elites. ⁴⁶And the name of the daughter of Asher was Serah. ⁴⁷These are the families of the sons of Asher according to their number, fifty-three thousand four hundred.

⁴⁸The sons of Naphtali according to their families: of Jahzeel, the family of the Jahzeelites; of Guni, the family of the Gunites; ⁴⁹of Jezer,

the family of the Jezerites; of Shillem, the family of the Shillemites. ⁵⁰These are the families of Naphtali according to their families; and their number was forty-five thousand four hundred.

⁵¹This was the number of the people of Israel, six hundred and one thousand seven hundred and thirty.

⁵²The Lord said to Moses: ⁵³"To these the land shall be divided for inheritance according to the number of names. ⁵⁴To a large tribe you shall give a large inheritance, and to a small tribe you shall give a small inheritance; every tribe shall be given its inheritance according to its numbers. ⁵⁵But the land shall be divided by lot; according to the names of the tribes of their fathers they shall inherit. ⁵⁶Their inheritance shall be divided according to lot between the larger and the smaller."

⁵⁷These are the Levites as numbered according to their families: of Gershon, the family of the Gershonites; of Kohath, the family of the Kohathites; of Merari, the family of the Merarites. ⁵⁸These are the families of Levi: the family of the Libnites, the family of the Hebronites, the family of the Mahlites, the family of the Mushites, the family of the Korahites. And Kohath was the father of Amram. ⁵⁹The name of Amram's wife was Jochebed the daughter of Levi, who was born to Levi in Egypt; and she bore to Amram Aaron and Moses and Miriam their sister. ⁶⁰And to Aaron were born Nadab, Abihu, Eleazar and Ithamar. ⁶¹But Nadab and Abihu died when they offered unholy fire before the Lord. ⁶²And those numbered of them were twenty-three thousand, every male from a month old and upward; for they were not numbered among the people of Israel, because there was no inheritance given to them among the people of Israel.

⁶³These were those numbered by Moses and Eleazar the priest, who numbered the people of Israel in the plains of Moab by the Jordan at Jericho. ⁶⁴But among these there was not a man of those numbered by Moses and Aaron the priest, who had numbered the people of Israel in the wilderness of Sinai. ⁶⁵For the Lord had said of them, "They shall die in the wilderness." There was not left a man of them, except Caleb the son of Jephunneh and Joshua the son of Nun.

(i)

It is interesting to compare this census with the one in chapter 1:

First Census	Tribe	Second Census
46,500	Reuben	43,730
59,300	Simeon	22,200
45,650	Gad	40,500
74,600	Judah	76,500
54,400	Issachar	64,300

57,400	Zebulun	60,500
32,200	Manasseh	52,700
40,500	Ephraim	32,500
35,400	Benjamin	45,600
62,700	Dan	64,400
41,500	Asher	53,400
53,400	Naphtali	45,400
603,550	Total	601,730

The overall number of healthy adult males was slightly down, even if we allow for the unresolved question of whether the term for one thousand means "a brigade" or the like (see commentary on 1:5–19). The largest and most influential tribe was then and remained still that of Judah, even though it did not grow significantly. The tribe of Simeon, on the one hand, from being in the top three tribes numerically has plummeted to being the smallest of them all, a collapse also reflected in Gen. 34:25–31 and 49:5–7. The tribe that had grown most was that of Manasseh, with a meteoric rise of over 60%.

Perhaps the most important thing for us to learn from such lists is that they deal with real human beings, not demi-gods who, because they appear in the pages of the Bible, must be essentially different from the rest of us. They died and were born on the journey; there were plagues and other natural disasters and setbacks; some tribes were more aggressive, some more withdrawn, keeping themselves intact; some stayed close to the Lord and his directions for their common life, and some rebelled. It was exactly the same with the New Testament Church, the Church of the first generations of believers. We too often regard these individuals and their congregations as glowing examples of all that is right and beautiful in the Church as God envisions it; and yet they were only human beings too. There would be no letters of Paul in the New Testament were it not for the fact that they were not super-human, since these letters were written for encouragement and correction, warning and rebuke, comfort and restraint.

(ii)

In vv. 52–56 are found two distinct criteria for dividing up the land once they settle in it: (a) by *prestige*, i.e. the larger the tribe the more territory to be given; and (b) by *lot*, i.e. without bias, with equal opportunities for all. If the two methods are to be reconciled, then either the general area of the country was to be allocated by lot and within that area size and prestige were to be taken into account in deciding particular locations, or vice versa. These verses come before the count of the Levites (up from 22,000 to 23,000) to emphasize that they inherited no land (see v. 62). They also highlight an important distinction between the two censuses—this second one was not only for military purposes, but also for settlement purposes.

Finally, the last verses indicate the writer's view of the necessity for such a census at this time. In fulfilment of 14:26–30, only Caleb and Joshua remained from the generation that set out from Sinai, so this was, in a sense, a new people of God, though in continuity with the original people. We are none of us indispensable, least of all the leaders of the Church under Jesus, the King and the Head, but the people of God will go on, and the very gates of Hell will not prevail against them.

THE LAW OF INHERITANCE

Numbers 27:1–11

[1]Then drew near the daughters of Zelophehad the son of Hepher, son of Gilead, son of Machir, son of Manasseh, from the families of Manasseh the son of Joseph. The names of his daughters were: Mahlah, Noah, Hoglah, Milcah, and Tirzah. [2]And they stood before Moses, and before Eleazar the priest, and before the leaders and all the congregation, at the door of the tent of meeting, saying, [3]"Our father died in the wilderness; he was not among the company of those who gathered themselves together against the Lord in the company of Korah, but died for his own sin; and he had no sons. [4]Why should the name of our father be taken away from his family, because he had no son? Give to us a possession among our father's brethren."

⁵Moses brought their case before the Lord. ⁶And the Lord said to Moses, ⁷"The daughters of Zelophehad are right; you shall give them possession of an inheritance among their father's brethren and cause the inheritance of their father to pass to them. ⁸And you shall say to the people of Israel, 'If a man dies, and has no son, then you shall cause his inheritance to pass to his daughter. ⁹And if he has no daughter, then you shall give his inheritance to his brothers. ¹⁰And if he has no brothers, then you shall give his inheritance to his father's brothers. ¹¹And if his father has no brothers, then you shall give his inheritance to his kinsman that is next to him of his family, and he shall possess it. And it shall be to the people of Israel a statute and ordinance, as the Lord commanded Moses.'"

(i)

These verses, involving the women mentioned in 26:33, are quite remarkable. Following the settlement plans of the previous chapter, they present a case-study of the least powerful of all those preparing to settle, those with no established rights at all to territory. What happened when a father of a clan died leaving no male heirs? Could his daughters be given land? This was the situation facing the daughters of a certain Zelophehad, the father of a clan within the tribe of Manasseh. There were five daughters without a brother, and their names were Mahlah, Noah, Hoglah, Milcah, and Tirzah. They must have been strong women and proud Israelites to speak out in such a bold fashion at an official gathering of the leaders and camp (v. 2). But their father's confidence in them, as he named them, was justified, since they won their case. Their names mean respectively "gentleness, flattery, magpie, counsel, delight".

Their case was that their father had died a natural death. He had not been among those judged by the Lord, but just a member of the camp who died on the journey; a sinner, but not an apostate or a rebel. The daughters therefore make their seemingly reasonable request for the sake of the family, not personal gain. But of course it was not a reasonable request in the context of the ancient East where all social pressures were against women inheriting property. The case was so exceptional that

Moses, as in the case of those unable to celebrate the Passover and the man who wilfully violated the Sabbath (9:8; 15:34), had to seek the Lord.

The Lord decided in favour of the rightness of the case of the daughters, and instructed Moses to draw up a system of priorities for the future to ensure that the property and territory of a family stay within that family.

(ii)

The relationship of land and people under God is of fundamental importance for understanding the Old Testament and the Jewish people. The reasoning behind this decision is contained in Lev. 25:23, where the Lord says: "The land shall not be sold in perpetuity, for the land is mine; for you are strangers and sojourners with me." In other words, the Promised Land was a gift from God, not an inalienable right of anyone's to sell or incorporate as they wished. Families were given their share of the land for them alone. In a real sense we could say that the faith of Israel was concerned with *families*, not just the heads of families.

The passage also gives us a valuable glimpse of the way revelation came to the people and how the laws and codes interspersed throughout the Old Testament were drawn up. Our encounter with the God of the Bible is rooted in the here and now. He may have chosen us from all eternity, but our experience is *firmly* part of our earthly lives. So we see here the historical faith of Israel growing a bit more as she saw a need, took it to the Lord, received his Torah or "Direction", and moved on.

Our faith too will grow, and we will mature, as we recognize our needs, take them to the Lord, receive his direction, and move on rejoicing. As our hymn has it: "What a Friend we have in Jesus . . . Take it to the Lord in prayer."

MOSES CONFIRMS JOSHUA

Numbers 27:12–23

[12]The Lord said to Moses, "Go up into this mountain of Abarim, and

see the land which I have given to the people of Israel. [13] And when you have seen it, you also shall be gathered to your people, as your brother Aaron was gathered, [14] because you rebelled against my word in the wilderness of Zin during the strife of the congregation, to sanctify me at the waters before their eyes." (These are the waters of Meribah of Kadesh in the wilderness of Zin.) [15] Moses said to the Lord, [16] "Let the Lord, the God of the spirits of all flesh, appoint a man over the congregation, [17] who shall go out before them and come in before them, who shall lead them out and bring them in; that the congregation of the Lord may not be as sheep which have no shepherd." [18] And the Lord said to Moses, "Take Joshua the son of Nun, a man in whom is the spirit, and lay your hand upon him; [19] cause him to stand before Eleazar the priest and all the congregation, and you shall commission him in their sight. [20] You shall invest him with some of your authority, that all the congregation of the people of Israel may obey. [21] And he shall stand before Eleazar the priest, who shall inquire for him by the judgment of the Urim before the Lord; at his word they shall go out, and at his word they shall come in, both he and all the people of Israel with him, the whole congregation." [22] And Moses did as the Lord commanded him; he took Joshua and caused him to stand before Eleazar the priest and the whole congregation, [23] and he laid his hands upon him, and commissioned him as the Lord directed through Moses.

(i)

This passage contains the first firm hint that Moses' time of parting company with the earthly camp of the Israelites was drawing near. In 20:10–12 it was stated clearly that neither he nor Aaron would be the one to lead the people into the Promised Land, and in 20:22–29 there occurred the death of his brother Aaron. Moses is reminded of both incidents by the Lord. Verses 12–13 are almost identical with Deut. 32:48–50, except that there the particular peak, Mount Nebo, is mentioned. Moses would be able to see all the Promised Land stretched out before him from the peak on which he died, but yet would not be able to enter it. When the present writer stood on top of the traditional site of Jebel-en-Neba in modern Jordan, he could see the light of the sun reflected on the Sea of Galilee during the day, and the lights of Jerusalem at night—all with the naked eye. The view is truly commanding and breathtaking. And there Moses was to die.

Moses shows no bitterness nor depression, but seeks the Lord for the Lord's man. Again (compare 16:22) he appeals to him as the Lord of all life and destinies to secure the life and destiny of his people. His successor must be one who can "go out . . . come in . . . lead . . . out . . . bring . . . in". This is an idiom for being fully occupied in everyday work. In the present context it means someone able to take charge of all of the camp's movements, settlements, battles, etc. Compare Micaiah's vision in 1 Kings 22:13–17, where he too sees Israel "scattered upon the mountains, as sheep that have no shepherd".

(ii)

The man chosen is Joshua (or Hoshea, a shorter form), the son of Nun. There is of course a book of the Scriptures named after him, but the words of God which most testify to his stature are found here where it is said that he is the one "in whom is the spirit". What this means is that God has already chosen him and given gifts so that he can fulfil God's plan for him; and has already given him tasks to use those gifts and mature in them. He has in fact been favourably mentioned before in Numbers in connection with exploring the land of Canaan, when only he and Caleb were truly able to report with the Lord's perspective (13:8,16; 14:6, 30, 38; 26:55). It is an interesting insight into what having God's spirit really involves.

Moses is to "lay" his "hands upon him", which made him "full of the spirit of wisdom" according to Deut. 34:9. In this context it is not strictly speaking an act of ordination like that of the laying on of hands by the elders, for instance. Rather Moses is carrying out a public act of ratifying what God had already done and was about to do through Joshua, an act of confirmation and affirmation. The symbolic action was common enough, and is found in several different contexts in the Old Testament: the blessing of Ephraim and Manasseh (Gen. 48:14); the cursing of a blasphemer (Lev. 24:14); the sanctifying of a sacrifice (2 Chron. 29:23); the choosing of the Levites to serve the Lord in the sanctuary (Num. 8:10). The words of this chapter, however, were, according to the Mishnah, to be used in the "ordination" of rabbis. The idea was continued and developed in the synagogues, and from there it was adapted by the apostles. We come across it in Acts 6:6 for the setting aside of the seven men to serve the community, and in 1 Tim. 4:14 referring to the setting apart of Timothy for his distinctive ministry. To that extent it marked Joshua as one of God's special men, set aside for service.

Moses is to "commission" him, i.e. "give him a charge" and "invest" him with "some of" his own "authority". This is the only place in the Pentateuch where this term for "authority" occurs. So what is special about it? It is used for the sovereignty and majesty of a king (e.g. Jer. 22:18; Ps. 45:3), but especially for that of God, the King (e.g. Ps. 104:1). We are therefore catching a glimpse of the esteem in which Moses was held—his was the authority of the King. There could never be another like him (Deut. 34:9–12), and so Joshua could only receive a portion of this greatness. As such, Joshua might not go straight to the Lord, but had to consult the High Priest and go through the priestly machinery.

Fortunately we don't have to rely on such a system, having instead Jesus as our intercessor and mediator. He is the one immeasurably greater than either Moses or Joshua, who will ensure that we are never without a Shepherd.

GOD'S CALENDAR: DAYS, WEEKS, MONTHS

Numbers 28:1–15

[1]The Lord said to Moses, [2]"Command the people of Israel, and say to them, 'My offering, my food for my offerings by fire, my pleasing odour, you shall take heed to offer to me in its due season.' [3]And you shall say to them, This is the offering by fire which you shall offer to the Lord: two male lambs a year old without blemish, day by day, as a continual offering. [4]The one lamb you shall offer in the morning, and the other lamb you shall offer in the evening; [5]also a tenth of an ephah of fine flour for a cereal offering, mixed with a fourth of a hin of beaten oil. [6]It is a continual burnt offering, which was ordained at Mount Sinai for a pleasing odour, an offering by fire to the Lord. [7]Its drink offering shall be a fourth of a hin for each lamb; in the holy place you shall pour

out a drink offering of strong drink to the Lord. [8]The other lamb you shall offer in the evening; like the cereal offering of the morning, and like its drink offering, you shall offer it as an offering by fire, a pleasing odour to the Lord.

[9]"On the sabbath day two male lambs a year old without blemish, and two tenths of an ephah of fine flour for a cereal offering, mixed with oil, and its drink offering: [10]this is the burnt offering of every sabbath, besides the continual burnt offering and its drink offering.

[11]"At the beginnings of your months you shall offer a burnt offering to the Lord: two young bulls, one ram, seven male lambs a year old without blemish; [12]also three tenths of an ephah of fine flour for a cereal offering, mixed with oil, for each bull; and two tenths of fine flour for a cereal offering, mixed with oil, for the one ram; [13]and a tenth of fine flour mixed with oil as a cereal offering for every lamb; for a burnt offering of pleasing odour, an offering by fire to the Lord. [14]Their drink offerings shall be half a hin of wine for a bull, a third of a hin for a ram, and a fourth of a hin for a lamb; this is the burnt offering of each month throughout the months of the year. [15]Also one male goat for a sin offering to the Lord; it shall be offered besides the continual burnt offering and its drink offering.

(i)

The next two chapters of the book contain the procedures for public sacrificial worship to be offered in the course of every year by the community, once they had entered the Promised Land. Many of the details probably come from a later time, but we will not concern ourselves with that problem here (see *Additional Note* 1). Personal worship and sacrifices are also encouraged, as the note at the end of these two chapters shows (29:39), but the emphasis here is on the obligatory worship of the people as a whole. The account begins at the least spectacular but the basic level of the daily sacrifices. This was good sense. Only when the daily walk with the Lord was right could the big occasions under God also be right.

Look at v. 2: "My... my... my... my... to me", says the Lord. He is a jealous God, and expects everything we have to give to be given to him. "My offering" is really the shorthand way of saying "all that is due to me", and the people are here commanded to take care to give him his due. Many of the technical terms will be found discussed in the commentary on 15:1–16.

In v. 3 is found the backbone of the sacrificial system. This daily round of sacrifices is called by the RSV "a continual offering", yet the term is used in Ezek. 39:14 in a context where the words obviously mean "men in regular employment", set apart to bury the dead. "Regular" is a more accurate translation than "continual" here too. It was something to be done every day.

The place for this daily offering was the "holy place", in later times probably the court where the altar stood for the burnt offerings (see Exod. 28:43; Ezek. 44:27). Snaith says of this court: "Whatever went into this area never came out again; it was either burnt on the altar or eaten by the priests." All of this was intended to produce "a pleasing odour to the Lord", a poetic way of saying "please him".

Christians no longer conduct sacrifices. What then must we do to please God? We are told by John that he and his brothers and sisters "keep his commandments and [so] do what pleases him" (1 John 3:22). But it is put at its most basic in the Letter to the Hebrews 11:6 where we are told clearly that "without faith it is impossible to please him". What is this faith? It is "the assurance of things hoped for, the conviction of things not seen" (Heb. 11:1). So if we accept such a gift from the Lord and use it in all our dealings with him and with his world, we will please him.

(ii)

At the end of every week comes the day of rest, the "sabbath day", inspired by the story of Gen. 2:1–3. In a sense this day is the crown of Judaism. It is the God-ordained day of rest and worship. The central point of the inauguration of the modern Sabbath is the chanting of a piece which begins: "Come, my friend, to meet the bride; let us welcome the presence of the Sabbath." Such is the reverence for it among the people that one sage once remarked: "Even more than the Jews have kept the Sabbath, has the Sabbath kept the Jews."

It has also been called by the great Jewish theologian, Heschel, a "temple in time". What a glorious phrase! The Lord himself inaugurated the day at Sinai: "You shall keep the sabbath, because it is holy for you." It was the only specific matter to do with worship enshrined in the Ten Commandments: "Remember the sabbath day, to keep it holy" (Exod. 20:8). The day was to be one of rest, and the version of this commandment in Deut. 5:14f. makes explicit its motive of providing a time of "re-creation" for all, even slaves and domestic animals.

During the Exile, Second Isaiah singled out the Sabbath as the "pre-condition of individual and national restoration" in a remarkable passage, 56:1–8. It was then, when no temple sacrifices were possible, that it came into its own. It is not surprising, therefore, that after the Temple was destroyed in A.D. 70, the Sabbath emerged as the chief public witness of the Jews to their faith in the company of their non-Jewish neighbours. A Rabbinic treatise on Exod. 31:14 comments: "Furthermore, whoever keeps the Sabbath testifies of him at whose word the world came into being; that he created the world in six days and rested on the seventh."

For Christians too it is important to honour the "Lord's day" (Rev. 1:10). In the early Church, where there was a mix of Jewish and Gentile believers, the day to be celebrated was a matter of strong dispute. Paul refers to it, and other similar disputes of conviction and tradition, in Rom. 14, and lays down the principle that whatever we decide to do, it should be done "in honour of the Lord" (vv. 5–9). Christians have chosen another day for their "Sabbath", but that principle still stands. It is a chance for us to proclaim to others that we are the Lord's.

(iii)

In vv. 11–15 are found the sacrifices appropriate for the first day of each month as it comes by. Great prominence is given to the new moon by these massive sacrifices. The calendar was (and the Jewish calendar still is) based on the moon's cycles, not on the earth's journey around the sun. It is clear from elsewhere that the new moon was a popular and important celebration (1 Sam. 20:4–5, 18; 2 Kings 4:23; Ezek. 26:1; 29:17; 32:1), though the prophets did not always approve of it (Isa. 47:13; Amos 8:4–5).

Although the Church never seems to have adopted this Jewish tradition, the significance of it was well known, and questions as to its observance or not were keenly disputed (see Col. 2:16–17). Perhaps the reader will best appreciate the witness of the feast (and to this day in orthodox synagogues it is, though without the sacrifices, very joyfully kept) if he or she reads three of the Psalms appointed to be sung and chanted at it. These are: (1) Ps. 104— "Bless the Lord, O my soul! O Lord my God, thou art very great!... Thou didst set the earth on its foundations... Thou makest springs gush forth in the valleys... Thou hast made the moon to mark the seasons... O Lord, how manifold are thy works!... may the Lord rejoice in his works... Praise the Lord!"; (2) Ps. 8—"O Lord, our Lord, how majestic is thy name in all the earth!... When I look at thy heavens... what is man that thou art mindful of him?"; and (3) Ps. 148—"Praise the Lord!... all his angels... all his host... sun and moon... you highest heavens... Praise the Lord!"

There was a common belief in antiquity that just before the new moon the demons of the world were especially active (we may compare the traditions behind All Hallows and All Hallows Eve). Perhaps this partly lies behind the special "sin offering" (v. 15) and behind the prophetic disapproval of the feast as well. The offering of a "male goat" recalls the sacrifices of the Day of Atonement, and to this day a fast is held before this feast and is called the "little Day of Atonement". The celebration therefore also carried an undertone of redemption from the evil realms of life.

PASSOVER AND PENTECOST

Numbers 28:16–31

[16]"On the fourteenth day of the first month is the Lord's passover. [17]And on the fifteenth day of this month is a feast; seven days shall unleavened bread be eaten. [18]On the first day there shall be a holy convocation: you shall do no laborious work, [19]but offer an offering by fire, a burnt offering to the Lord: two young bulls, one ram, and seven

male lambs a year old; see that they are without blemish; 20also their cereal offering of fine flour mixed with oil; three tenths of an ephah shall you offer for a bull, and two tenths for a ram; 21a tenth shall you offer for each of the seven lambs; 22also one male goat for a sin offering, to make atonement for you. 23You shall offer these besides the burnt offering of the morning, which is for a continual burnt offering. 24In the same way you shall offer daily, for seven days, the food of an offering by fire, a pleasing odour to the Lord; it shall be offered besides the continual burnt offering and its drink offering. 25And on the seventh day you shall have a holy convocation; you shall do no laborious work.

26"On the day of the first fruits, when you offer a cereal offering of new grain to the Lord at your feast of weeks, you shall do no laborious work, 27but offer a burnt offering, a pleasing odour to the Lord: two young bulls, one ram, seven male lambs a year old; 28also their cereal offering of fine flour mixed with oil, three tenths of an ephah for each bull, two tenths for one ram, 29a tenth for each of the seven lambs; 30with one male goat, to make atonement for you. 31Besides the continual burnt offering and its cereal offering, you shall offer them and their drink offering. See that they are without blemish.

(i)

Passover was the formative festival of the nation recalling the creation of Israel under the redeeming power of the Lord at the Exodus, and under the covenanting grace of the Lord at Mount Sinai. See further the commentary on 9:1–5.

For the first evening of the seven-day feast no sacrifice is mentioned, as essentially Passover was a family feast celebrated in homes with the extended families gathered. In this respect also it is a unique festival. Exod. 12:21–22 makes it clear that at the first Passover the original generation stayed at home, prepared at home, and ate at home before setting off hurriedly; and Exod. 12:3–14 authorizes succeeding generations to honour this memory by celebrating also at home.

During the succeeding days (properly the public feast of Un-leavened Bread) each day had its sacrifices, and these daily offerings were quite substantial, consisting of two young bulls, a ram, and seven male yearling lambs, all without physical blemishes or defects, as well as the appropriate cereal offerings. A male goat was also to be offered daily as a "sin offering" to "make atonement". On the first and seventh days, no "laborious work" was to be done. This term came to be used for any work forbidden on the Sabbath (Lev. 23:3; Deut. 5:13–14) or special assemblies (here; Num. 29:7; Lev. 16:29).

The reason for the complete rest is that the first and seventh days are called "a holy convocation" (see also 28:25, 26; 29:1, 7, 12). The phrase literally means a "holy calling", i.e. calling together, so perhaps "holy assembly" would be a good translation. It was a call to all Israel to show herself to be God's holy people, and was fundamental not only to Passover, but to the other pilgrim feasts of Weeks and Booths, as well as to the Day of Atonement and the Sabbaths. The same term is used in another sense in Neh. 8:8 for "the reading" of the Law, and became the later Rabbinic term for "Scripture".

(ii)

For the feast of "first fruits" it became the law that all Jews had to travel to Jerusalem to worship together (compare Paul's desire, as a Jew, to worship there at that time in Acts 20:16). On the first day the people brought the first crops of the new harvest as an offering to the Lord, symbolically returning to him in gratitude what was his already, and symbolically dedicating themselves anew to his service. The feast is also know as the "feast of harvest" (Exod. 23:16), and the "feast of weeks" (Exod. 34:22).

The offerings were substantial, and equivalent to those for the new moon and Passover. It was in fact an agricultural festival to celebrate the closing of the barley harvest and the starting of the wheat harvest. In modern Judaism it keeps the title of "Weeks" (*Shavuot*) since it falls one week of weeks, i.e. 49 days, after Passover.

Note again the stress on repentance and the need for reconciliation, with the "male goat, to make atonement".

The word Pentecost is from the Greek term for "fiftieth", and was used among Greek-speaking Jews for the feast since it fell on the fiftieth day after the Passover Sabbath. The institution is given in Lev. 23:15ff. with the words: ". . . counting fifty days to the morrow after the seventh sabbath; then you shall present a cereal offering of new grain to the Lord." In other words this feast, with its offering of "two loaves of bread to be waved" from the first of the wheat crop, was a kind of harvest thanksgiving in advance, expressing before the whole crop was in grateful dependence on God for "daily bread".

But a change in the significance of the feast came about during the Exile, when the Jews had no harvests to reap. The teachers, basing their reckoning on Exod. 19:1 ("On the third new moon after the people of Israel had gone forth out of the land of Egypt, on that day they came into the wilderness of Sinai"), concluded that this was also the very day on which the Lord gave the Torah to Israel. So the feast became known also as "the season of the giving of the Law". As with Passover, the original festival was overlaid with a historical meaning. The passage Exod. 19:1–20:26 was read. Also read was the book of Ruth, perhaps because its events revolved around harvest time, or because Ruth was an ancestress of King David, who died on this day, as tradition has it; but perhaps also because Ruth's acceptance of the faith of Israel was felt to be appropriate for the festival which celebrated the giving of that faith to Israel, or because Ruth's faithfulness to her mother-in-law was taken to be symbolic of Israel's loyalty to the Torah.

In short, it might be said that Pentecost marks the birthday of Judaism as the people of Torah. Many centuries were to pass before Jesus, the expected Messiah, came to Israel and the world. After his resurrection, and before his ascension, he commanded his disciples to wait until the Holy Spirit came upon them in the full power of God, before going out to be witnesses to him. They waited a full forty-nine days after the Passover meal they shared with him. Then, "when the day of Pentecost had come, they were all together in one place . . . and they were all filled with the Holy Spirit . . . and there were added that day about three thousand souls" (Acts 2:1, 4, 41). Pentecost therefore also marks the birthday of the Church, the birthday of Christianity.

Just as that first generation of people with Moses were the "first fruits" of Judaism, so that first generation of people with Peter were the "first fruits" of Christianity. Let us thank God that we are part of his great harvest, in a continuous line from Abraham to today, and let us resolve to offer him only the best of our lives in gratitude.

NEW YEAR AND ATONEMENT

Numbers 29:1–11

[1]"On the first day of the seventh month you shall have a holy convocation; you shall do no laborious work. It is a day for you to blow the trumpets, [2]and you shall offer a burnt offering, a pleasing odour to the Lord: one young bull, one ram, seven male lambs a year old without blemish; [3]also their cereal offering of fine flour mixed with oil, three tenths of an ephah for the bull, two tenths for the ram, [4]and one tenth for each of the seven lambs; [5]with one male goat for a sin offering, to make atonement for you; [6]besides the burnt offering of the new moon, and its cereal offering, and the continual burnt offering and its cereal offering, and their drink offering, according to the ordinance for them, a pleasing odour, an offering by fire to the Lord.

[7]"On the tenth day of this seventh month you shall have a holy convocation, and afflict yourselves; you shall do no work, [8]but you shall offer a burnt offering to the Lord, a pleasing odour: one young bull, one ram, seven male lambs a year old; they shall be to you without blemish; [9]and their cereal offering of fine flour mixed with oil, three tenths of an ephah for the bull, two tenths for the one ram, [10]a tenth for each of the seven lambs: [11]also one male goat for a sin offering, besides the sin offering of atonement, and the continual burnt offering and its cereal offering, and their drink offerings.

(i)

Here is a passage that seems to say nothing in particular. On the first day of the "seventh month", i.e. a new moon feast, as well as the accepted offerings for the new month there were to be offered an extra "young bull . . . ram, seven male lambs a year old". Again, they must be spotless, and must be accompanied by the

appropriate cereal offerings. And again there is the "male goat"
as a "sin offering". It is perhaps striking to the reader only in that
it is to be inaugurated by those who will "blow the trumpets". In
this respect it is like the inauguration of the great Jubilee Year
(Lev. 25:9).

Strangely enough the name of this feast is not given, but it is
"New Year's Day" in Jewish tradition. New Year's Day, then, as
suggested by the large sacrifices needed, became for the Jews a
solemn time of repentance and confession of sins. It was the time
when, they believed, God rewarded the righteous and punished
the wicked. Now Judaism is a healthily realistic religion, which
knows that no one is either fully righteous or wicked, rather all
are in between. So there followed after the call to repentance by
the blast of the trumpets a period of ten days, called the "days of
awe". During this time people had the chance to convince God of
their "godly sorrow" leading to "repentance". They confessed to
those they had wronged, forgave those who confessed to them,
and as they were able made up all quarrels of the past year.

The apostle John puts the same truth this way: "If anyone says,
'I love God', and hates his brother, he is a liar; for he who does
not love his brother whom he has seen, cannot love God whom he
has not seen" (1 John 4:20). Jesus, if anything, goes further when
he says: "So if you are offering your gift at the altar, and there
remember that your brother has something against you, leave the
gift there before the altar and go; first be reconciled to your
brother, and then come and offer your gift" (Matt. 5:23–24).
Indeed, he may well have had the Jewish New Year in mind when
he taught his disciples that the fulfilment of our prayers to God for
forgiveness is in part linked with our willingness to forgive others
(Matt. 6:12).

(ii)

On the tenth day of the seventh month came the holiest of the
special days—the Day of Atonement. The sacrifices reflect its
gravity, and bring to a climax the stress on repentance and the
need for reconciliation that is seen in all the sacrifices of these
feast and fast days. In vv. 8–10 are found the usual offerings, with

v. 11 including the "male goat for a sin offering". But this is *as well as* "the sin offering of atonement", i.e. a bullock (see Exod. 29:36; 30:10; Lev. 16:11). And also *as well as* the regular offerings. These sacrifices then were very costly to the people.

This day is the only fast day commanded plainly in the Torah, and is known simply as "the fast" in Acts 27:9. It comes ten days after the New Year's Day call for repentance and confession, and concludes the ten "days of awe". It also came to be known, from Lev. 23:26–32 and Lev. 25:9, as the Day of Atonement (Hebrew *Yom Kippur*). On this day only could the High Priest—and only he—enter the holiest inner chamber of the sanctuary, the "Holy of Holies", after special cleansing rites, and sacrifice there.

He offered a bull as a "sin offering" for himself and his house, and then a male goat for a "sin offering" for the place. Another male goat was then brought live to the High Priest, who laid hands on it, transferring with appropriate prayer the sins of the people of the year past to it. It was then sent out into the wilderness to take their sins away, thus giving the English language its term "scapegoat". Finally a ram was offered as a "burnt offering" for the people. This is all spelled out in Lev. 16, with the purpose revealed in 16:30: "For on this day shall atonement be made for you, to cleanse you; from all your sins you shall be clean before the Lord."

The Hebrew term *kippur* comes from a root meaning "to cover", and the belief was that God "covered" the people's sins by the blood of the sacrifice. The Talmud says clearly: "There can be no atonement save by blood". Nor does the New Testament disagree. We find in Heb. 9:22 that "without the shedding of blood there is no forgiveness of sins". We should read all of that ninth chapter if we wish to appreciate how indispensable the Old Testament is for understanding the way in which the death of Jesus is described in the New Testament. To the Christian, atonement is not an annual affair, nor can it be established by the sacrifice of animals' blood. Rather, "Christ, having been offered *once* to bear the sins of many, will appear a second time, not to deal with sin, but to save those who are eagerly waiting for him" (Heb. 9:28).

TABERNACLES

Numbers 29:12–40

12"On the fifteenth day of the seventh month you shall have a holy convocation; you shall do no laborious work, and you shall keep a feast to the Lord seven days; 13and you shall offer a burnt offering, an offering by fire, a pleasing odour to the Lord, thirteen young bulls, two rams, fourteen male lambs a year old; they shall be without blemish; 14and their cereal offering of fine flour mixed with oil, three tenths of an ephah for each of the thirteen bulls, two tenths for each of the two rams, 15and a tenth for each of the fourteen lambs; 16also one male goat for a sin offering, besides the continual burnt offering, its cereal offering and its drink offering.

17"On the second day twelve young bulls, two rams, fourteen male lambs a year old without blemish, 18with the cereal offering and the drink offerings for the bulls, for the rams, and for the lambs, by number, according to the ordinance; 19also one male goat for a sin offering, besides the continual burnt offering and its cereal offering, and their drink offerings.

20"On the third day eleven bulls, two rams, fourteen male lambs a year old without blemish, 21with the cereal offering and the drink offerings for the bulls, for the rams, and for the lambs, by number, according to the ordinance; 22also one male goat for a sin offering, besides the continual burnt offering and its cereal offering and its drink offering.

23"On the fourth day ten bulls, two rams, fourteen male lambs a year old without blemish, 24with the cereal offering and the drink offerings for the bulls, for the rams, and for the lambs, by number, according to the ordinance; 25also one male goat for a sin offering, besides the continual burnt offering, its cereal offering and its drink offering.

26"On the fifth day nine bulls, two rams, fourteen male lambs a year old without blemish, 27with the cereal offering and the drink offerings for the bulls, for the rams, and for the lambs, by number, according to the ordinance; 28also one male goat for a sin offering; besides the continual burnt offerings and its cereal offering and its drink offering.

29"On the sixth day eight bulls, two rams, fourteen male lambs a year old without blemish, 30with the cereal offering and the drink offerings for the bulls, for the rams, and for the lambs, by number, according to the ordinance; [31]also one male goat for a sin offering; besides the continual burnt offering, its cereal offering, and its drink offerings.

[32]"On the seventh day seven bulls, two rams, fourteen male lambs a year old without blemish, [33]with the cereal offering and the drink offerings for the bulls, for the rams, and for the lambs, by number, according to the ordinance; [34]also one male goat for a sin offering; besides the continual burnt offering, its cereal offering, and its drink offering.

[35]"On the eighth day you shall have a solemn assembly: you shall do no laborious work, [36]but you shall offer a burnt offering, an offering by fire, a pleasing odour to the Lord: one bull, one ram, seven male lambs a year old without blemish, [37]and the cereal offering and the drink offerings for the bull, for the ram, and for the lambs, by number, according to the ordinance; [38]also one male goat for a sin offering; besides the continual burnt offering and its cereal offering and its drink offering.

[39]"These you shall offer to the Lord at your appointed feasts, in addition to your votive offerings and your freewill offerings, for your burnt offerings, and for your cereal offerings, and for your drink offerings, and for your peace offerings."

[40]And Moses told the people of Israel everything just as the Lord had commanded Moses.

(i)

Tabernacles is the last of the great feasts. Its name is found in the corresponding passage in Lev. 23:33–36 as "the feast of booths", although the RSV footnote has the traditional "tabernacles". It is described at far greater length than the other occasions. Lev. 23:39 shows that this *was* the greatest of the feasts in public acclaim since it is called simply "the feast of the Lord". In John's Gospel it is known merely as "the feast" (7:37). It was the final thanksgiving at the end of the fruit harvest. Hence it was also called the "Feast of Ingathering", when the fruit of the fields and the orchards and the groves was safely in.

A summary table of the sacrifices made at the various festivals is very illuminating:

	Young Bulls	Rams	Male Lambs	Goats
Daily:				
(Morning and Evening)			2	
Additional For:				
Sabbaths			2	
New Moons	2	1	7	1
Passover	2×7=14	1×7=7	7×7=49	1×7=7
Pentecost	2	1	7	1
New Year	1	1	7	1
Day of Atonement	1	1	7	1
Tabernacles	13+12+11 +10+9+8+7 +1=71	2×7+1 =15	14×7+7 =105	1×8=8

It must have been a great time in Jerusalem when all the pilgrims came there in the days of the monarchy, bringing animals and crops and wines and oils for the massive festival. And of course this was in addition to any personal sacrifices and vows to be fulfilled (v. 39). No wonder the Talmud states: "He who has not seen Jerusalem during the Feast of Tabernacles does not know what rejoicing is."

The Jewish traditions have it that the seventy bulls offered on the first seven days represented the seventy nations of the world (found in Gen. 10), being sacrificed for them in anticipation of their conversion to the God of Israel; the ninety-eight lambs of the first seven days avert the ninety-eight curses found in Deut. 28:15–68. On the eighth day the sacrifices were for Israel alone, the Rabbis interpreting the term of v. 35 to mean a "restricted" day for Israel. In the same way that a king might arrange a huge banquet and afterwards invite a close friend for a modest feast so as to enjoy his company, so the Lord set aside the last day for Israel. In Jesus' time this tradition was widespread. Jesus' use of it in his great address in John 7 (see v. 2) we shall see shortly.

(ii)

In the passage in Lev. 23:39–43 the reason for the name of the feast is explained. We read there: "You shall dwell in booths for

seven days; all that are native in Israel shall dwell in booths."
Quite apart from the original agricultural purpose of the festival it
became the time for recalling and identifying with the time of
God's great care of and disciplining of his people in the Wilderness—the time of the events in the book of Numbers. During this
time they lived in easily assembled, easily dismantled tents or
rough booths, and so all Jews at this time had to—and many still
do—assemble booths and live in them, thus professing iden-
tity with their ancestors and their essential nature as pilgrims
on the earth. However, the two characteristic customs of the
feast in Jesus' time were the water ceremony and the lights
ceremony.

On every day of the feast a golden jug was filled with water
from the Pool of Siloam and poured into a basin at the altar by the
High Priest. With this was mixed a jug of wine, and the mixture
flowed back via a pipeline to the Brook of Kidron. This was a
symbolic gesture in the prayers for abundant rain during the
coming winter, without which there would be no fruitful new
seasons. Israel's rainfall comes in a very short season indeed, and
up to the present day there are special prayers for rain during the
feast. On the last and greatest day the trumpets sounded, the
Levites sang triumphantly, and the people chanted the Pss.
113–118, while the water was poured out, and blessing was
anticipated.

At this point of the service Jesus stepped forward from the
crowd and called out: "If anyone thirst, let him come to me and
drink . . ." (John 7:37–39). Jesus was making a clear Messianic
claim, and in effect was saying that their hope for blessing,
refreshment, unity with all the world under God was to be
fulfilled in him. What a furore this must have caused in the
Temple! We are told of this in vv. 40–52, but also that he achieved
a breakthrough with some; for John says laconically: "So there
was a division among the people over him."

Another aspect of the feast was the dimming of all the lights in
Jerusalem until four great candelabra were lit in the Temple,
after which all the torches and lamps were lit, transforming the
Temple into a huge "focus of light", after which all of Jerusalem

was lit up. It was still in the context of the feast, and with this ceremony in mind, that Jesus again stood up and called out: "I am the light of the world; he who follows me will not walk in darkness, but will have the light of life" (John 8:12). Jesus is telling us all that he only is the true dwelling-place on earth of God.

It is impossible to fully appreciate Jesus and the New Testament witness to him without knowing the Old Testament and the Jewish customs that derived from it.

WOMEN'S VOWS

Numbers 30:1–16

[1]Moses said to the heads of the tribes of the people of Israel, "This is what the Lord has commanded. [2]When a man vows a vow to the Lord, or swears an oath to bind himself by a pledge, he shall not break his word; he shall do according to all that proceeds out of his mouth. [3]Or when a woman vows a vow to the Lord, and binds herself by a pledge, while within her father's house, in her youth, [4]and her father hears of her vow and of her pledge by which she has bound herself, and says nothing to her; then all her vows shall stand, and every pledge by which she has bound herself shall stand. [5]But if her father expresses disapproval to her on the day that he hears of it, no vow of hers, no pledge by which she has bound herself, shall stand; and the Lord will forgive her, because her father opposed her. [6]And if she is married to a husband, while under her vows or any thoughtless utterance of her lips by which she has bound herself, [7]and her husband hears of it, and says nothing to her on the day that he hears; then her vows shall stand, and her pledges by which she has bound herself shall stand. [8]But if, on the day that her husband comes to hear of it, he expresses disapproval, then he shall make void her vow which was on her, and the thoughtless utterance of her lips, by which she bound herself; and the Lord will forgive her. [9]But any vow of a widow or of a divorced woman, anything by which she has bound herself, shall stand against her. [10]And if she vowed in her husband's house, or bound herself by a pledge with an oath, [11]and her husband heard of it, and said nothing to her, and did not oppose her; then all her vows shall stand, and every pledge by

which she bound herself shall stand. [12]But if her husband makes them null and void on the day that he hears them, then whatever proceeds out of her lips concerning her vows, or concerning her pledge of herself, shall not stand: her husband has made them void, and the Lord will forgive her. [13]Any vow and any binding oath to afflict herself, her husband may establish, or her husband may make void. [14]But if her husband says nothing to her from day to day, then he establishes all her vows, or all her pledges, that are upon her; he has established them, because he said nothing to her on the day that he heard of them. [15]But if he makes them null and void after he has heard of them, then he shall bear her iniquity."

[16]These are the statutes which the Lord commanded Moses, as between a man and his wife, and between a father and his daughter, while in her youth, within her father's house.

This is a self-contained chapter, dealing with a subject not treated elsewhere. It is concerned with the validity of any "vow . . . oath . . . pledge", but particularly with the problem that, whereas men were considered to be responsible for their own decisions and vows, women were only considered as personally responsible if they were widowed or divorced. Otherwise their fathers or husbands possessed the ultimate authority. For other passages giving the Old Testament teaching on vows, reference should be made to Num. 6 (see the commentary); Lev. 5:4–6; 27; Deut. 23:21ff.

At the outset comes the law that a man is bound by unconditional rules to vows made. This is an important part of the background to the New Testament teachings on vows, especially the teaching of Jesus in Matt. 5:33–37. Jesus wasn't making a mountain out of a mole-hill, but was speaking to a significant and vulnerable area of religious life. We who take vows and promises lightly ought to listen to what he says and to be aware of its very Jewish background.

In Jewish law, based on the Old Testament, the age at which a "boy" becomes a "man" is thirteen years and one day. After a thirteen-year-old's *bar mitzvah* (a phrase meaning "son of the commandment") the young man can make binding contracts and vows for himself. This is the background to the incident recorded only by Luke in 2:41–52, when at the right age Jesus went with his parents to the Temple in Jerusalem to be dedicated as a *bar mitzvah*. And as soon as he became a "man" before God he was to be found "in the temple, sitting among the teachers, listening to them and asking them questions."

However, any woman, of whatever age, but not yet married, was under the responsible authority of her father (vv. 3–5). This chapter lays it down that she could make vows or enter contracts but her father could annul them, as long as he did so on the same day he heard of them. He did not need to hear them made, nor yet annul them on the day they were made, but only on the day someone informed him of them. Presumably this informant was usually the other person or persons involved who would want to know as soon as possible whether the word stood or not. Silence meant approval, or at least assent. If, however, a woman made a vow and then married before the father heard of it, or had time to annul it, then responsibility fell to the husband as soon as he heard of it (vv. 6–8). Only a widow or divorced woman was directly responsible for her own vows (v. 9).

The remaining case involves vows made by women established in marriage, where the husband has that final authority (vv. 10–15). His silence will establish a vow and his annulment will annul it. But here an important point is made (v. 15), that if after the allotted period of a day he tries to revoke the vow, then he "shall bear her iniquity", i.e. he will bear the consequences of breaking a vow as if it were one *he* had made. This penalty was probably set to ensure speedy decision by the husband so that the other party or parties involved could act with assurance and security.

These laws reflect the lowly position of women in Israelite as in every other ancient eastern society, and have little to teach us on that score. If there is a lesson in this chapter, it is to be found in the strong emphasis on a man's—and we might add a woman's—word being his bond. It is a rebuke to our modern societies, where the law seems more concerned with the "small print" of an agreement than with honestly striking a bargain and keeping to it.

DESTROY MIDIAN!

Numbers 31:1–24

¹The Lord said to Moses, ²"Avenge the people of Israel on the Midianites; afterward you shall be gathered to your people." ³And Moses said to the people, "Arm men from among you for the war, that they may go against Midian, to execute the Lord's vengeance on Midian. ⁴You shall send a thousand from each of the tribes of Israel to the war." ⁵So there were provided, out of the thousands of Israel, a thousand from each tribe, twelve thousand armed for war. ⁶And Moses sent them to war, a thousand from each tribe, together with Phinehas the son of Eleazar the priest, with the vessels of the sanctuary and the trumpets for the alarm in his hand. ⁷They warred against Midian, as the Lord commanded Moses, and slew every male. ⁸They slew the kings of Midian with the rest of their slain, Evi, Rekem, Zur, Hur, and Reba, the five kings of Midian; and they also slew Balaam the son of Beor with the sword. ⁹And the people of Israel took captive the women of Midian and their little ones; and they took as booty all their cattle, their flocks, and all their goods. ¹⁰All their cities in the places where they dwelt, and all their encampments, they burned with fire, ¹¹and took all the spoil and all the booty, both of man and of beast. ¹²Then they brought the captives and the booty and the spoil to Moses, and to Eleazar the priest, and to the congregation of the people of Israel, at the camp on the plains of Moab by the Jordan at Jericho.

¹³Moses, and Eleazar the priest, and all the leaders of the congregation, went forth to meet them outside the camp. ¹⁴And Moses was angry with the officers of the army, the commanders of thousands and the commanders of hundreds, who had come from service in the war. ¹⁵Moses said to them, "Have you let all the women live? ¹⁶Behold, these caused the people of Israel, by the counsel of Balaam, to act treacherously against the Lord in the matter of Peor, and so the plague came among the congregation of the Lord. ¹⁷Now therefore, kill every male among the little ones, and kill every woman who has known man by lying with him. ¹⁸But all the young girls who have not know man by lying with him, keep alive for yourselves. ¹⁹Encamp outside the camp seven days; whoever of you has killed any person, and whoever has touched any slain, purify yourselves and your captives on the third day and on the seventh day. ²⁰You shall purify every garment, every article of skin, all work of goats' hair, and every article of wood."

²¹And Eleazar the priest said to the men of war who had gone to battle: "This is the statute of the law which the Lord has commanded Moses: ²²only the gold, the silver, the bronze, the iron, the tin, and the lead, ²³everything that can stand the fire, you shall pass through the fire, and it shall be clean. Nevertheless it shall also be purified with the water of impurity; and whatever cannot stand the fire, you shall pass through the water. ²⁴You must wash your clothes on the seventh day, and you shall be clean; and afterward you shall come into the camp."

(i)

According to v. 5 only 12,000 Israelites marched on the Midianites, and although the number of Midianite fighting men is not given, v. 35 puts the number of virgin captives at 32,000, so that there must have been a vast number of men. What is more, v. 7 tells that all the enemy's men were killed, while according to v. 49 not a single Israelite warrior was lost.

We cannot take these figures literally. They have obviously been exaggerated to point up the glorious victory of weak Israel over a vastly stronger foe. We get the same impression in Judg. 7:2–8, where a mere three hundred Israelites were enough to defeat—remarkably it is again—the Midianites, who were supposed in this chapter to have been wiped out!

No doubt it was a memorable victory. Note how it is emphasized that *all* Israel took part, with each tribe represented by a thousand men (though probably this means a "battalion" containing many fewer; see commentary on 1:5–19). Moses is told to "arm" these men for the fight (v. 3), but a better translation would be to "conscript" or (NEB) to "draft". The meaning is to draw men out of normal social life to take part in a special mission. Like Gideon's three hundred, these twelve battalions were specially picked for this odds-against battle.

But with the Lord on their side, the outcome was not in doubt. Women, children, livestock and goods were taken as spoils of war, while all the men were put to the sword. The Midianite cities and nomadic camps were destroyed, and Moses and Eleazar went out to meet the heroes as they returned.

(ii)

This is "holy war" with a vengeance, far removed from Jesus' command to love our enemies (Matt. 5:44). We can understand that Israel in this early period had constantly to fight for very existence. But it is not the fighting that distresses us, but the vindictiveness and boasting. It is not surprising that a leading scholar has described the whole concept as "one of the vestiges of ancient Semitic religion that remained chaff amidst the wheat of ancient Israelite faith." (See further the discussion at 21:1–3.)

A small point to notice is the reference to the death of Balaam (v. 8). We were reminded when dealing with the Balaam and Balak cycle that there were traditions—the more powerful in influence as it has turned out—that interpreted Balaam as a villain. We have here in vv. 8 and 16 examples of these traditions. Whatever happened to Balaam after he left Balak, and wherever he went, he sinned against Israel and brought the Lord's judgement on himself.

There is another possibility worth pursuing, though, and that is that the apostasies of 25:1–18, which are accredited in v. 16 to the inspiration of Balaam, all took place *before* Balak summoned him, although the Bible has them happening *after* the cycle involving Balak. Balaam would then indeed have worked against the people of Israel for the Midianites, and it would have been this that convinced Balak that he would do the same for Moab (22:1–6). Note also that Balak involved the "elders of Midian" (22:4, 7) in his plans, and that he could not believe that Balaam would not destroy Israel. So by the time of chs. 22–24 he already had a bad reputation, and this stayed on in spite of his full and, according to the text, happy blessing of Israel. In this way we can at least make sense of the contrary traditions about him.

But returning to the present passage, it is worth pausing to wonder at the total determination of Moses and Eleazar to keep ritual uncleanness out of the camp. Perhaps if we were so insistent on keeping sin out of our lives and homes, we would be better people.

THE SPOILS OF WAR

Numbers 31:25–54

[25]The Lord said to Moses, [26]"Take the count of the booty that was taken, both of man and of beast, you and Eleazar the priest and the heads of the fathers' houses of the congregation; [27]and divide the booty into two parts, between the warriors who went out to battle and all the congregation. [28]And levy for the Lord a tribute from the men of war who went out to battle, one out of five hundred, of the persons and of the oxen and of the asses and of the flocks; [29]take it from their half, and give it to Eleazar the priest as an offering to the Lord. [30]And from the people of Israel's half you shall take one drawn out of every fifty, of the persons, of the oxen, of the asses, and of the flocks, of all the cattle, and give them to the Levites who have charge of the tabernacle of the Lord." [31]And Moses and Eleazar the priest did as the Lord commanded Moses.

[32]Now the booty remaining of the spoil that the men of war took was: six hundred and seventy-five thousand sheep, [33]seventy-two thousand cattle, [34]sixty-one thousand asses, [35]and thirty-two thousand persons in all, women who had not known man by lying with him. [36]And the half, the portion of those who had gone out to war, was in number three hundred and thirty-seven thousand five hundred sheep, [37]and the Lord's tribute of sheep was six hundred and seventy-five. [38]The cattle were thirty-six thousand, of which the Lord's tribute was seventy-two. [39]The asses were thirty thousand five hundred, of which the Lord's tribute was sixty-one. [40]The persons were sixteen thousand, of which the Lord's tribute was thirty-two persons. [41]And Moses gave the tribute, which was the offering for the Lord, to Eleazar the priest, as the Lord commanded Moses.

[42]From the people of Israel's half, which Moses separated from that of the men who had gone to war—[43]now the congregation's half was three hundred and thirty-seven thousand five hundred sheep, [44]thirty-six thousand cattle, [45]and thirty thousand five hundred asses, [46]and sixteen thousand persons—[47]from the people of Israel's half Moses took one of every fifty, both of persons and of beasts, and gave them to the Levites who had charge of the tabernacle of the Lord; as the Lord commanded Moses.

[48]Then the officers who were over the thousands of the army, the captains of thousands and the captains of hundreds, came near to Moses, [49]and said to Moses, "Your servants have counted the men of

war who are under our command, and there is not a man missing from us. [50]And we have brought the Lord's offering, what each man found, articles of gold, armlets and bracelets, signet rings, earrings, and beads, to make atonement for ourselves before the Lord." [51]And Moses and Eleazar the priest received from them the gold, all wrought articles. [52]And all the gold of the offering that they offered to the Lord, from the commanders of thousands and the commanders of hundreds, was sixteen thousand seven hundred and fifty shekels. [53](The men of war had taken booty, every man for himself.) [54]And Moses and Eleazar the priest received the gold from the commanders of thousands and of hundreds, and brought it into the tent of meeting, as a memorial for the people of Israel before the Lord.

In this section Moses is given instructions about the sharing of the "booty" captured from the Midianites. It was a custom among the peoples of the ancient Near East to divide the spoils of war so that the non-combatants also shared in the glory and material benefits of victory. In this passage only one half of the spoils went to the "warriors", with the rest of the "congregation" (i.e. the women, the children, those unfit for military service, etc.) also receiving one half. Thereafter there was a levy on behalf of the priests and Levites. From the warriors was taken only one part in five hundred from their half, but from the people's half one part in fifty. The priests benefited from the combatants' tribute, while the Levites benefited from that of the non-combatants.

The Levites therefore received ten times the revenue of the priests, who must then have been many fewer in number. The figures are as follows:

Total Spoils	Warriors' Spoils	Priests' Spoils	Congregation's Spoils	Levites' Spoils
675,000 Sheep	337,500 Sheep	675 Sheep	337,500 Sheep	6,750 Sheep
72,000 Cattle	36,000 Cattle	72 Cattle	36,000 Cattle	720 Cattle
61,000 Assses	30,500 Asses	61 Asses	30,500 Asses	610 Asses
32,000 Virgins	16,000 Virgins	32 Virgins	16,000 Virgins	320 Virgins

The value of the gold and other precious items came to 16,750 shekels—a small fortune in worldly terms. What is not altogether clear is how this related to the total booty, since v. 53 is far from explicit in meaning. It can mean: (a) this booty was part of the total booty collected by the men and brought back to the camp, while on top of this there was their personal booty which the men did not have to hand over to the camp; (b) this booty was not normally part of the total booty of sheep, cattle, asses and virgins, split between warriors and congregation, but was nevertheless offered by the soldiers rather than be kept by them; or (c) only the officers gave what booty they claimed as an atonement for counting the heads of the men, whereas the men kept what they claimed. The second choice is probably the right one.

All of this costly offering of gold and jewellery was given to the Lord as a permanent reminder to his people Israel, "a memorial for the people of Israel before the Lord". It was a fine gesture, but the Christian can now see further. We know that the costliest offering of all, the life of Jesus, which was the winning of the victory over everything that is opposed to God and his people, was not given by us at all, but by God himself. This is what is meant by the term the "grace of God". Our offering, our sacrifice, is not meant to be one that will effect atonement, nor is it meant in any way to earn our salvation or sanctification. Rather our offering is made in grateful acceptance of God's acceptance of us—it is our worship of the Lord because we are already within the family of his victory. "I appeal to you therefore, brethren, by the mercies of God, to present your bodies as a living sacrifice, holy and acceptable to God, which is your spiritual worship" (Rom. 12:1).

There are not many spiritual lessons in this primitive chapter, but that at least is one.

C. THE PEOPLE OF ISRAEL AND THE TRIALS OF SETTLEMENT

GAD AND REUBEN: FRIEND OR FOE?

Numbers 32:1–32

¹Now the sons of Reuben and the sons of Gad had a very great multitude of cattle; and they saw the land of Jazer and the land of Gilead and behold, the place was a place for cattle. ²So the sons of Gad and the sons of Reuben came and said to Moses and to Eleazar the priest and to the leaders of the congregation, ³"Ataroth, Dibon, Jazer, Nimrah, Heshbon, Elealeh, Sebam, Nebo, and Beon, ⁴the land which the Lord smote before the congregation of Israel, is a land for cattle; and your servants have cattle." ⁵And they said, "If we have found favour in your sight, let this land be given to your servants for a possession; do not take us across the Jordan."

⁶But Moses said to the sons of Gad and to the sons of Reuben, "Shall your brethren go to the war while you sit here? ⁷Why will you discourage the heart of the people of Israel from going over into the land which the Lord has given them? ⁸Thus did your fathers, when I sent them from Kadesh-barnea to see the land. ⁹For when they went up to the Valley of Eshcol, and saw the land, they discouraged the heart of the people of Israel from going into the land which the Lord had given them. ¹⁰And the Lord's anger was kindled on that day, and he swore, saying, ¹¹'Surely none of the men who came up out of Egypt, from twenty years old and upward, shall see the land which I swore to give to Abraham, to Isaac, and to Jacob, because they have not wholly followed me; ¹²none except Caleb the son of Jephunneh the Kenizzite and Joshua the son of Nun, for they have wholly followed the Lord.' ¹³And the Lord's anger was kindled against Israel, and he made them wander in the wilderness forty years, until all the generation that had done evil in the sight of the Lord was consumed. ¹⁴And behold, you have risen in your fathers' stead, a brood of sinful men, to increase still more the fierce anger of the Lord against Israel! ¹⁵For if you turn away

from following him, he will again abandon them in the wilderness; and you will destroy all this people."

16Then they came near to him, and said, "We will build sheepfolds here for our flocks, and cities for our little ones, 17but we will take up arms, ready to go before the people of Israel, until we have brought them to their place; and our little ones shall live in the fortified cities because of the inhabitants of the land. 18We will not return to our homes until the people of Israel have inherited each his inheritance. 19For we will not inherit with them on the other side of the Jordan and beyond; because our inheritance has come to us on this side of the Jordan to the east." 20So Moses said to them, "If you will do this, if you will take up arms to go before the Lord for the war, 21and every armed man of you will pass over the Jordan before the Lord, until he has driven out his enemies from before him 22and the land is subdued before the Lord; then after that you shall return and be free of obligation to the Lord and to Israel; and this land shall be your possession before the Lord. 23But if you will not do so, behold, you have sinned against the Lord; and be sure your sin will find you out. 24Build cities for your little ones, and folds for your sheep; and do what you have promised." 25And the sons of Gad and the sons of Reuben said to Moses, "Your servants will do as my lord commands. 26Our little ones, our wives, our flocks, and all our cattle, shall remain there in the cities of Gilead; 27but your servants will pass over, every man who is armed for war, before the Lord to battle, as my lord orders."

28So Moses gave command concerning them to Eleazar the priest, and to Joshua the son of Nun, and to the heads of the fathers' houses of the tribes of the people of Israel. 29And Moses said to them, "If the sons of Gad and the sons of Reuben, every man who is armed to battle before the Lord, will pass with you over the Jordan and the land shall be subdued before you, then you shall give them the land of Gilead for a possession; 30but if they will not pass over with you armed, they shall have possessions among you in the land of Canaan." 31And the sons of Gad and the sons of Reuben answered, "As the Lord has said to your servants, so we will do. 32We will pass over armed before the Lord into the land of Canaan, and the possession of our inheritance shall remain with us beyond the Jordan."

The tribes, having come via the route forced upon them by their own disobedience and then by the opposition of certain neighbouring kingdoms, are now approaching Canaan from the general direction of the south east. They have established control of much of the territory east of the river Jordan. As they prepare to cross into Canaan some are obviously beginning to appreciate the advantages of staying where they are. So they ask to be allowed to forgo the satisfaction of occupying and settling in the land to the west of the river. However, Moses makes it clear that that would be to the disadvantage of the remaining tribes whose task would be made considerably more difficult without them. In the end a compromise is reached. The two tribes concerned (Reuben and Gad) pledge themselves to take part in the coming campaign, ensuring that the conquest is one of all Israel; only after that would they return to their favoured lands for settlement.

Note that the two tribes politely and deferentially come to Moses and the other leaders. It must have been a surprise to them when what they thought was a reasonable request was peremptorily turned down. Moses passionately implies that they are forsaking the blessing of the three great Patriarchs (strangely enough, this is the only mention in the whole book of them). He accuses them of being no whit better than the evil generation who had been condemned to the forty years' wandering. He calls them a "brood of sinful men", and although this term "brood" is only used here, the meaning is quite clear since the related verb is that used in the famous command in Genesis to mankind to "be fruitful and multiply". The idea is that the previous wicked generation has bred an equally wicked generation. It is a hard speech, but it works.

The leaders of the two tribes appreciate the point and agree to leave their families and livestock secure while they take full part in the campaign to take Canaan. We are reminded of Jesus' words to us that if we seek the true will of God and follow it, then all the things we need to live on earth will also be given to us by our Father who is the giver of all good gifts to his children (see Matt. 6:25–33; James 2:17; Luke 11:11–13).

CITIES REBUILT

Numbers 32:33–42

> ³³ And Moses gave to them, to the sons of Gad and to the sons of Reuben and to the half-tribe of Manasseh the son of Joseph, the kingdom of Sihon king of the Amorites and the kingdom of Og king of Bashan, the land and its cities with their territories, the cities of the land throughout the country. ³⁴ And the sons of Gad built Dibon, Ataroth, Aroer, ³⁵ Atroth-shophan, Jazer, Jogbehah, ³⁶ Beth-nimrah and Beth-haran, fortified cities, and folds for sheep. ³⁷ And the sons of Reuben built Heshbon, Elealeh, Kiriathaim, ³⁸ Nebo, and Baal-meon (their names to be changed), and Sibmah; and they gave other names to the cities which they built. ³⁹ And the sons of Machir the son of Manasseh went to Gilead and took it, and dispossessed the Amorites who were in it. ⁴⁰ And Moses gave Gilead to Machir the son of Manasseh, and he settled in it. ⁴¹ And Jair the son of Manasseh went and took their villages, and called them Havvoth-jair. ⁴² And Nobah went and took Kenath and its villages, and called it Nobah, after his own name.

This small section gives some notes about the eventual settlement of Transjordan by Gad and Reuben and (not mentioned earlier in the chapter) Machir, a subdivision of Manasseh.

Scholars are divided over which of three terms to use for Israel moving in to live in Canaan, the land promised her. These are *settlement, conquest*, and *occupation*.

The period of the *settlement* of the tribes was really one of constant guerrilla warfare, campaigns to take and occupy settlements, and efforts to defend these settlements. The first impression of the texts, especially in Josh. 1–12, however, is that the correct term to use is *conquest* and that it was a single strategic and military operation of all Israel under Joshua. But a closer look, especially when we compare the early chapters of Judges, shows that it was far from that, and far from easy. There was probably a long drawn-out series of gradually stepped-up campaigns moving from the non-urban to the urban areas, sometimes by one tribe, sometimes by a few acting in concert. When this *occupation* was complete, if never totally secure, there was an entity called Israel, people and land under God. It is not surprising that when a united Israel looked back on that period to record it, as here in Numbers, instead of speaking about this tribe or that group doing something, they spoke (with theological insight if not historical precision) of *Israel* doing it, and doing it quickly.

There is a small hint of the true course of events in v. 34, although it is obscured by the RSV translation. This says the Gadites "built" several cities. A better translation would be "rebuilt". These cities were there long before Israel came along and fought over them. See 1 Kings 16:34, where Jericho is *built* in Ahab's time when *rebuilt* is the obvious meaning.

It is the same verb that is used in many Old Testament passages describing the last days, when the Messiah shall come. The Lord promises to Israel that: "your ancient ruins shall be rebuilt". Those who are then disheartened in Israel "shall build up the ancient ruins . . . repair the ruined cities." The Lord will vindicate Israel: "I will restore the fortunes of my people Israel, and they shall rebuild the ruined cities and inhabit them." And this will be done so that all the other nations "shall know that I, the Lord, have rebuilt the ruined places" (Isa. 58:12; 61:4; Amos 9:14; Ezek. 36:36). For the Lord, building and rebuilding, planting and re-planting, healing and re-healing, are all part of the one process of bringing his creation to fulfilment. We can rest in the knowledge of that and give thanks for the hand of God in all events involving us and around us. Jesus has come and taken our ruined lives over. He has begun the rebuilding of our lives, and can be trusted to present us whole to his and our Father. May his "occupation" of us be soon complete!

RÉSUMÉ OF THE PILGRIMAGE

Numbers 33:1–49

[1]These are the stages of the people of Israel, when they went forth out of the land of Egypt by their hosts under the leadership of Moses and Aaron. [2]Moses wrote down their starting places, stage by stage, by command of the Lord; and these are their stages according to their starting places. [3]They set out from Rameses in the first month, on the

fifteenth day of the first month; on the day after the passover the people of Israel went out triumphantly in the sight of all the Egyptians, ⁴while the Egyptians were burying all their first-born, whom the Lord had struck down among them; upon their gods also the Lord executed judgments.

⁵So the people of Israel set out from Rameses, and encamped at Succoth. ⁶And they set out from Succoth, and encamped at Etham, which is on the edge of the wilderness. ⁷And they set out from Etham, and turned back to Pi-ha-hiroth, which is east of Baal-zephon; and they encamped before Migdol. ⁸And they set out from before Hahiroth, and passed through the midst of the sea into the wilderness, and they went a three days' journey in the wilderness of Etham, and encamped at Marah. ⁹And they set out from Marah, and came to Elim; at Elim there were twelve springs of water and seventy palm trees, and they encamped there. ¹⁰And they set out from Elim, and encamped by the Red Sea. ¹¹And they set out from the Red Sea, and encamped in the wilderness of Sin. ¹²And they set out from the wilderness of Sin, and encamped at Dophkah. ¹³And they set out from Dophkah, and encamped at Alush. ¹⁴And they set out from Alush, and encamped at Rephidim, where there was no water for the people to drink. ¹⁵And they set out from Rephidim, and encamped in the wilderness of Sinai. ¹⁶And they set out from the wilderness of Sinai, and encamped at Kibroth-hattaavah. ¹⁷And they set out from Kibroth-hattaavah, and encamped at Hazeroth. ¹⁸And they set out from Hazeroth, and encamped at Rithmah. ¹⁹And they set out from Rithmah, and encamped at Rimmon-perez. ²⁰And they set out from Rimmon-perez, and encamped at Libnah. ²¹And they set out from Libnah, and encamped at Rissah. ²²And they set out from Rissah, and encamped at Kehelathah. ²³And they set out from Kehelathah, and encamped at Mount Shepher. ²⁴And they set out from Mount Shepher, and encamped at Haradah. ²⁵And they set out from Haradah, and encamped at Makheloth. ²⁶And they set out from Makheloth, and encamped at Tahath. ²⁷And they set out from Tahath, and encamped at Terah. ²⁸And they set out from Terah, and encamped at Mithkah. ²⁹And they set out from Mithkah, and encamped at Hashmonah. ³⁰And they set out from Hashmonah, and encamped at Moseroth. ³¹And they set out from Moseroth, and encamped at Bene-jaakan. ³²And they set out from Bene-jaakan, and encamped at Hor-haggidgad. ³³And they set out from Hor-haggidgad, and encamped at Jotbathah. ³⁴And they set out from Jotbathah, and encamped at Abronah. ³⁵And they set out

from Abronah, and encamped at Ezion-geber. [36]And they set out from Ezion-geber, and encamped in the wilderness of Zin (that is, Kadesh). [37]And they set out from Kadesh, and encamped at Mount Hor, on the edge of the land of Edom.

[38]And Aaron the priest went up Mount Hor at the command of the Lord, and died there, in the fortieth year after the people of Israel had come out of the land of Egypt, on the first day of the fifth month. [39]And Aaron was a hundred and twenty-three years old when he died on Mount Hor.

[40]And the Canaanite, the king of Arad, who dwelt in the Negeb in the land of Canaan, heard of the coming of the people of Israel.

[41]And they set out from Mount Hor, and encamped at Zalmonah. [42]And they set out from Zalmonah, and encamped at Punon. [43]And they set out from Punon, and encamped at Oboth. [41]And they set out from Oboth, and encamped at Iye-abarim, in the territory of Moab. [45]And they set out from Iyim, and encamped at Dibon-gad. [46]And they set out from Dibon-gad, and encamped at Almon-diblathaim. [47]And they set out from Almon-diblathaim, and encamped in the mountains of Abarim, before Nebo. [48]And they set out from the mountains of Abarim, and encamped in the plains of Moab by the Jordan at Jericho; [49]they encamped by the Jordan from Beth-jeshimoth as far as Abel-shittim in the plains of Moab.

In this section we find a description of the route taken by Moses and the people from the place of their misery and bondage in Egypt to the very edge of their land of promise and plenty across the river Jordan. It records the various stop-over sites in their pilgrimage; unfortunately very few except at the beginning and end of the list can now be located with any certainty. When it comes to the time of the year when this portion of the Torah is read aloud in the synagogues, it is welcomed with great excitement and joy. Israel loves to recount the pilgrimage from oppression to liberty, from hopelessness to promise. Israel has always loved to remember and remind herself and others that the Lord has been good to her in all his dealings with her, even in spite of her response to him.

Perhaps the most wonderful example of this is to be found in Ps. 106, which is composed exactly around this theme. The Psalmist longs that he too "may see the prosperity of thy chosen ones . . . may glory with thy heritage" (v. 5). Then he goes over the record of Israel's life with the Lord, not forgetting either their infidelity or his faithfulness. This recounting includes Israel's "wanton craving in the wilderness", the death of Dathan and Abiram, the fearful report of the scouts, the apostasy to the Baal of Peor, the episode of Phinehas, all recorded in the book of Numbers. The grace of the Lord is affirmed at the close, with the whole congregation encouraged to say "Amen! Praise the Lord!"

Here in 33:1–49 we have a more prosaic summary. Yet we can imagine the atmosphere of expectation mounting as the various "stages" of the journey are recounted. This child-like enthusiasm is encouraged by the use of the literary device of naming each stage twice—once as the people reach it and once as they leave. The term "stages" is literally "pluckings up", i.e. it refers to the striking of camp, ready for the next journey. Forty-two are mentioned, including the first at Rameses in Egypt. The number seems to reflect a special criterion of selection, although we no longer know it, since in Matt. 1:17 the generations from Abraham to Christ are also said to be forty-two. Is Matthew implying that through these generations from Abraham to Jesus we see a real movement, or pilgrimage, to liberty and peace and plenty?

Coming to v. 9 we find one of the favourite texts to this day among religious Jews. "Elim" is the great place of refreshment, and the "twelve springs of water and seventy palm trees" are allegorized to represent the twelve tribes of Israel and the seventy elders in the Sanhedrin of post-Exilic times, who were the supreme spiritual and legal court for the Jewish people.

The people of Israel are now ready to move into the Promised Land. All of this is by the grace of God. So in a sense this section forms a type of testimony for Israel. Anyone who can say that the Lord has done something for him or her has a testimony to give. Israel clearly thought she had. Do we?

> Bless the Lord, O my soul; and all that is within me, bless his holy name!
> Bless the Lord, O my soul, and forget not all his benefits.
>
> (Ps. 103:1–2)

THE PILGRIMS' TASK

Numbers 33:50–56

[50] And the Lord said to Moses in the plains of Moab by the Jordan at Jericho, [51]"Say to the people of Israel, When you pass over the Jordan into the land of Canaan, [52]then you shall drive out all the inhabitants of the land from before you, and destroy all their figured stones, and destroy all their molten images, and demolish all their high places; [53]and you shall take possession of the land and settle in it, for I have given the land to you to possess it. [54]You shall inherit the land by lot according to your families; to a large tribe you shall give a large inheritance, and to a small tribe you shall give a small inheritance; wherever the lot falls to any man, that shall be his; according to the tribes of your fathers you shall inherit. [55]But if you do not drive out the inhabitants of the land from before you, then those of them whom you let remain shall be as pricks in your eyes and thorns in your sides, and they shall trouble you in the land where you dwell. [56]And I will do to you as I thought to do to them."

(i)

Moses tells the people that failure to carry out the will of God will not mean that Israel will be unable to settle in the land, but it will mean that they will be unable to have a peaceful and relaxed life there. But more of this later. These words were spoken while the people were still east of the river Jordan.

The task ahead is narrowed down to a command to "drive out" the existing inhabitants of Canaan. This is not presented, however, as an arbitrary whim of God. The rationale is added that the Canaanites and their religious faith and practices are such that their continued presence in the land will be dangerous for Israel's faith and life. Such a command seems to us ruthless, and there is doubtless much of selfish and proud Israel mixed up in it. But in a real sense it also comes from the very heart of a God who is holy and jealous for his people's love and loyalty. Because of this holiness he can tolerate neither perversion of his faith nor desertion to other gods and cults.

We find this in the Ten Commandments, heading everything else: "I am the Lord your God . . . You shall have no other gods before me . . . You shall not make for yourself a graven image...for I the Lord your God am a jealous God" (Exod. 20:3–6). The command to drive the Canaanites out is given for the first time shortly after this, "lest they make you sin against me" (Exod. 23:23–33), and is repeated not only in Numbers but in Deuteronomy (e.g. 7:1–6; 12:29ff.).

The "figured" (i.e. inscribed) "stones" and "molten images" of the inhabitants were to be destroyed along with their "high places". These were cultic sites for sacrifice and related rituals, set on raised ground for identification and vantage point. Thereafter, when their creators had been expelled, Israel was to settle and grow uninhibitedly. As v. 53 makes quite clear, the land belonged to the Lord, and it was his sovereign right to use it as he willed. And his intention was that it would be given to his people Israel as a "possession". The land was to be distributed to the "families" in each "tribe" in the way laid down already in 26:53–56, i.e. "by lot", but taking into account the relative numbers involved.

If the Israelites did not carry out this command, then the Canaanites left remaining in the land would be a constant threat to Israel's peace with the Lord (compare the even harsher words of Josh. 23:11ff.). The threat of v. 56 was later applied to the Exile in Babylonia when Israel was in her turn removed from the land.

(ii)

These are not pretty verses. But there are three positive points well worth making, even if we have to spiritualize a little:

(a) *Dangers of assimilation.* The warning is clearly given that to try to take the things of the world into our Christian lives is to court disaster. Rather we must drive out all that identifies us with the world and begin again with Christ so as to be easily identified with him by the world. Our business practices, philosophies, family care, worship, must be transformed altogether. As John writes: "If anyone loves the world, love for the Father is not in him" (1 John 2:15). God loves the world, yes, and we are to have his kind of love, i.e. not a seeking to participate but a seeking to redeem and transform, a more Christian rooting out of evil. In the words of the modern spiritual: "Don't let the devil ride; 'cause if you do he'll want to drive."

(b) *Image and likeness*—Gen. 1:26. We—you and I and everyone, whether believer or not—are created in the image of God. There are to be no images of other gods, and none either of the Lord; there is no need for them, since the Lord is the only God, and he is real enough in the here and now not to need substitutes nor mediators. People are his images, or rather, should be, if they follow the one man who succeeded in being the very image of the Living God (Col. 1:15). Jesus came as a human being, as the fulfilment therefore of all that is human and at the same time the one in whom we see God. For us living in the world, the best place to see the Lord is in each other, and the best way to love God is by loving him in each other.

(c) *Grace in spite of disobedience.* It is a supreme encouragement to know that even failure to do God's will does not mean that we are removed for ever from rest in him. We can still remain in the Lord though we may not yet experience the fulness of the joy of total surrender to him. He can allow for our disobedience and still create order out of our chaos, beauty out of our ugliness, hope out of our despair. And he will.

ISRAEL'S BOUNDARIES

Numbers 34:1–29

[1]The Lord said to Moses, [2]"Command the people of Israel, and say to them, When you enter the land of Canaan (this is the land that shall fall to you for an inheritance, the land of Canaan in its full extent), [3]your south side shall be from the wilderness of Zin along the side of Edom, and your southern boundary shall be from the end of the Salt Sea on the east; [4]and your boundary shall turn south of the ascent of Akrabbim, and cross to Zin, and its end shall be south of Kadesh-barnea; then it shall go on to Hazar-addar, and pass along to Azmon; [5]and the boundary shall turn from Azmon to the Brook of Egypt, and its termination shall be at the sea.

⁶"For the western boundary, you shall have the Great Sea and its coast; this shall be your western boundary.

⁷"This shall be your northern boundary: from the Great Sea you shall mark out your line to Mount Hor; ⁸from Mount Hor you shall mark it out to the entrance of Hamath, and the end of the boundary shall be at Zedad; ⁹then the boundary shall extend to Ziphron, and its end shall be at Hazar-enan; this shall be your northern boundary.

¹⁰"You shall mark out your eastern boundary from Hazar-enan to Shepham; ¹¹and the boundary shall go down from Shepham to Riblah on the east side of Ain; and the boundary shall go down, and reach to the shoulder of the sea of Chinnereth on the east; ¹²and the boundary shall go down to the Jordan, and its end shall be at the Salt Sea. This shall be your land with its boundaries all round."

¹³Moses commanded the people of Israel, saying, "This is the land which you shall inherit by lot, which the Lord has commanded to give to the nine tribes and to the half-tribe; ¹⁴for the tribe of the sons of Reuben by fathers' houses and the tribe of the sons of Gad by their fathers' houses have received their inheritance, and also the half-tribe of Manasseh; ¹⁵the two tribes and the half-tribe have received their inheritance beyond the Jordan at Jericho eastward, toward the sunrise."

¹⁶The Lord said to Moses, ¹⁷"These are the names of the men who shall divide the land to you for inheritance: Eleazar the priest and Joshua the son of Nun. ¹⁸You shall take one leader of every tribe, to divide the land for inheritance. ¹⁹These are the names of the men: Of the tribe of Judah, Caleb the son of Jephunneh. ²⁰Of the tribe of the sons of Simeon, Shemuel the son of Ammihud. ²¹Of the tribe of Benjamin, Elidad the son of Chislon. ²²Of the tribe of the sons of Dan a leader, Bukki the son of Jogli. ²³Of the sons of Joseph: of the tribe of the sons of Manasseh a leader, Hanniel the son of Ephod. ²⁴And of the tribe of the sons of Ephraim a leader, Kemuel the son of Shiphtan. ²⁵Of the tribe of the sons of Zebulun a leader, Elizaphan the son of Parnach. ²⁶Of the tribe of the sons of Issachar a leader, Paltiel the son of Azzan. ²⁷And of the tribe of the sons of Asher a leader, Ahihud the son of Shelomi. ²⁸Of the tribe of the sons of Naphtali a leader, Pedahel the son of Ammihud. ²⁹These are the men whom the Lord commanded to divide the inheritance for the people of Israel in the land of Canaan."

This chapter lays down the ideal boundaries of the Holy Land.

Like the passages Gen. 15:18ff. and Exod. 23:31, it presents what might be called the providential boundaries of Israel's territories and only briefly did Israel ever actually exercise control over all this area, even although she claimed sovereignty over it.

All of this was to be for only nine and a half tribes since Gad, Reuben and the part of the half tribe of Manasseh were going to settle to the east of the river Jordan (see section 32:1–33), and accordingly, ten representatives were chosen, one per tribe, to supervise the allotment of territory. The other part of Manasseh is included in the list, since its territory straddled the Jordan in later times. Levi is omitted, since there are to be special provisions for this priestly tribe (see ch. 35). All this was done under the authority of Eleazar, the High Priest, and Joshua, Moses' successor and commander-in-chief elect. None of the leaders named in the early census is to be found here, and only Caleb and Joshua's names remain from those of the twelve scouts sent out by Moses.

The ten leaders, apart from Caleb, are unknown. But the meanings of their names are strong and clear: "Shemuel", *Name of God*; "Elidad", *My God loves*; "Bukki", *Proved*; "Hanniel", *Grace of God*; "Kemuel", *Raised by God*; "Elizaphan", *My God protects*; "Paltiel", *God is my deliverance*; "Ahihud", *My Brother is majestic*; "Pedahel", *God delivers*. They reflect the sense of security the Israelites had in the Lord and in the fact that they were his army in the occupation of Canaan.

God has many gifts he wants to give each of us, and he has a plan for each of our lives. In a sense, all of us and each of us are being called to take part in occupying the land of promise given to us, in whatever area of life it is found. Yet so few of us actually reach out to the boundaries graciously allowed by the Lord; so few of us really claim his Lordship over *all* of our lives and then work hard at controlling all those areas under the Lord's sovereignty, by the grace of God. Our prayer must be that the Lord will really become Lord of each dimension of our lives, so that the boundaries are as much his as the central areas.

REFUGE CITIES

Numbers 35:1-34

[1]The Lord said to Moses in the plains of Moab by the Jordan at Jericho, [2]"Command the people of Israel, that they give to the Levites, from the inheritance of their possession, cities to dwell in; and you shall give to the Levites pasture lands round about the cities. [3]The cities shall be theirs to dwell in, and their pasture lands shall be for their cattle and for their livestock and for all their beasts. [4]The pasture lands of the cities, which you shall give to the Levites, shall reach from the wall of the city outward a thousand cubits all round. [5]And you shall measure, outside the city, for the east side two thousand cubits, and for the south side two thousand cubits, and for the west side two thousand cubits, and for the north side two thousand cubits, the city being in the middle; this shall belong to them as pasture land for their cities. [6]The cities which you give to the Levites shall be the six cities of refuge, where you shall permit the manslayer to flee, and in addition to them you shall give forty-two cities. [7]All the cities which you give to the Levites shall be forty-eight, with their pasture lands. [8]And as for the cities which you shall give from the possession of the people of Israel, from the larger tribes you shall take many, and from the smaller tribes you shall take few; each, in proportion to the inheritance which it inherits, shall give of its cities to the Levites."

[9]And the Lord said to Moses, [10]"Say to the people of Israel, When you cross the Jordan into the land of Canaan, [11]then you shall select cities to be cities of refuge for you, that the manslayer who kills any person without intent may flee there. [12]The cities shall be for you a refuge from the avenger, that the manslayer may not die until he stands before the congregation for judgement. [13]And the cities which you give shall be your six cities of refuge. [14]You shall give three cities beyond the Jordan, and three cities in the land of Canaan, to be cities of refuge. [15]These six cities shall be for refuge for the people of Israel, and for the stranger and for the sojourner among them, that any one who kills any person without intent may flee there.

[16]"But if he struck him down with an instrument of iron, so that he died, he is a murderer; the murderer shall be put to death. [17]And if he struck him down with a stone in the hand, by which a man may die, and he died, he is a murderer; the murderer shall be put to death. [18]Or if he struck him down with a weapon of wood in the hand, by which a man

may die, and he died, he is a murderer; the murderer shall be put to death. [19]The avenger of blood shall himself put the murderer to death; when he meets him, he shall put him to death. [20]And if he stabbed him from hatred, or hurled at him, lying in wait, so that he died, [21]or in enmity struck him down with his hand, so that he died, then he who struck the blow shall be put to death; he is a murderer; the avenger of blood shall put the murderer to death, when he meets him.

[22]"But if he stabbed him suddenly without enmity, or hurled anything on him without lying in wait, [23]or used a stone, by which a man may die, and without seeing him cast it upon him, so that he died, though he was not his enemy, and did not seek his harm; [24]then the congregation shall judge between the manslayer and the avenger of blood, in accordance with these ordinances; [25]and the congregation shall rescue the manslayer from the hand of the avenger of blood, and the congregation shall restore him to his city of refuge, to which he had fled, and he shall live in it until the death of the high priest who was anointed with the holy oil. [26]But if the manslayer shall at any time go beyond the bounds of his city of refuge to which he fled, [27]and the avenger of blood finds him outside the bounds of his city of refuge, and the avenger of blood slays the manslayer, he shall not be guilty of blood. [28]For the man must remain in his city of refuge until the death of the high priest; but after the death of the high priest the manslayer may return to the land of his possession.

[29]"And these things shall be for a statute and ordinance to you throughout your generations in all your dwellings. [30]If any one kills a person, the murderer shall be put to death on the evidence of witnesses; but no person shall be put to death on the testimony of one witness. [31]Moreover you shall accept no ransom for the life of a murderer, who is guilty of death; but he shall be put to death. [32]And you shall accept no ransom for him who has fled to his city of refuge, that he may return to dwell in the land before the death of the high priest. [33]You shall not thus pollute the land in which you live; for blood pollutes the land, and no expiation can be made for the land, for the blood that is shed in it, except by the blood of him who shed it. [34]You shall not defile the land in which you live, in the midst of which I dwell; for I the Lord dwell in the midst of the people of Israel."

(i)

Two separate strands have been woven together into this chapter by the editors of the book. The first is the subject of vv. 1–8: each

of the secular tribes, according to its territory, and therefore its
wealth (v. 8), is to apportion cities (towns might be more accurate) and land to the Levites who were not included in the land
allocations (ch. 34) as a tribe. In all, forty-eight cities (v. 7) and
surrounding pasture land are to be assigned to the Levites. The
idea was that this tribe, especially consecrated to the Lord's
service, would by its distribution among the tribes be able to serve
them and the Lord's sanctuaries, and also be maintained as a
tribe, with its own sense of cohesion and integrity, by the fact that
communities of them lived together in these cities. The Rabbinic
traditions say that the practice of "Levitical cities" only stopped
with the destruction of Solomon's Temple. According to Josh. 21
there were thirteen given to the Aaronic priests, and thirty-five
given to the Levitical priests as "cities to dwell in".

We are still expected to give from our plenty to those who serve
God full-time in his ministry. We must insist that our churches
actively and sacrificially give to what is referred to as the maintenance of the ministry, whether at home or in missions abroad. Any
church which spends only on itself will struggle for ever.

(ii)

The second strand in the chapter is the establishing of six "cities
of refuge" as places for the protection under law of those who
were responsible in some way for the death of another person.
The point of contact between the two strands is to be found in v. 6
where it is stated that six of the forty-eight cities to be given to the
Levites are in fact those six refuge cities. They are not named
here, but Josh. 20:7–8 gives them as Kedesh, Shechem,
Kiriatharba, Bezer, Ramoth and Golan.

The point to note about these cities (v. 11) is that they were
specifically for the guaranteed legal protection of those who kill
"without intent" (compare 15:24). This was a reform of the
highest order: (a) *only the killer with intent may be killed* and the
family feuds characteristic of tribal society are not entertained;
(b) *monetary substitutions for life are forbidden*. In short, it was a
milestone in the search for adequate and sufficient justice, recog-
nizing and affirming the difference between manslaughter and

culpable homicide, or between premeditated and unpremeditated murder. The older law is reflected in Gen. 9:6 where motive is not taken into account in determining the avenger's right to revenge.

The assumption is that the "avenger of blood" has the full right and authority to seek revenge and carry it out if possible. The term here is the word used for the Lord as "Redeemer" (see commentary on 5:5–10). But ideally he was a restorer of balance rather than a vengeance hunter in any barbaric sense. The balance sought by such a "redeemer" could take the form of marrying a brother's widow to give "him" sons (Ruth 3:13), or of buying a relative back from slavery (Lev. 25:48), but there was always the right to take life for life (as here).

In this chapter it is laid down that anyone who has killed another without malice or forethought may seek asylum in one of these six cities to await protection from the "avenger of blood" until objective judgement is given. A trial is to be arranged "before the congregation" to establish the presence or absence of an intent to kill. If he is judged innocent of malice then he may stay safely *in the city*. The elders who decide the matter are presumably those of the city to which the killer fled, rather than those of his home community. This law of guaranteed justice protected the innocent and yet took seriously the fact of killing by limiting the freedom of the killer to that particular city.

So to the important last two verses (compare 5:1–4). The Lord is in his own mystical and detectable way present in the land, and therefore it must be kept holy. Yet blood "pollutes" the land and it must therefore be de-polluted, an act only possible by an "expiation" made by the killer. But how much more wonderful for the world to know now that the Lord really is present with us through the incarnation of his Son as Jesus of Nazareth, and by the ministry of the Holy Spirit making him alive in his followers! And more—that expiation for all humanity's crimes was totally and freely made through the innocent blood of such a "Redeemer"!

HEIRESSES AND MARRIAGE

Numbers 36:1–13

[1]The heads of the fathers' houses of the families of the sons of Gilead the son of Machir, son of Manasseh, of the fathers' houses of the sons of Joseph, came near and spoke before Moses and before the leaders, the heads of the fathers' houses of the people of Israel; [2]they said, "The Lord commanded my lord to give the land for inheritance by lot to the people of Israel; and my lord was commanded by the Lord to give the inheritance of Zelophehad our brother to his daughters. [3]But if they are married to any of the sons of the other tribes of the people of Israel then their inheritance will be taken from the inheritance of our fathers, and added to the inheritance of the tribe to which they belong; so it will be taken away from the lot of our inheritance. [4]And when the jubilee of the people of Israel comes, then their inheritance will be added to the inheritance of the tribe to which they belong; and their inheritance will be taken from the inheritance of the tribe of our fathers."

[5]And Moses commanded the people of Israel according to the word of the Lord, saying, "The tribe of the sons of Joseph is right. [6]This is what the Lord commands concerning the daughters of Zelophehad, 'Let them marry whom they think best; only, they shall marry within the family of the tribe of their father. [7]The inheritance of the people of Israel shall not be transferred from one tribe to another; for every one of the people of Israel shall cleave to the inheritance of the tribe of his fathers. [8]And every daughter who possesses an inheritance in any tribe of the people of Israel shall be wife to one of the family of the tribe of her father, so that every one of the people of Israel may possess the inheritance of his fathers. [9]So no inheritance shall be transferred from one tribe to another; for each of the tribes of the people of Israel shall cleave to its own inheritance.'"

[10]The daughters of Zelophehad did as the Lord commanded Moses; [11]for Mahlah, Tirzah, Hoglah, Milcah, and Noah, the daughters of Zelophehad, were married to sons of their father's brothers. [12]They were married into the families of the sons of Manasseh the son of Joseph, and their inheritance remained in the tribe of the family of their father.

[13]These are the commandments and the ordinances which the Lord commanded by Moses to the people of Israel in the plains of Moab by the Jordan at Jericho.

(i)

In 27:1–11 a direction was given to allow daughters to inherit their fathers' property if no male heir was produced, in order to keep the property in the tribe. The very same daughters who requested that decision appear again in this final chapter with an additional problem. If they married men of other tribes, they would be obeying the law at the cost of this property staying within their tribes, since it would pass into the tribes of their husbands. Any male children born to them would also be identified with their fathers' tribes, not their mothers'.

In the opening verses we see again the way people brought issues to Moses as they arose, so that he could seek the Lord's will. It is worth emphasizing again that the Lord did not give a package-deal of directions before the people set out from Sinai. Rather, he gave the core of his teaching and, as the pilgrimage progressed, he gave more and more in answer to the needs of the moment. It is exactly the same in our pilgrimage through life. God will not give us everything at the start. We have our core in the Bible and in our spiritual fellowship with God and his Church, but the making it our own, the real learning of discipleship, the genuine process of becoming like Jesus, is and must be a growth process. As we daily turn to God for the day's grace and insight he will give to us what direction we need.

There is a difficulty of interpretation in this section, in v. 4. According to Lev. 25 the cycle of "seven weeks of years" was to be marked as a "jubilee", a time to: (a) *rejoice* in God's faithfulness in the past; (b) *rest* in God's blessings in the present; and (c) *be released* for God's call in the future. At this time, property that had been sold was to be returned to its original owner, so that man and land, family and land, were reunited under God. However, *inherited* land, such as in the case here, was outside the scope of this festal time. It has puzzled commentators that v. 4 should be here at all since it does seem to be "an irrelevant addition" (Noth). It would be better to translate: "And when the jubilee . . . comes, *even* then their inheritance will still be added". The point is that there will be no way, not even under the wonderful jubilee system, to reclaim such property lost through marriage. So a particular judgement was made, which then became the general law, that daughters who inherited property should marry within the tribe of their father. This was not normally favoured since the relationships were too close, but in this case was enjoined so that the tribe might keep its land.

(ii)

So, with a problem about the beloved land of promise before our eyes, the book of Numbers comes to an end. The people have been brought from Mount Sinai to "the plains of Moab by the Jordan at Jericho". A long and vital stage in Israel's pilgrimage with God is closed. What will happen next?

We can be sure of two things, which more than most have been stressed throughout the book: (a) *The Lord will still have the initiative*; and (b) *The Lord will work his purpose out in the here and now*.

For us today, the message is clear and strong. The end of this book is only the end of one stage in Israel's pilgrimage. Indeed, it is from another view only a beginning—the prologue to moving in to take possession of the Promised Land. We too are all at various stages in our pilgrimages, and most of us still have not really moved in to take possession of the wonderful promises given to us by our Father through Jesus. But God still has the initiative in our lives, and if we will only let him lead us, let him work out his purposes in our *here and now*, a great future stretches ahead of us.

ADDITIONAL NOTES

1. This is not the place to go into theories about how the Old Testament and in particular the first five books, the Pentateuch, reached their present form. A tradition arose early that Moses wrote it all down. But the Pentateuch itself never claims Moses or any single person as its author. There are a few passages claiming Mosaic authorship for this or that part, e.g. Num. 33:2, but that is all. And not a few passages seem to presuppose a time much later than Moses'. Most obviously there is Deut. 34:5–10, "So Moses . . . *died* there": but there are also many places (we point out some of them in the commentary) where what is said seems to relate to events or practices that happened or developed long after Israel had settled in Canaan.

   The use in various contexts of distinctive phrases, names and interests, has led scholars to argue that behind the Pentateuch lie many more than a single mind and hand. The story of their detective work in isolating and analyzing such sources is an involved but fascinating one; and the reader is encouraged to read the accounts in any of the standard introductions to the Old Testament. Of course, some scholars have gone too far in searching for minutiae; some wrongly look for evidence of exact dates; some are even sceptical and deny supernatural inspiration or direction to the Bible. We do not need to follow their example. On the other hand, we would be foolish to ignore the broad results of their researches. We even have hints in the Biblical text itself of some of these earlier sources, e.g. Num. 21:14ff., 27ff. A similar testimony can be found in Luke 1:1–4 about sources for Jesus of Nazareth's life which were used by the writers of our Gospels.

   Many different groups or schools of thought were probably active in keeping Israel's memories alive, preserving her records, interpreting and reinterpreting events. It is surely possible to think of these groups as just as inspired as any single author. One such school of thought was particularly concerned with priestly matters and records, with genealogies and liturgies, with the holiness and transcendence of God. The bulk of the book of Numbers seems to have come from such a group, though other interests and emphases can also sometimes be detected.

   We have to think, therefore, of the book of Numbers as coming gradually into being, having its rise in the era of Moses but reflecting

God's continuing revelation to his people over many generations following the specific events it records.

2. On the Day of Atonement all of Israel's worship was climaxed: (a) The High Priest was divinely anointed and appointed, and represented all Israel; (b) he consecrated himself to act for all Israel; (c) he took the sacrificial animal, confessed the sins of Israel and slew the animal; (d) he ascended to the Holy of Holies to intercede for Israel; (e) he returned, raising his hands in the blessing of peace.

In Jesus we see this fulfilled: (a) he was divinely anointed and appointed, and represented all Israel and all the world (John 1:29, 34); (b) he consecrated himself (John 17); (c) he offered himself as the sacrifice (John 18–19); (d) he ascended to the very presence of the Father (John 20:1–18); (e) he returned with the blessing, "Peace be with you" (John 20:19–29).

3. "Spirit" in the Bible is a terribly powerful and dynamic thing, revealing in itself the character of God's spirit. God is reminding us in these days, as he pours out his Spirit on the Church, that we must not try to domesticate him. He is neither passive nor timid. Is it not strange that almost every time hymns are sung by believers and there is a verse calling on the Holy Spirit, they drop their voices and hold back as if there were undertones of ghosts? We should sing such verses as Charles Wesley's powerfully and passionately:

> Come, Holy Ghost, our hearts inspire;
> Let us Thine influence prove,
> Source of the old prophetic fire,
> Fountain of life and love.

4. In the Old Testament we find references to: (a) burnt offering; (b) whole burnt offering; (c) cereal offering; (d) drink offering; (e) peace offering; (f) thank offering; (g) votive offering; (h) free-will offering; (i) sin offering; (j) guilt offering; (k) fire offering; (l) heave offering; (m) wave offering; (n) memorial portion.

5. The Old Testament word for an "angel" means basically "a messenger" or "one sent". The most important occurrences for study are as follows: Gen. 16:7–14; 18:1–22; 19; 21:17–19; 22:9–18; 31:11–13; 32:24–30; 48:15–16; Exod. 3:2–6; 14:19–22; Josh. 5:13–15; Judg. 2:1–5; 6:11–14; 13:2–23; Zech. 1–8 *passim*. In all of these there is a great fluidity of movement between the angels talking as if messengers

and talking as if God himself; the very pronouns move from person to person, or from singular to plural. This is not the place to examine the matter in detail. Suffice it to say that in a real sense the Lord was "in" the angel. A person's character and personality were held to be in their *name*, as we have seen early in this commentary, and one of the most poignant passages in the Old Testament is Exod. 23:20f. where the Lord says of his angel that "My name is in him".

6. Compare "the Book of Jashar" (Josh. 10:13; 2 Sam. 1:18); "the book of the law" (2 Kings 22:8); "the book of the covenant" (Exod. 24:7); "the Book of the Chronicles of the Kings of Israel" (1 Kings 14:19); "the Book of the Chronicles of the Kings of Judah" (1 Kings 14:29); "the Book of the Chronicles" (Neh. 12:23); "the Book of the Kings of Israel and Judah" (2 Chron. 27:7); "the Book of the Kings of Israel" (1 Chron. 9:1); "the Book of the Kings of Judah and Israel" (2 Chron. 16:11); "the Commentary on the Book of the Kings" (2 Chron. 24:27); "the book of the acts of Solomon" (1 Kings 11:41); "the book of the law of God" (Josh. 24:26); general references to "a book" or "this book" (Josh. 18:9; 1 Sam. 10:25; Isa. 30:8; Jer. 25:13); "a book of remembrance (Mal. 3:16); see also Isa. 4:3; Dan. 12:1. The New Testament carries on this idea of a metaphorical "book" of life with the saints' names inscribed therein Phil. 4:3; Rev. 3:5, etc.

7. There are three Jewish Aramaic versions of the Old Testament, and they read as follows for 24:17–24; also given are the Greek Septuagint readings, and finally a single reading from the Latin Vulgate:

Version	*Present Text*	*Version's Text*
Targum Onkelos:	v. 17 star	king
	and a sceptre shall rise	anointed the Messiah
	v. 20 the first of the nations	the first to wage war against Israel
	v. 24 Kittim	Romans

(The Messiah is seen in this version as a military figure who will destroy the power of Rome, and is probably based on a great figure like Bar Kochba.)

Version	Present Text	Version's Text
Targum Pseudo-Jonathan:	v. 17 star	mighty king
	and a sceptre shall rise	shall be anointed Messiah
	v. 19 cities	Constantinople and Caesarea
	v. 20 the first of the nations	the first to wage war against Israel
	in the end	shall be the last ones, together with all the sons of the East, to wage war against Israel, in the days of the King Messiah
	v. 23 when God does this	when the Memra (Word) of the Lord reveals itself (i.e. in the Messianic Age)
	v. 24 Kittim	Italy . . . Rome . . . Constantinople
	shall come to destruction	shall come to destruction by the hand of the King Messiah

(This version is even more explicitly Messianic; references to God and his armies are also brought in.)

Fragmentary Targum:	v. 19 by Jacob shall dominion be exercised	a king shall rise from the House of Jacob
	v. 24 Kittim	Italy/Rome

(No specific mention of the Messiah is found, but this version is eschatologically in sympathy with the other two Targums.)

Version	*Present Text*	*Version's Text*
Septuagint:	v. 17 I see him	I will point to him
	I behold him	I will bless him
	sceptre	man
	forehead	princes
	v. 19 by Jacob shall dominion be exercised	one shall arise out of Jacob
	v. 24 ships shall come	one shall come forth

(The tone is markedly eschatalogical and Messianic.)

Vulgate:	v. 24 Kittim	Italy

From the time of Matthew (2:2, 9) and John (Rev. 22:16) this is seen as a Messianic passage by the Church too, referring to Jesus. There are many such interpretations in the Greek and Latin Fathers.

FURTHER READING

Y. Aharoni and M. Avi-Yonah, *The Macmillan Bible Atlas* (The Macmillan Company, 1968)

S. Herrmann, *A History of Israel in Old Testament Times* (SCM Press, 1975)

G. B. Gray, *The International Critical Commentary—Numbers* (T. and T. Clark, 1903)

A. R. S. Kennedy, *The Century Bible—Leviticus and Numbers* (Nelson, n.d.)

J. Marsh, *The Interpreter's Bible—Numbers* (Abingdon Press, 1953)

M. Noth, *Old Testament Library—Numbers* (SCM Press, 1966)

N. H. Snaith, *The New Century Bible—Leviticus and Numbers* (Nelson, 1967)

J. Sturdy, *The Cambridge Bible Commentary (NEB)—Numbers* (Cambridge UP, 1976)